T0301485

Thirlwall's Law at 40

Thirlwall's Law at 40

Edited by

Thomas Palley

Founding Editor, Review of Keynesian Economics *and Independent Economist*

Esteban Pérez Caldentey

Editor, Review of Keynesian Economics, *Economic Commission for Latin America and the Caribbean (CEPAL), Chile*

Matías Vernengo

Founding Editor, Review of Keynesian Economics, *Professor, Bucknell University, USA*

A SPECIAL ISSUE OF THE REVIEW OF KEYNESIAN ECONOMICS

Edward Elgar
PUBLISHING

Cheltenham, UK • Northampton, MA, USA

Originally published in 2019 as part of Volume 7 Issue 4 of *Review of Keynesian Economics*

Published by
Edward Elgar Publishing Limited
The Lypiatts
15 Lansdown Road
Cheltenham
Glos GL50 2JA
UK

Edward Elgar Publishing, Inc.
William Pratt House
9 Dewey Court
Northampton
Massachusetts 01060
USA

For further information on the *Review of Keynesian Economics*
see www.elgaronline/roke

A catalogue record for this book is available from the British Library

Library of Congress Control Number: 2021932452

This book is available electronically in the **Elgar**online
Economics subject collection
http://dx.doi.org/10.4337/9781800881471

ISBN 978 1 80088 146 4 (cased)
ISBN 978 1 80088 147 1 (eBook)
Printed and bound in Great Britain by TJ Books Limited, Padstow, Cornwall

Contents

Review of Keynesian Economics, Vol. 7 No. 4, Winter 2019, pp. 1–2

Thirlwall's law at 40

Esteban Pérez Caldentey
Chief, Financing for Development Unit, Economic Development Division, Economic Commission for Latin America and the Caribbean, Santiago, Chile

Matías Vernengo
Professor, Bucknell University, Lewisburg, PA, USA

The year 2019 marked the 40th anniversary of the publication of Anthony P. Thirlwall's classic paper titled 'The balance-of-payments constraint as an explanation of international growth rate differences' (Thirlwall 1979). This article introduced and provided empirical evidence in favor of the proposition that the long-run rate of growth of an economy compatible with balance-of-payments equilibrium can be approximated by the simple rule of the ratio of the growth of exports to the income elasticity of demand for imports.

This simple proposition known as Thirlwall's law is the dynamic analogue of the static Harrod trade multiplier result. In his book *International Economics* (1933), Roy Harrod had shown that the level of income equaled the level of exports divided by the propensity to import, based on the same assumptions as those of Thirlwall, that is, exports are the only component of autonomous demand, trade is balanced, and the real exchange rate (or terms of trade) does not change (Thirlwall 1997; 2018; McCombie and Thirlwall 1994). It is also similar to the model discussed by Raúl Prebisch in his *American Economic Review* paper (Prebisch 1959). These ideas were further developed by Nicholas Kaldor, who developed a demand-driven theory of cumulative causation, based on the supermultiplier (Kaldor 1970). Thirlwall's contribution follows in the Keynesian and Structuralist tradition of these authors.

Thirlwall's law focuses on aggregate demand as the key constraint to economic growth. According to Thirlwall's law, countries face an external constraint when

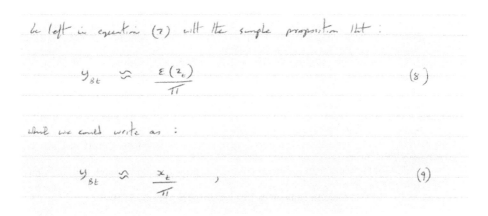

Figure 1 Thirlwall's law in the original draft

Journal compilation © 2019 Edward Elgar Publishing Ltd
The Lypiatts, 15 Lansdown Road, Cheltenham, Glos GL50 2JA, UK
and The William Pratt House, 9 Dewey Court, Northampton MA 01060-3815, USA

their performance in foreign markets and the response of the financial markets to this performance restrict growth to a rate lower than internal conditions would warrant. In this sense, Thirlwall's approach is an alternative framework to mainstream theory (whether framed in terms of exogenous or endogenous growth theory) which places the focus on endowments and technology to explain growth differences between countries and for which there are no demand constraints. According to mainstream theory, which abides by Say's law, demand simply adapts to supply.

Thirlwall's law provides a theoretical underpinning for several of the arguments traditionally espoused by the heterodox followers of Keynes, which since the 1970s have been often referred to as Post-Keynesian. These include the fact that equilibrium coexists with less than full employment, that income effects prevail over substitution effects, that international payment imbalances can have negative consequences on growth, and also that, as with the case of the closed economy, money in an open economy is not neutral in the long run. In addition, Thirlwall's law can also be viewed as a guide to policy-making. Real exchange-rate variations and capital-flow movements will not guarantee an improvement in the long-run rate of the growth of an economy. The external constraint can only be eased through structural change, thereby altering the relationship between the income import and export demand elasticities.

Thirlwall's law has spurred a rich research agenda at both the theoretical and empirical levels (Thirlwall 2011). Theoretically the core model has been extended to include the different components of the current account of the balance of payments. Empirically, it has withstood the test of time and has been corroborated, with perhaps a few exceptions, for a variety of developed and developing countries under different historical contexts and different periods of time.

This special issue brings together a series of known experts and researchers to present the latest developments and debates on Thirlwall's law and to reflect and discuss how some of the latest developments in theory and those related to the evolution and workings of capitalist economies relate to the external sector and, in particular, to the concept of the balance-of-payments constraint underpinning the formulation of Thirlwall's law.

REFERENCES

Harrod, R.F. (1933), *International Economics*, New York: Harcourt, Brace and Company.
Kaldor, N. (1970 [1989]), 'The case for regional policies,' in F. Targetti and A.P. Thirlwall (eds), *The Essential Kaldor*, London: Duckworth, pp. 311–326.
McCombie, J.S.L. and A.P. Thirlwall (1994), *Economic Growth and the Balance-of-Payments Constraint*, New York: St Martin's Press.
Prebisch, R. (1959), 'Commercial policy in the underdeveloped countries,' *American Economic Review Papers and Proceedings*, 49(2), 251–273.
Thirlwall, A.P. (1979), 'The balance-of-payments constraint as an explanation of international growth rate differences,' *BNL Quarterly Review*, 32, 45–53.
Thirlwall, A.P. (1997), 'Reflections on the concept of balance-of-payments-constrained growth,' *Journal of Post Keynesian Economics*, 19(3), 377–385.
Thirlwall, A.P. (2011), 'Balance of payments constrained growth models: history and overview,' *PSL Quarterly Review*, 64, 307–351.
Thirlwall, A.P. (2018), 'A life in economics,' *PSL Quarterly Review*, 71, 9–39.

Review of Keynesian Economics, Vol. 7 No. 4, Winter 2019, pp. 3–17

Why Thirlwall's law is not a tautology: more on the debate over the law

J.S.L. McCombie*
University of Cambridge, UK

This paper reconsiders the argument first debated in the 1980s and revisited by Blecker (2016) and Razmi (2016), inter alios, that Thirlwall's law is nothing but a near-identity. It is shown theoretically and by simulation analysis that this proposition is erroneous. It is also demonstrated that Razmi's (2016) specification of the balance-of-payments-constrained growth model is problematical. The paper concludes by assessing the effectiveness of the rate of change of relative prices for export and import growth. Recent evidence provides further support for the importance of non-price competitiveness in international trade and, hence, for Thirlwall's law.

Keywords: *Thirlwall's law, balance-of-payments-constrained growth, tautology, price and non-price competitiveness*

JEL codes: *E12, F32, F43*

1 INTRODUCTION

Thirlwall's law (1979) is now 40 years old and since the publication of the seminal article there have been numerous papers both confirming Thirlwall's law and extending it theoretically and empirically. When Thirlwall's paper was first published there were a number of early criticisms and lively debates. One was concerned with whether or not the law is merely a tautology (McCombie 1981; Thirlwall 1981; McCombie 2011). The outcome of the debate is that the criticism is invalid: the law is not a tautology. However, ironically, the same argument criticizing the law has recently been put forward again. See, *inter alios*, Blecker (2016) and Razmi (2016).

This paper first shows that the earlier conclusion that the criticism is untenable is confirmed with respect to Blecker's restatement of it. It is further shown that Razmi's reformulation of Thirlwall's model suffers from a number of problems. The paper concludes with an assessment of the effectiveness of changes in relative prices with respect to Thirlwall's law.

2 THIRLWALL'S LAW IS NOT A TAUTOLOGY

The standard test of Thirlwall's law, which goes back to Thirlwall's (1979) seminal paper, is to test the closeness of the fit between $y_b = \left(\frac{\hat{\varepsilon}}{\pi}\right)w$ and y, where y_b is the

---

* I am grateful to Jesus Felipe, Rafael Ribeiro, João Romero, Tony Thirlwall and a referee for their helpful comments. The usual disclaimer applies.

Journal compilation © 2019 Edward Elgar Publishing Ltd
The Lypiatts, 15 Lansdown Road, Cheltenham, Glos GL50 2JA, UK
and The William Pratt House, 9 Dewey Court, Northampton MA 01060-3815, USA

balance-of-payments-constrained growth rate of income, y is the actual rate of growth and w is the growth of world income. $\hat{\varepsilon}$ and $\hat{\pi}$ are the econometric estimates of the income elasticities of demand for exports and imports respectively. They are the values derived from the estimation of the standard macroeconomic export and import demand functions. These regressions include a relative price term and normally use annual data. w and y used in the test mentioned above are the average exponential growth rates of world and domestic income respectively, calculated using the terminal and initial level figures of the period. The law is considered to be not refuted if the estimate of y_b is sufficiently close to y. A corollary of this test is that the estimated income elasticities should both be statistically significant. (See Thirlwall 2011 for a history of the development of the law.)

However, Blecker (2016, p. 276) claims that 'in recent years a number of heterodox critics … have questioned both the theoretical logic of Thirlwall's law and the empirical evidence in its favour'. He contends that 'tests of Thirlwall's law are testing a near-identity that is likely to be satisfied for almost any country regardless of whether its growth is BP- [balance-of-payments] constrained in the sense of Thirlwall or not' (ibid., p. 277). The implication is that the law is likely to be confirmed for any data set where the 'the quantities of exports and imports grow at approximately the same rate in the long run' (ibid., p. 277). Razmi (2016) takes a similar view, concluding that the 'the traditional approach to testing the BPCG [balance-of-payments-constrained growth] model is really a test of whether or not exports and imports grow at similar rates' (ibid., p. 1585).[1] Razmi assumes that changes in relative prices are negligibly small. We return to this point below. Consequently, Blecker terms Thirlwall's law a 'near-tautology' or 'near-identity'.

However, in this section, which is an elaboration of the argument in Thirlwall (1981) and McCombie (1981; 2011, sec. 2), we show that the error is entirely on the part of the current critics. They have made the mistake of assuming that the mathematical calculation of a total income elasticity, using the long-run average growth rates, *must* give a value that is always the same (or nearly the same) as the value of the statistical estimation of that coefficient. It does not.

We concentrate on the argument espoused by Blecker (2016), who follows Clavijo Cortes and Ros Bosch (2015), and show that it rests on a fundamental confusion between the *mathematical* calculation of an elasticity and its *econometric* estimation. Of course, the principle of testing and determining whether or not relationships in economics are statistically significant is the whole rationale for econometric analysis. Regression coefficients are statistically estimated and not merely arithmetically (or deterministically) calculated from the data. We will show that the failure to make this important distinction is the reason why it is erroneous to assume that Thirlwall's law is a near-identity.

To see this, let us consider Blecker's argument about the law being a tautology. For reasons of generality, we confine ourselves to discussing what is known as the 'strong version' of Thirlwall's law. As we have seen, Thirlwall's law is given by:

$$y_b = \left(\frac{\varepsilon}{\pi}\right)w. \tag{1}$$

1.   In the monetary approach to the balance of payments, the law of one price is assumed to hold, the growth of exports equals imports (which is ultimately determined by the growth of base money) and output is at its maximum potential (Frenkel and Mussa 1985). This is the antithesis of Thirlwall's approach. It shows that whereas the equality of the growth of imports and the growth of exports is a necessary condition for Thirlwall's law to hold, it is not a sufficient condition.

Blecker's argument that the law is merely a tautology is based on using the calculated (not statistically estimated) values of ε and π, namely, $\varepsilon^* = x/w$ and $\pi^* = m/y$. x and m are the growth rates of exports and imports. x, m, w and y are the average exponential growth rates calculated over a period of years. In other words, for example, $x = (1/T)(lnX_T - lnX_0)$, where X is the level of exports and T is the length of the period in years and the subscripts T and 0 denote the terminal and base year.

Substitution of these two equations for ε^* and π^* into equation (1) and rearranging gives:

$$y_b \equiv \frac{x}{m} y. \tag{2}$$

Hence, the assertion is that, so long as $x = m$, Thirlwall's law is unambiguously a tautology, namely, $y_b \equiv y$.

Blecker seeks to justify this result by arguing that:

> According to the near-tautology (or near-identity) argument, the *econometric* estimates of [$\hat{\varepsilon}$] and [$\hat{\pi}$] are likely to approximate the ratios of the growth rates of each trade variable (the volume of exports and imports) to the corresponding income growth rate (foreign or domestic), that is, [$\hat{\varepsilon} \approx \frac{x}{w}$] and [$\hat{\pi} \approx \frac{m}{y}$] ... – especially if relative price effects are negligible in the long run. (Blecker 2016, p. 277, emphasis added)

Blecker (2016, p. 278) concedes that the inclusion of the relative price term means the law is not an identity. Nevertheless he argues that, as a matter of logic, 'if relative prices are small or insignificant, then the estimated income elasticities should be *closer* to the observed ratios [x/w] and [m/y] than if relative prices were large and significant' (ibid., p. 278, emphasis in the original). Hence, this is seen as reinforcing the argument that Thirlwall's law is a 'near identity'.[2]

However, there is no econometric reason why, in a regression of a variable on (say) two regressors, if one regressor is statistically insignificant, this will necessarily make the other regressor better-determined or will significantly affect its estimated value.

The fundamental flaw in the argument that Thirlwall's law is a near-identity, even if changes in relative prices are statistically insignificant, is that there is nothing in econometric theory that necessarily implies $\varepsilon^* \approx \hat{\varepsilon}$ and $\pi^* \approx \hat{\pi}$. Whether or not they do is an empirical matter. ε^* and π^* are both derived from a deterministic calculation based on two data points and there is no error term. It is also a calculation of a total, rather than a partial, elasticity.

Consequently, for a given x, w and y, there is a precise value of ε^*. $\hat{\varepsilon}$, however, is an estimated partial elasticity using numerous observations. There is no reason why it should not be statistically significantly different from ε^* or indeed from zero, at the chosen confidence level. To put this another way, there is no *a priori* reason, for example, why $\varepsilon^* \approx \hat{\varepsilon}$. The reason why this may be likely to occur is because the results of the estimation of the export and import demand functions empirically confirm Thirlwall's law. There is no *logical* reason why ε^* and $\hat{\varepsilon}$ (or π^* and $\hat{\pi}$) should be approximately equal. It is an empirical issue.

---

2.   Blecker argues that if the relative price term is endogenous, its estimated coefficient may be biased downwards. Romero and McCombie (2016; 2018) and Christodoulopoulou and Tkačevs (2016) control for simultaneity and find that the relative price term is quantitively unimportant and/or statistically insignificant for a wide range of developed countries.

                                    Journal compilation © 2019 Edward Elgar Publishing Ltd

We may see this, at the risk of some repetition, by further considering the argument. The supposed tautological nature of Thirlwall's law stems from the use of the numerical *calculations* of export and import income elasticities calculated using only data at the end and beginning of the period. Consequently,

$$\varepsilon^* \equiv \frac{ln(X_T/X_0)/T}{ln(W_T/W_0)/T} \equiv \frac{x}{w}, \tag{3}$$

where W is the level of world income.

It will be recalled that the star on the elasticities serves to remind us that this estimate is an arithmetical value and not an estimated value, which, as above, we denote by $\hat{\varepsilon}$.

The same argument applies to the income elasticity of demand for imports

$$\pi^* \equiv \frac{ln(M_T/M_0)/T}{ln(Y_T/Y_0)/T} \equiv \frac{m}{y}, \tag{4}$$

where M and Y are the levels of imports and domestic income.

Thirlwall's law, as we have seen, according to Blecker's argument, is given by the equation:

$$y_b^* \equiv \frac{\varepsilon^*}{\pi^*} w \equiv y, \tag{5}$$

where y_b^* is the balance-of-payments-constrained growth rate using the mathematically calculated elasticities.

Thus, if we substitute equations (3) and (4) into (5), we do indeed derive a quasi-identity because of the way ε^* and π^* have been calculated, namely:

$$y_b^* \equiv \frac{x/w}{m/y} w \equiv y. \tag{6}$$

This derivation is, as Blecker correctly notes, a tautology provided that the growth of x and m, mathematically calculated over the long run, are equal, which empirically holds for many countries.

However, in practice, the estimates of the elasticities are obtained by estimating the following equations, in their simplest form:

$$lnX_t = c_1 + b_1 lnW_t + b_2 lnP_t + \mu_t \tag{7}$$

and

$$lnM_t = c_2 + b_3 lnY_t + b_4 P'_t + \varphi_t, \tag{8}$$

where P_t and P'_t are the appropriately defined relative price terms. μ_t and φ_t are the error terms and c_1 and c_2 are constants.[3] The subscript t denotes the year and we assume, for comparability with equations (1) and (2), that t runs from the base year to T.

---

3.   The seminal empirical papers of Houthakker and Magee (1969) and Goldstein and Khan (1978) omit the time trend. The autonomous growth of exports and imports of the various countries are captured in the (differing) estimates of the respective income elasticities of demand.

                    Journal compilation © 2019 Edward Elgar Publishing Ltd

The econometric and consequently *correct* test of Thirlwall's law is whether or not $y_b = \frac{\hat{\varepsilon}}{\hat{\pi}} w$ closely approximates to y, and $\hat{\varepsilon}$ and $\hat{\pi}$ are both statistically significant. In this test, w and y are again the long-run exponentially calculated growth rates of world and domestic income.

We are now in a position easily to see the problem with Blecker's argument. Blecker uses the calculated values of the elasticities, whereas the correct test is to use the econometric estimates of the partial elasticities, the values for which we have no *a priori* information. For Blecker's tautological argument to have any meaning it is necessary for ε^* and π^* not just to be empirically the same as $\hat{\varepsilon}$ and $\hat{\pi}$ respectively, but for these equalities to be due to a *definitional* relationship.

Suppose we estimate equation (7). There is nothing in econometric theory that states that, using the same data set, the estimate of $\hat{\varepsilon}$ should be equal to ε^*. The same is true for equation (8). They are not identities. There is no *a priori* reason why $\hat{\varepsilon}/\hat{\pi}$ should equal ε^*/π^* .

One reason why the estimates of the income elasticities could be statistically insignificant is that the variance of the logarithm of exports (or imports) is almost completely explained by the logarithm of the relative price term; for example, the Neoclassical law of one price empirically holds. In this case, the estimates of the income elasticities are likely to be *statistically* insignificant. There is no necessary reason why the estimated income elasticities should always be statistically significant. Thirlwall (1981) made this point nearly 40 years ago.

The issue is actually more general than this. There is no econometric reason why the estimated coefficients in a regression equation should not *all* be statistically insignificant. After all, they are derived from behavioural relationships and this is why elasticities are estimated econometrically and not simply calculated arithmetically.

As has been shown, the argument that Thirlwall's law is simply a tautology is based on a confusion between a statistically estimated elasticity and an arithmetically calculated one. In order to illustrate this argument, we estimated some export and import demand functions in a simulation analysis.

3   THIRLWALL'S LAW AND A SIMULATION EXERCISE

It should be emphasized that the simulations have no implications as to whether or not Thirlwall's law actually empirically holds. But what they do show is that the issue is an empirical, and not a tautological, one. This is in spite of the fact that in all the simulation exercises we impose the condition that, over the period of the data set, the average growth rates of exports and imports are exactly equal. It will be recalled that, according to Blecker, *inter alios*, this relationship is *all* that is necessary to ensure that Thirlwall's law is a tautology.

We report the results of only five regressions of export and import demand functions out of the many that have been run, but they all have the same implications for the theoretical argument.

The various five simulation databases consist of annual indices of the volumes of imports, exports, world income domestic income and relative prices. The data consist of ten years' annual observations.[4] The long-run average growth of world income and domestic income were set equal to 3 per cent per annum in all the databases.

---

4.   We ran other simulations with 20 and 30 observations. Our argument, though, is not dependent on the sample size.

These specific figures do not have any significant role to play in the argument and we could equally have used any values. But what does matter is the fact that the long-run growth of imports and exports are constrained to be equal and average 6 per cent per annum. The data were constructed so that the volume of exports equals the volume of imports at the beginning of the sample, and there is no long-term growth of capital flows.

From all five databases, the numerical calculation of the elasticities is $\varepsilon^* \equiv 6\%/3\% = 2$ and $\pi^* \equiv 6\%/3\% = 2$. These equalities consequently hold for all the simulations, although the annual observations of the variables differ between the databases. Nothing depends on the particular values of the elasticities.

Thirlwall's law, using this numerical method, is given by $y_b \equiv \varepsilon^* w/\pi^* = 3\%$ per year, which, given the way it is calculated, is indeed a tautology. However, the whole point of obtaining statistical values for the income elasticities of export and import demand functions, since Houthakker and Magee (1969), is to determine whether or not the estimates are statistically significant and what predictive power they have.

Consequently, we estimated the export and import demand functions using the very different annual values from the five simulation databases. We obtain the results reported in Table 1. Equations 1(a) and 1(b) refer to the results using database 1, equations 2(a) and (2b) using database 2, etc. Table 2 reports a summary of the elasticities and the calculation of Thirlwall's law. The results are based on the use of ordinary least squares regression analysis. As the point we are making is about the difference in effect of using statistical estimates of the elasticities, *per se*, compared with their numerical calculation, the exact method of estimation is unimportant. Hence, we also do not report the usual regression diagnostic tests.

As the *estimation* of the various coefficients is an econometric matter, it is not possible to predict the values of the coefficients *a priori*. Using database 1, the results are given by equations 1(a) and 1(b) and the estimated coefficients of both lnW (that is, $\hat{\varepsilon}$) and lnY (that is, $\hat{\pi}$) are statistically insignificant. The variation in the logarithms of exports and imports are statistically significantly explained by variations in the logarithms of the indices of the relative price terms (lnP and lnP') and not by the logarithms of the income terms.

Using databases 2, 3, 4 and 5, the relative price terms are insignificant and, consequently, are dropped from the specifications of the regressions. This has the advantage that we are now comparing the different ways of determining the values for the total, and not partial, income elasticities. Using database 2, the estimate of $\hat{\varepsilon}$ is just significant and $\hat{\pi}$ is statistically at the 95 per cent confidence level. However, using database 3, the income elasticities are both statistically significant (a necessary, but not sufficient condition, for the non-refutation of Thirlwall's law). Using databases 4 and 5, the elasticities are statistically significant, but their values are very different from ε^* and π^*.

For convenience, these estimates are summarized in Table 2, together with the estimates of y_b. As the estimates of the import and export functions are independent of each other, we also report Thirlwall's law using the estimates of the income elasticities from equations 1(a) and 3(b) and also 3(a) and 1(b).

It should be noted that equations 1(a) and 3(b) use the export and import statistics from databases 1 and 3 respectively. Similarly, equations 3(a) and 1(b) use the export and import statistics from databases 3 and 1.

It can be seen that Thirlwall's law using ε^* and π^* in all five databases is not, and cannot, be refuted because of the way that the elasticities are arithmetically calculated. In other words, $y_b^* \equiv (\varepsilon^*/\pi^*)w \equiv y$. Furthermore, in the light of previous discussion, they not surprisingly give identical results for all five databases. *This is Blecker's tautology and is not a test of Thirlwall's law.*

Table 1   Estimated export and import demand functions: results using the five databases

1(a)	$lnX = 13.911 + 0.191lnW - 2.205lnP$ (9.15) (1.17) (−10.30)	$\bar{R}^2 = 0.959$
1(b)	$lnM = 13.186 + 0.248lnY - 2.088lnP'$ (9.15) (0.89) (−5.06)	$\bar{R}^2 = 0.828$
2(a)	$lnX = 0.129 + 1.010lnW$ (0.05) (1.98)	$\bar{R}^2 = 0.245$
2(b)	$lnM = 1.342 + 0.739lnM$ (0.08) (1.40)	$\bar{R}^2 = 0.197$
3(a)	$lnX = -4.437 + 1.971lnW$ (0.08) (27.39)	$\bar{R}^2 = 0.989$
3(b)	$lnM = -3.886 + 1.845lnY$ (−6.92) (15.69)	$\bar{R}^2 = 0.968$
4(a)	$lnX = -0.495 + 1.117lnW$ (−0.25) (2.65)	$\bar{R}^2 = 0.467$
4(b)	$lnM = 0.034 + 1.001lnY$ (0.03) (4.13)	$\bar{R}^2 = 0.680$
5(a)	$lnX = 0.741 + 0.861lnW$ (0.35) (1.97)	$\bar{R}^2 = 0.243$
5(b)	$lnM = -3.836 + 1.851lnY$ (−3.43) (7.86)	$\bar{R}^2 = 0.871$

Notes: In all regressions the long-run growth of exports equals the growth of imports and is 6 per cent per annum. The long-run growth of world and domestic income equals 3 per cent per annum. The values of cumulative imports equal cumulative exports over the period. The annual values of exports and imports differ between the databases. Figures in parentheses are *t*-values.

Table 2   Income elasticities and Thirlwall's law

Equations	$\hat{\varepsilon}$	$\hat{\pi}$	$\tilde{y}_b$	ε^*	π^*	y_b^*	y
1(a) and 1(b)	0.191[§]	0.248[§]	2.310	2.0	2.0	3.0	3.0
2(a) and 2(b)	1.010[#]	0.739[§]	4.100	2.0	2.0	3.0	3.0
3(a) and 3(b)	1.971[#]	1.845[#]	3.205	2.0	2.0	3.0	3.0
4(a) and 4(b)	1.117[#]	1.001[#]	3.348	2.0	2.0	3.0	3.0
5(a) and 5(b)	0.861[#]	1.851[#]	1.395	2.0	2.0	3.0	3.0
1(a) and 3(b)	0.191[§]	1.845[#]	0.311	2.0	2.0	3.0	3.0
3(a) and 1(b)	1.971[#]	0.248[§]	23.843	2.0	2.0	3.0	3.0

Notes: § denotes the estimated coefficient is not significant at the 95 per cent confidence level and # that it is. $\tilde{y}_b$ is the output growth calculated from estimate income elasticities of the export and import demand functions. y_b^* is the predicted output growth from the tautology and y is the actual growth of output.

In four of the databases the calculated income elasticities are not even close to the estimated values. These are the estimates of databases 1, 2, 4 and 5 reported in Table 1. Thirlwall's law is refuted in databases 1 and 2 where one of the values of the elasticities is statistically insignificant. This is true for the combinations of equations 1(a) and 3(b) as well as 3(a) and 1(b). This is not the case for database 3 where the estimated income elasticities are very close to the arithmetically calculated ones. But there is nothing that ensures, *a priori*, this must be the case. Database 4 is an interesting case because Thirlwall's law is not refuted even though the values of $\hat{\varepsilon}$ and $\hat{\pi}$ are not close to ε^* and π^*. This is because the *ratio* of the estimated elasticities is close to the *ratio* of the calculated one. The regressions using database 5 give estimates of both export and import elasticities that are statistically significant but give a value of $\tilde{y}_b$, the estimated balance-of-payments equilibrium growth rate that is very different from the actual growth rate, y.

These various estimates, of course, do not have any implications for the actual estimates of Thirlwall's law. They are merely designed to demonstrate that the law is not a tautology. The empirical testing of the law usually confirms the law, but can in principle refute it. The tautology, by definition, must always confirm it, but this should not be confused with the results of the regressions that also confirm the law. The latter results are not because of the tautology.

4   SOME PROBLEMS WITH RAZMI'S (2016) MODEL

As a result the erroneous interpretation of Thirlwall's law as a tautology, Razmi (2016) has proposed a theoretical respecification of the balance-of-payments equilibrium growth equation, which explicitly incorporates the supply side. The revised theoretical equation for the balance-of-payments equilibrium growth rate is given by a hybrid of demand and supply variables, namely:

$$y_b = \beta_1 w + \beta_2 k + \beta_3 e, \tag{9}$$

where the β coefficients consist of various demand and supply price elasticities of imports and exports, e is the growth of the nominal exchange rate, and k is the *exogenous* growth of the capital stock of the export sector. (In the subsequent empirical analysis, k is proxied by the growth of the total capital stock.) w is again the exogenous growth of world income. Razmi estimates a specification similar to equation (9) using panel-data and single-equation methods for a number of developed and developing countries. The first generally uses growth rates and the second uses log levels. We shall concentrate on the former. The growth of the nominal exchange rate is excluded from the regressions. The logarithm of Rodrik's (2008) measure of the real exchange-rate undervaluation,[5] the growth of relative export and import prices and the logarithm of external debt-to-income ratio are also included as control variables. (The equation is similar to Thirlwall's law, but with the growth of the capital stock included as an additional regressor.) Razmi finds that, empirically, the estimated coefficient of k is statistically significant and that of w is often significant, but the size of its coefficient is reduced when k is included. Consequently, the regression results mean that an exogenous increase in the growth of the capital stock, due to, say, an increase in entrepreneurs' 'animal spirits', raises the growth of exports and hence the balance-of-payments equilibrium growth rate. This is holding the

---

5.   This is the divergence of the tradable from the non-tradable exchange rate, adjusted for the Balassa–Samuelson affect. It is not derived from the estimation of import and export demand functions. Rodrik (2008) found that it was only important for the low-income countries. Woodford (2008), Goncalves and Rodrigues (2017) and Ribeiro et al. (2019), *inter alios*, find little or no support for this result.

other independent variables constant, notably the relative price terms and the growth of world income. An autonomous increase in the growth of world income, via an induced increase in exports can, in turn, in the model, increase the growth of output, again holding the other regressors constant. These somewhat paradoxical results are derived from the underlying theoretical assumptions of the model.

Razmi's (2016, p. 1593, equ. (9)) theoretical specification of the export-supply function, in dynamic form, is a function of the *exogenous* growth of the export sector's capital stock, together with the growth of the *nominal* export price. Hence, the former is treated as autonomous in the specification of the theoretical model. Razmi (p. 1593, fn 19) cites Goldstein and Khan (1985) in support of the inclusion of an exogenous scaling factor, who consider either trend income or trend exports. However, Goldstein and Khan (1985, p. 1060) justify the latter in terms of the assumptions underlying the Lucas New Classical 'surprise' supply function. Furthermore, they explicitly state that they assume that long-run output growth is determined by the supply side. Both assumptions are the antitheses of those underlying the balance-of-payments-constrained growth model.

In the balance-of-payments-constrained growth model, the growth of the flow of export-capital services is more plausibly assumed to be endogenous, determined by the growth of exports. Williamson (1983, p. 153) argues that, in the short run, 'the [exporting] manufacturer sets the price and is pleased to sell everything that is demanded at that price'. Firms keep a planned margin of excess capacity (and inventories) to meet a short-term increase in demand, which, if sustained, is met by increased capacity and capital accumulation. As Lavoie (2014, p. 154) puts it, 'there are good theoretical as well as practical reasons, as well as good strategic and technical ones, to explain why corporations generally aim at operating much below their full capacity'.

In the long run, the Kaldorian approach is that

> [i]n the case of industrial activities ('manufactures') the impact effect of exogenous changes in demand will be on production rather than on prices. 'Supply', at any rate long-run supply, is normally in excess of demand – in the sense that producers would be willing to produce more, and to sell more, at the prevailing price (or even at a lower price) in response to an increased flow of orders. (Kaldor 1970, p. 485)

So, in this approach, it is the growth of demand for a country's exports that endogenously determines the growth of capital in the export sector, and not vice versa.

The use of the nominal price by Razmi in the theoretical specification of the export-supply (and the import-supply) functions is implausible as it implies firms are money illusioned. Goldstein and Khan (1978, p. 276; 1985, p. 1045) state that the correct variable is the price of a country's exports relative to its domestic price. As this increases, it becomes more profitable to export. If the country only produces one good, as Razmi assumes, then the relative price will be unity. Razmi cites Dornbusch (1975) and Isard (1995) as cases where nominal prices are used in the context of the standard derivation of the Marshall–Lerner conditions. But, having done this, both Dornbusch (1975, p. 860) and Isard (1995, p. 95) subsequently criticize the approach for not using relative prices.[6]

6.   Razmi (2016, p. 1593, fn 16) states that if the demand for imports and exports are also based on nominal prices, it makes no difference to the model. But this does not solve the problem that relative prices should be used.

As we have noted, the inclusion of the assumed exogenous growth of the total capital stock as a proxy for the export sector's capital stock is statistically significant in the various regression analyses. But this result does not necessarily provide evidence for the importance, or otherwise, of the supply side. This is because this result will always largely be determined by an underlying accounting identity and so does not necessarily reflect a behavioural relationship. The share of capital in the total value of output is given by $a \equiv K/Y$, where r is the rate of profit, K is the capital stock and Y is output. The growth of output is *definitionally* equal to $y \equiv (g_r - g_a) + k$, where g_r and g_a are the growth rates of r and a. If the share of capital and the rate of profit are approximately constant, which empirically is often the case, a regression of y on k must definitionally give a very close goodness of fit, with a value of the slope coefficient of about unity. (This is one of Kaldor's stylized facts.) Even if a and r do change over time, there is still likely be a close statistical fit between y and k because of the identity. This is true even when k is included in a multivariate regression such as Razmi's estimated model, although its coefficient may differ from unity.

Razmi takes a very different approach to the traditional approach to testing whether or not growth is balance-of-payments-constrained, originated by Thirlwall (1979). The latter is discussed below. Razmi describes equation (9) above as theoretically determining the balance-of-payments equilibrium growth rate, but he uses the actual growth of output as the regressor in his empirical approach. The interpretation of the regression results presumably seems to be that the magnitude of the coefficients of w and k reflects the relative contributions of the demand and supply side to the balance-of-payments-constrained growth rate. As we noted above, the results of the regression analysis mean that either an increase in the growth of world demand, *ceteris paribus*, or an increase in growth of the capital stock, holding the other regressors constant, will each independently increase the rate of growth of output. In the light of this, in what sense can this be interpreted as a test of whether or not growth is balance-of-payments-constrained or, alternatively, that the estimating equation is of the balance-of-payments-constrained growth rate? A country can always relax the balance-of-payments constraint (that is, increase the growth of output) in this approach simply by investing more in the export sector. This statistical result occurs because the growth of world income, the rate of change of relative prices and the other regressors are all held constant when considering the impact of the growth of the capital stock on the growth of output in the specification of the multiple regression. Likewise, a growth in world income (demand) in this regression specification can increase the growth of output, holding all the other independent variables constant, including, implausibly, the growth of the capital stock.

In Thirlwall's approach to balance-of-payments-constrained growth, the growth of the export-capital stock is endogenously determined by the growth of demand for exports. This is for the reasons discussed above. In this case, the growth of the capital stock should not appear as a regressor in the estimating equation, as in Razmi's model. As a simplification for expositional reasons, we have essentially the following model. First, the estimate of the balance-of-payments equilibrium growth rate of a country is determined by the growth of world demand, $y_b = f_1(w)$, calculated using the estimates of the elasticities from the export and import demand functions. As discussed in the next section, it is generally found that the rate of change of relative prices has a negligible effect on the growth of exports and imports and, hence, on y_b. y_b is then tested to determine whether or not it differs from the actual growth of output, which is a function of the supply-side factors.

                     Journal compilation © 2019 Edward Elgar Publishing Ltd

Second, the growth of the export-capital stock is determined by the growth of exports, that is, $k = f_2(x)$. It follows that k is also a function of the growth of world income, that is to say, $k = f_3(w)$, as x is a function of w. The last two equations are different specifications of the export-capital supply function.

Let us assume that $k = f_3(w)$ is estimated by regressing k on w and is found to be statistically significant. Consequently, we would expect that k could well be statistically significant if it is erroneously included as a regressor of y in the first equation ($y = f_1(w)$), as in Razmi's estimating equation. It should be noted that this inclusion is not a problem that can be overcome by the use of instrumental variable techniques, as it is a misspecification issue.

An important extension of the traditional Thirlwall approach is that of Lanzafame (2014). Lanzafame calculates y_b for a number of countries and tests whether it differs from the econometrically estimated endogenous natural (or maximum) rate of growth, y_n. (Lanzafame uses the methodology of León-Ledesma and Thirlwall 2002 to estimate the values of the natural rate of growth.) It proves generally not to differ. He further uses panel Granger causality estimation methods in this approach and finds that there is a unidirectional causality from export growth to output growth. Moreover, y_n adjusts to y_b, and thus it is 'supply that responds to demand. This gives robust support to the Keynesian notion of growth as primarily determined on the demand side, with BOP [balance-of-payments] equilibrium acting as a long-run constraint and productive capacity adapting *endogenously* when actual growth is above the natural rate of growth' (Lanzafame 2014, p. 833, emphasis added).

The use of the actual growth rate of output as the regressand in Razmi's individual country regression analyses makes it impossible to test which countries are, and which are not, balance-of-payments-constrained as in the traditional (Thirlwall) approach discussed above.

Consequently, the preferable approach to the testing of whether or not the growth of a country is balance-of-payments-constrained is still the original method using Thirlwall's law.

5   THE IMPACT OF RELATIVE PRICES AND THIRLWALL'S LAW

A *sine qua non* of the balance-of-payments-constrained growth model is that the rate of change of relative prices plays a quantitatively small role in the determination of the growth of exports and imports. The empirical evidence suggests that this is nearly always the case.

A recent comprehensive survey of estimates of the Marshall–Lerner condition found that 'the results of our analysis are clear: The M-L [Marshall–Lerner] condition does not [statistically] hold in a large fraction of cases in which it is claimed to do so' (Bahmani et al. 2013, p. 435). They also provided their own estimates and further concluded that 'those who draw on previous studies to support certain expected benefits from a currency depreciation should think twice before they rely too heavily on such estimates' (ibid., p. 439). Recall that even when the Marshall–Lerner condition is met, given the specification of the import and export demand functions discussed, it is necessary for the rate of change of relative prices to be continuous for it to affect the balance-of-payments-constrained growth rate. This is implausible. Even for relatively homogenous agricultural commodities the evidence that the Neoclassical law of one price holds is not convincing (Thursby et al. 1986; Ardeni 1989).

                    Journal compilation © 2019 Edward Elgar Publishing Ltd

There are now numerous estimations of Thirlwall's law (and other econometric estimations of export and import demand functions) that confirm the unimportance of relative prices for a wide range of countries. Recent studies include Lanzafame (2014),
which has been discussed above. Christodoulopoulou and Tkačevs (2016) find this
unimportance to be true for the euro area countries, using a variety of relative price
measures. Romero and McCombie (2016; 2018) also show this using export data
for industries and quality-adjusted relative prices for a number of developed countries.
As noted above, these three studies correct for any simultaneous equation bias.

There is the substantial research emanating from the European Central Bank's
Research Competitiveness Network which has confirmed the overwhelming importance of non-price competitiveness in explaining changes in both cumulative export
market shares and export performance. This analysis has become possible in recent
years with the construction of large data sets with highly disaggregated international
products and prices.

The approach, *inter alia*, is to construct two separate aggregate indices of trade
prices using data at a high level of disaggregation. The first is the 'conventional'
relative unit value (value per physical measure of goods such as tonnage), or conventional relative export price (RXP), and measures only price competitiveness. The
second is the relative export price adjusted for quality and taste. It is 'measure of
price per unit of utility'.[7] A comparison of the two indices reflects the contribution
of non-price factors to changes in export prices (Benkovskis and Wörz 2015; see also
Benkovskis and Wörz 2012; 2016).

The problem has been posed by Benkovskis and Wörz (2015) in their aptly titled
paper, 'Cost competitiveness: a dangerous obsession'. They ask: 'How can we recon-
cile real effective exchange rate (REER) – and hence an apparent deterioration in cost
competitiveness – with rising world market share – a clear sign of improved competitiveness?' (This is the Kaldor 1978 paradox.) They point out that many emerging market economies have increased their share of world markets with increasing relative
prices, while other countries have lost global market share despite increasing cost
competitiveness. They show that it is due to changes in non-price competitiveness.
The first result that is in accordance with Allard's (2009) findings for four Central
European economies, *inter alia*.

In the case of the US, for example, since about the year 2000 the conventional RXP
has depreciated, but so also has the US market share. What accounts for this paradox?
The answer, according to Benkovskis and Wörz (2015) is that the RXP, after it has
been adjusted for quality, has increased markedly over this period, suggesting a
decline in non-price competitiveness. The fall in the conventional real exchange rate
has been more than offset by a decline in the relative (although not absolute) quality
of US exports. Moreover, China, in particular, owes its export success to the substantial gains in its non-price competitiveness, and not to the increasing relative cheapness
of its exports. This confirms the conclusions of both Pula and Santabárbara (2011) and
Fu et al. (2012) using regression analysis.

This method quantifies and 'highlights the crucial importance of non-price competitiveness in assessing emerging countries' performance on external markets', as well as
for the developed countries (Benkovskis and Wörz 2016, p. 706). It also demonstrates
that the effect of non-price competitiveness differs from country to country.

Boggio and Barbieri (2017) find that the growth of export market shares of
33 countries are significantly determined by the levels of unit labour costs (ULCs),

---

7.   Some studies break these down into further indices including changes in tastes.

but not their growth rates. However, relative ULCs should have been used (that is, costs relative to those of a country's trading competitors). Moreover, the panel data estimation implausibly imposes the same value of the coefficient on both the developed and developing countries. When the level of per-capita GDP is introduced as a variable capturing technological capabilities, the coefficient of the ULC variable becomes insignificant, suggesting the importance of the former. However, Felipe and Kumar (2014) present sceptical reasons about the use of ULCs as a measure of cost competitiveness.

Overall, the evidence discussed above confirms the crucial importance of non-price competitiveness in determining trade flows, as originally emphasized by Thirlwall (1979).

6   CONCLUDING COMMENTS

The argument that the only thing that tests of Thirlwall's law are doing is estimating a tautology has been shown to be both theoretically and econometrically erroneous. This has been confirmed by a simulation analysis. This hare was set running in 1981 by McCombie, but who, as a result of an interchange with Thirlwall in 1981, subsequently changed his mind.

We have confirmed Thirlwall's view by showing that the test of the law is an econometric matter and this, by itself, is sufficient to show that the law is not a tautology. There is nothing, *a priori*, to stop the estimates of both the income elasticities and price elasticities being statistically insignificant. This would empirically refute the law and, of course, a tautology cannot be refuted.

We have further shown that Razmi's (2016) attempt to reformulate Thirlwall's law is not compelling, particularly as it includes both the demand-side and the supply-side variables at the same time in a single estimating equation.

The evidence of the importance of non-price competitiveness, emphasized by Thirlwall (1979) has also been confirmed by studies that adjust relative price changes to reflect quality changes. The latter play an important part in explaining a country's changes in its cumulative export shares. Generally, rates of changes in relative prices have little or no effect on the growth of exports and imports and the Marshall–Lerner conditions are usually not met. The balance-of-payments constraint is important in understanding why growth rates differ.

REFERENCES

Allard, C. (2009), 'Competitiveness in Central Europe: what has happened since EU accession?', IMF Working Paper, WP/09/121, International Monetary Fund.

Ardeni P.G. (1989), 'Does the law of one price really hold for commodity prices?', *American Journal of Agricultural Economics*, 71(3), 661–669.

Bahmani, M., H. Harvey and S.W. Hegerty (2013), 'Empirical tests of the Marshall–Lerner condition: a literature review', *Journal of Economic Studies*, 40(3), 411–443.

Benkovskis, K. and J. Wörz (2012), 'Evaluation of non-price competitiveness of exports from Central, Eastern and Southeastern European countries in the EU market', Bank of Latvia Working Paper 1/2012.

Benkovskis, K. and J. Wörz (2015), 'Cost competitiveness: a dangerous obsession', *VOX CEPR Policy Portal*, available at: http://voxeu.org/article/cost-competitiveness-obsession.

Benkovskis, K. and J. Wörz (2016), 'Non-price competitiveness of exports from emerging countries', *Empirical Economics*, 51(2), 707–735.

    Journal compilation © 2019 Edward Elgar Publishing Ltd

Blecker, R.A. (2016), 'The debate over "Thirlwall's Law": balance-of-payments-constrained growth reconsidered', *European Journal of Economics and Economic Policies: Intervention*, 13(3), 275–290.

Boggio, L. and L. Barbieri (2017), 'International competitiveness in post-Keynesian growth theory: controversies and empirical evidence', *Cambridge Journal of Economics*, 41(1), 25–47.

Christodoulopoulou, S. and O. Tkačevs (2016), 'Measuring the effectiveness of cost and price competitiveness in external rebalancing of euro area countries: what do alternative HCIs tell us?', *Empirica*, 43(3), 487–531.

Clavijo Cortes, P.H. and J. Ros Bosch (2015), 'La ley de Thirlwall: una lectura critica', *Investigación Económica*, 74(292), 11–40.

Dornbusch, R. (1975), 'Exchange rates and fiscal policy in a popular model of international trade', *American Economic Review*, 65(5), 859–871.

Felipe, J. and U. Kumar (2014), 'Unit labor costs in the eurozone: the competitiveness debate again', *Review of Keynesian Economics*, 2(4), 490–507.

Frenkel, J.A. and M.L. Mussa (1985), 'Asset markets, exchange rates and the balance of payments', in R. Jones and B.P. Kenen (eds), *Handbook of International Economics*, vol. 2, Amsterdam: New Holland, pp. 679–747.

Fu, X., R. Kaplinsky and J. Zhang (2012), 'The impact of China on low and middle income countries' export prices in industrial-country markets', *World Development*, 40(8), 1483–1496.

Goldstein, M. and M.S. Khan (1978), 'The supply and demand for exports: a simultaneous approach', *Review of Economics and Statistics*, 60(4), 275–286.

Goldstein, M. and M.S. Khan (1985), 'Income and price effects in foreign trade', in P.B. Kenen and R.W. Jones (eds), *Handbook of International Economics*, vol. 2, Amsterdam: North Holland, pp. 1041–1105.

Goncalves, C.E. and M. Rodrigues (2017), 'Exchange rate misalignment and growth: a myth?', IMF Working Paper, 17/283.

Houthakker, H.S. and S.P. Magee (1969), 'Income and price elasticities in world trade', *Review of Economics and Statistics*, 51(2), 111–125.

Isard, P. (1995), *Exchange Rate Economics*, Cambridge, UK: Cambridge University Press.

Kaldor, N. (1970), 'The case for regional policies', *Scottish Journal of Political Economy*, 17(3), 337–348.

Kaldor, N. (1978), 'The effect of devaluations on trade in manufactures', in N. Kaldor (ed.), *Further Essays on Applied Economics*, London: Duckworth, pp. 99–116.

Lanzafame, M. (2014), 'The balance of payments-constrained growth rate and the natural rate of growth: new empirical evidence', *Cambridge Journal of Economics*, 38(4), 817–838.

Lavoie, M. (2014), *Post-Keynesian Economics: New Foundations*, Cheltenham, UK and Northampton, MA: Edward Elgar Publishing.

León-Ledesma, M. and A.P. Thirlwall, A.P. (2002), 'The endogeneity of the natural rate of growth', *Cambridge Journal of Economics*, 26(4), 441–459.

McCombie, J.S.L. (1981), 'Are international growth rates constrained by the balance of payments? A comment on Professor Thirlwall', *Banca Nazionale del Lavoro Quarterly Review*, 34(139), 455–458.

McCombie, J.S.L. (2011), 'Criticism and defences of the balance-of-payments constrained growth model: some old, some new', *PSL Quarterly Review*, 64(259), 353–392.

Pula, G. and D. Santabárbara (2011), 'Is China climbing up the quality ladder? Estimating cross country differences in product quality using Eurostat's COMEXT trade database', ECB Working Paper, No 1310, European Central Bank.

Razmi, A. (2016), 'Correctly analysing the balance-of-payments constraint on growth', *Cambridge Journal of Economics*, 40(6), 1581–1608.

Ribeiro, R.S.M., J.S.L. McCombie and G.T. Lima (2019), 'Does real exchange rate undervaluation really promote economic growth?', *Structural Change and Economic Dynamics*, available at: https://doi.org/10.1016/j.strueco.2019.02.005.

Rodrik, D. (2008), 'The real exchange rate and economic growth', *Brookings Papers on Economic Activity*, (2), 365–412.

Romero, J.P. and J.S.L. McCombie (2016), 'The multi-sectoral Thirlwall's law: evidence from 14 developed European countries using product-level data', *International Review of Applied Economics,* 30(3), 301–325.

Romero, J.P. and J.S.L. McCombie (2018), 'Thirlwall's law and the specification of export and import functions', *Metroeconomica*, 69(2), 366–395.

Thirlwall, A.P. (1979), 'The balance of payments constraint as an explanation of international growth rate differences', *Banca Nazionale del Lavoro Quarterly Review*, 32(128), 45–53.

Thirlwall, A.P. (1981), 'Are international growth rates constrained by the balance of payments? A reply to Mr McCombie', *Banca Nazionale del Lavoro Quarterly Review*, 34(139), 458–459.

Thirlwall, A.P. (2011), 'Balance of payments constrained growth models: history and overview', *PSL Quarterly Review*, 64(259), 307–351.

Thursby, M.C., P.R. Johnson and T.J. Grennes (1986), 'The law of one price and the modelling of disaggregated trade flows', *Economic Modelling*, 3(4), 293–302.

Williamson, J. (1983), *The Open Economy and the World Economy*, New York: Basic Books.

Woodford, M. (2008), 'Comments on Dani Rodrik, "The real exchange rate and economic growth"', *Brookings Papers on Economic Activity*, 2, 420–439.

          Journal compilation © 2019 Edward Elgar Publishing Ltd

Review of Keynesian Economics, Vol. 7 No. 4, Winter 2019, pp. 18–36

Endogenous growth, capital accumulation and Thirlwall's dynamics: the case of Latin America

Ignacio Perrotini-Hernández*
National Autonomous University of Mexico, Mexico City, Mexico

Juan Alberto Vázquez-Muñoz**
Meritorious Autonomous University of Puebla, Puebla, Mexico

The article draws together the analyses of the interaction between economic capacity (ec), the endogeneity of the natural growth rate (g_n) and the growth rate consistent with balance-of-payments equilibrium (g_{tb}) that constrains economic activity. We identify two possible scenarios: the self-correcting scenario where g_{tb} is more elastic than the normal natural rate of growth (g_{nn}) vis-à-vis ec, and the self-aggravating scenario where g_{nn} is more elastic than g_{tb} with respect to ec. We empirically assess our central tenet (ec is a determinant of the relations between g_{tb}, g_w and g_{nn}) for the cases of Argentina, Brazil, Chile and Mexico, and found that, in all countries, the relationships between ec and g_{nn} and between ec and g_{tb} are positive, except in the case of Argentina where the relation between g_{tb} and ec was negative in the sub-period 1975–1990.

Keywords: *growth, capital accumulation, balance of payments, Latin America*

JEL codes: *E22, N16, 041*

> *'There is nothing natural about the natural rate of growth … the natural rate of growth is endogenous, not exogenous, and responds to the actual rate of growth.'*
> Kevin S. Nell and A.P. Thirlwall (2017, p. 215)

1 INTRODUCTION

Harrod (1936; 1939; 1948) carried Keynes's (1936 [1964]) static short-run analysis of the principle of effective demand over the long period by considering the effect of investment on income (the multiplier) and productive capacity (the acceleration principle). He established the foundations of dynamic analysis while introducing three fundamental concepts: the actual growth rate (g) given by the ratio of the savings rate (s) to the actual capital accumulation (c) or incremental capital–output ratio ($\Delta K/\Delta Y$); the warranted growth rate (g_w) defined as the growth rate that leaves 'all parties satisfied' as induced investment equals planned investment when firms 'have produced neither more nor less than the right amount' (Harrod 1939, p. 16); and the natural growth rate,

* Email: iph@unam.mx.
** Email: juan.vazquez@correo.buap.mx.

Journal compilation © 2019 Edward Elgar Publishing Ltd
The Lypiatts, 15 Lansdown Road, Cheltenham, Glos GL50 2JA, UK
and The William Pratt House, 9 Dewey Court, Northampton MA 01060-3815, USA

which represents a full-employment equilibrium growth path determined by the full-employment of the labour force plus the growth rate of technological progress.

Harrod recognized that the existence of a full-employment equilibrium growth path is a mere coincidence, since there is no built-in mechanism whereby g and g_w would necessarily tend to converge, nor is there any automatic tendency for g_w to coincide with g_n.

Harrod's instability principle can be summarized as follows: suppose investment increases faster (slower) than g_w; the income effect of investment will be greater (less) than the effect on the economic capacity. This will in all probability quicken (slow down) the growth rate of investment, which will widen the rising (descending) deviation of g vis-à-vis g_w and expand the disequilibrium. If g rises above (falls below) g_w, g will tend to increase (decrease) without limits and will aggravate the initial inflationary (depressive) disequilibrium. Furthermore, if the natural growth rate exceeds (falls short of) the warranted rate there will be a tendency for g to exceed (fall short of) g_w, and thus for the economy to experience chronic inflation (depression). Therefore, according to Harrod's instability principle, it appears that once g deviates from g_w, an ever-worsening stagnation or an ever-rising inflation will prevail, unless an anti-cyclical economic policy prevents the system from collapsing or exploding.

Harrod (1939) solved the first instability problem through endogenous changes of both the propensity to save and g_w coupled with the upper limit set on g by g_n. He solved the second instability problem through a reduction of the growth rate of population (when $g_n > g_w$) or through a decreasing savings propensity (when $g_n < g_w$).

Seminal as his contribution was, Harrod (1939) did not analyse the influence of the balance of payments in his extension of Keynes's (1936 [1964]) short period analysis of effective demand problems. In his seminal article 'The balance of payments constraint as an explanation of the international growth rate differences', Thirlwall (1979) bridged the gap by extending Harrod's dynamic analysis for an open-economy setting. In Thirlwall's model the growth rate consistent with balance-of-payments equilibrium (g_{tb}) depends on the growth rate of exports (x) and the income elasticity of the demand for imports (Ψ). Elaborating on his g_{tb} model, Thirlwall (2001) reconsidered Harrod's instability principle to show six scenarios with different disequilibrium positions which are summarized in two self-aggravating scenarios and one self-correcting scenario.

Following Thirlwall (1979), Vázquez-Muñoz (2018) has put forth a model where, given the gross capital elasticity of the demand for imports (Ψ_I) and Ψ, g_{tb} is a function of both x and the growth rate of economic capacity (ec). Similarly, Perrotini and Vázquez-Muñoz (2017) ponder depressive, normal and expansive growth regimes to argue that g_n is endogenous to both effective demand (à la León-Ledesma and Thirlwall 1998; 2000) and the growth rate of economic capacity (à la Lewis 1954). Perrotini and Vázquez-Muñoz (2017) also maintain that in the normal growth regime case g_n is equal to g_w.

The purpose of this paper is to reappraise Harrod's instability problems from a Thirlwallian perspective, so to speak, where all the involved growth rates, g_{nn}, g_w and g_{tb}, are functions of ec. We found two scenarios. In the first scenario, the disequilibrium between g_{tb} and g_{nn} is self-aggravating; in the second, the disequilibrium is self-correcting. However, in both of them the economic policy aimed at altering capital accumulation (k) –the main determinant of ec – can either aggravate or improve the unstable case, or else make the stable case slower or faster. It is also found that when g_{nn} is higher than g_{tb}, either in the self-correcting or in the self-aggravating cases, the economy may face external financial fragility, inducing a restrictive economic policy and hindering the self-correcting or the self-aggravating processes.

    Journal compilation © 2019 Edward Elgar Publishing Ltd

The rest of the paper is organized as follows: Section 2 describes our theoretical models where ec is a determinant of g_{tb}, g_{nn}, and g_w. Section 3 briefly discusses Thirlwall's assessment of Harrod's instability problem. Section 4 presents the empirical analysis for the main Latin American economies, namely Argentina, Brazil, Chile and Mexico.[1] Section 5 contains our final remarks.

2   ECONOMIC CAPACITY, BALANCE-OF-PAYMENTS EQUILIBRIUM, THE NATURAL AND THE WARRANTED GROWTH RATES

Capital accumulation affects a country's demand for imports positively (some capital goods must be imported) and negatively (capital accumulation adds to economic capacity,[2] making room for an import substitution effect) (Vázquez-Muñoz 2018). The same is true of exports: their direct effect improves the trade balance, while their indirect effect may tend to increase imports as a result of the increased income generated by export revenues.

It appears that these dual consequences of capital accumulation and exports should be made explicit in a model in which the adjustment process hinges upon quantity changes rather than price or real exchange-rate fluctuations. Our demand-for-imports equation is meant to capture such dual effects:

$$lnM_t = \alpha_0 + \Psi_{KB}lnKB_t + \alpha_2(lnID_t - lnEC_t) + \alpha_3(lnX_t - lnEC_t), \tag{1}$$

where ln, M, KB, ID, X, EC, α_0, Ψ_{KB}, α_2 and α_3 stand for the natural logarithm operator, the imports level, the gross capital stock, the level of domestic demand for domestic goods, the exports level, the level of economic capacity, a constant, the gross capital elasticity of the demand for imports, the income elasticity of the demand for imports weighted by the share of total imports financed by domestically generated income and the income elasticity of the demand for imports weighted by the share of total imports financed by the increased income generated by exports, respectively, and the subscript t is a time index. Therefore, $\alpha_2 + \alpha_3$ are the overall income elasticity of the demand for imports (Ψ). EC is that part of output that covaries with the net capital stock over the long run, given as:

$$lnEC_t = \beta_0 + \beta_1 lnK_t + \beta_2 t, \tag{2}$$

where K is the net capital stock measured in domestic output, β_0 is a constant, β_1 is the long-run net capital stock elasticity of the economic capacity and β_2 is the growth rate of the exogenous productivity of net capital.

Now, assuming that the real exchange rate is constant ($q = 1$), the value of the trade balance (F) is equal to:

$$F_t = M_t - X_t. \tag{3}$$

As shown by Thirlwall and Hussain (1982; see also McCombie and Thirlwall 1997; Moreno-Brid 1998/1999; Barbosa-Filho 2001), the dynamic condition to maintain a

---

1.   The rationale for our choice of countries is as follows: Argentina, Brazil and Mexico, according to the World Development Indicators, are the largest Latin American economies in terms of GDP, whilst Chile holds the largest GDP per capita in the region.
2.   Economic capacity is defined as the desired level of output, given the economy's net capital stock (Shaikh and Moudud 2004).

                    Journal compilation © 2019 Edward Elgar Publishing Ltd

constant position of the trade balance as a percentage of the level of output (Y), can be decomposed as follows:

$$\phi x_t + (1 - \phi)g_t = m_t \qquad \text{if } \phi < 1 \qquad (4)^3$$

or

$$\phi x_t - (1 - \phi)g_t = m_t \qquad \text{if } \phi > 1, \qquad (4')$$

where x, g and m stand for the growth rates of exports, output and imports, respectively, and ϕ is the ratio X to M. Since we are explicitly considering the specific effect of ID and X on the demand for imports, disaggregating g into the growth rates of ID (id) and x, we can rewrite equations (4) and (4') and obtain:

$$\phi x_t + \{[1 - \phi][\lambda id_t + (1 - \lambda)x_t]\} = m_t \qquad \text{if } \phi < 1 \qquad (5)$$

or

$$\phi x_t - \{[1 - \phi][\lambda id_t + (1 - \lambda)x_t]\} = m_t \qquad \text{if } \phi > 1. \qquad (5')$$

Taking time derivatives of equation (1), substituting the result in equations (5) and (5') and solving for id obtains the growth rate of the internal demand for domestic output consistent with a constant position of the trade balance as a percentage of the level of output:

$$id_{tbt} = \frac{[\phi + (1 - \phi)(1 - \lambda) - \alpha_3]x_t - \Psi_{KB}kb_t + \Psi ec_t}{\alpha_2 - (1 - \phi)\lambda} \qquad \text{if } \phi < 1 \qquad (6)$$

or

$$id_{tbt} = \frac{[\phi - (1 - \phi)(1 - \lambda) - \alpha_3]x_t - \Psi_{KB}kb_t + \Psi ec_t}{\alpha_2 + (1 - \phi)\lambda} \qquad \text{if } \phi > 1, \qquad (6')$$

where kb is the growth rate of gross capital stock and ec is the growth rate of economic capacity. Using equations (6) and (6'), we obtain the growth rate of output consistent with a constant position of the trade balance as a percentage of the output level:

$$g_{tbt} = \lambda id_{tbt} + (1 - \lambda)x_t. \qquad (7)$$

Hence g_{tb} is obtained as a function of ec and x, given Ψ_{KB} and Ψ.

Now, following Perrotini and Vázquez-Muñoz (2017), we argue that the natural growth rate is endogenous both to effective demand (*à la* León-Ledesma and Thirlwall 1998; 2000) and to economic capacity (*à la* Lewis 1954). This reasoning is consistent with León-Ledesma and Thirlwall (1998; 2000), who, using Okun's law, estimated the next equation to get the normal natural growth rate (g_{nn}):

$$g_t = \theta_0 + \theta_1 u_t + v_{gt} \qquad (\theta_0 > 0, \theta_1 < 0), \qquad (8)$$

where u is the percentage variations of the unemployment rate, θ_1 is the elasticity of output vis-à-vis the rate of unemployment and v_{gt} is an error term.[4] According to León-Ledesma and Thirlwall (1998 and 2000), θ_0 is equal to g_{nn}; to obtain the

---

3. The ratio F/Y will be constant if the growth rates of F and Y (f and g) are equal.
4. See Boggio and Seravalli (2002) for a critic of the endogeneity of the natural growth rate and the rejoinder by León-Ledesma and Thirlwall (2002).

Journal compilation © 2019 Edward Elgar Publishing Ltd

expansive natural growth rate, León-Ledesma and Thirlwall (1998; 2000) used a dummy variable for the upward shift of the intercept of equation (8) when the economy expands.[5] Here we are concerned with a twofold endogeneity of g_n, that is, with respect to effective demand and ec, which may be written as:

$$g_t = \theta_2 ec_t \sigma_t + \theta_3 u_t + v_{2gt} \qquad (\theta_2 > 0, \theta_3 < 0), \qquad (9)$$

where σ is the utilization ratio of EC (Y/EC) and θ_2 measures the positive or negative shifts of the intercept of equation (9) in the $u - g$ quadrant owing to increases or decreases of σ and/or ec (see Figure 1). We define g_{nn} as the growth rate that keeps the unemployment rate constant and σ is equal to its average value.

Now we can obtain g_n as $\theta_2 ec_t \sigma_t$, from which the normal natural growth rate is defined (g_{nn}) as:

$$g_{nn} = \theta_2 ec_t \sigma_{ave},$$

where σ_{ave} is the average value of σ.

Harrod (1939) defined the warranted growth rate (g_w) as the g for which induced investment is equal to planned investment. Therefore, it is fair to say that g_w is equal to g_{nn} as it implies a particular g for which σ is equal to its normal value; in other words, it entails a g equal to ec, so there are no incentives to modify planned investment. Further, it can be argued that g_w, g_{nn}[6] and g_{tb} are functions of ec:

$$g_w = g_{nn} = f(ec) \qquad (f' > 0)$$
$$g_{tb} = h(ec) \qquad (h' > 0),$$

where f and h denote functions and ′ stands for the first derivative.

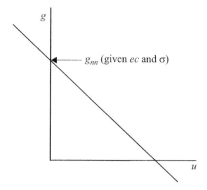

Source: Authors' elaboration.

Figure 1   Determination of the natural growth rate

5.   Empirical estimations of the endogeneity of the natural growth rate are found in León-Ledesma and Thirlwall (1998; 2000), Perrotini and Tlatelpa (2003), León-Ledesma (2006), Ciriaci (2007), Oreiro et al. (2007), Lanzafame (2009; 2010; 2014), Libânio (2009), Vogel (2009), Dray and Thirlwall (2011) and Perrotini and Molerés (2012).
6.   Harrod's definition of the natural growth rate considered the stock of capital: '[t]his is the maximum rate of growth allowed by the increase of population, *accumulation of capital*, technological improvement and the work/leisure preference schedule, supposing that there is always full employment in some sense' (Harrod 1939, p. 30, emphasis added).

3   THE RELATIONSHIP BETWEEN g_w, g_{nn} AND g_{tb}

According to Thirlwall (2001), given the existence of g_w, g_n and g_{tb}, there exist six possible dynamic disequilibrium scenarios which, in turn, can be summarized into two self- aggravating scenarios and one self-correcting scenario. Thirlwall (2001, p. 87) concludes that

> [f]or most countries, it must be true, however, that as long as some countries run payments surpluses through choice, or are literally supply constrained (such as some oil producing countries), the ultimate constraint on growth must be its balance of payments equilibrium growth rate, not the Harrodian natural rate of growth.

In keeping with this view, given that ec determines g_{nn} (g_w) and g_{tb}, we argue that countries are constrained by g_{tb} according to two different possible scenarios shown in Figure 2.

In scenario (a), g_{tb} is more elastic than g_{nn} to ec, in the second g_{nn} is more elastic than g_{tb} to ec. Scenario (a) is self-correcting whilst scenario (b) is self-aggravating. If the economy falls in the scenario (a) and ec is higher (lower) than ec^*, the full employment position is reached while running an increasing trade balance surplus (deficit) and capital outflows (capital inflows). Therefore, the initial disequilibrium gets reduced. On the other hand, if the economy falls in the scenario (b) and ec is higher (lower) than ec^{**}, the economy runs an increasing trade balance deficit (surplus) and capital inflows (capital outflows). Therefore, the initial disequilibrium gets aggravated.

However, it is worth mentioning that, in both cases, the self-correcting and the self-aggravating scenarios, the processes could be interrupted if, in scenario (a), ec happens to be lower than ec^0 or if, in scenario (b), ec is higher than ec^1. In both cases the interruption is brought about by an increase in the economy's external financial fragility, which is a positive function of the discrepancy between g_{nn} and g_{tb}. Should such a situation occur, it could be necessary to implement restrictive economic policies to rein in economic expansion, although in the self-correcting scenario the result of this course of action can be a vicious circle of even greater external financial fragility, the adoption of further restrictive economic policies, an inducement of a larger gap between g_{nn} and g_{tb}, and so on and so forth. Now we turn to an empirical assessment of the preceding theoretical discussion for the cases of Argentina, Brazil, Chile and Mexico.

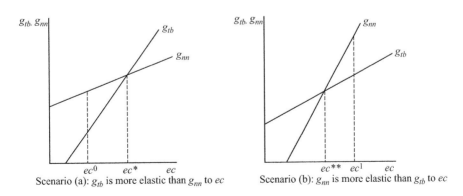

Scenario (a): g_{tb} is more elastic than g_{nn} to ec Scenario (b): g_{nn} is more elastic than g_{tb} to ec

Source: Authors' elaboration.

Figure 2   The relation between g_{nn} (g_w), g_{tb} and ec

4   EMPIRICAL EVIDENCE

We estimate the demand for imports (equation (1))[7] for each of the countries of our sample study using the Bound Test Approach (Pesaran et al. 2001) and information from the World Development Indicators database of the World Bank, the CEPAL-STAT database of the Economic Commission for Latin America and the Caribbean and the Penn World Table version 9.0. All the series are measured in constant local currency; the internal demand for domestic goods was taken as the difference between GDP and exports, the gross capital stock is the sum of the net capital stock (K) in period $t-1$[8] plus the gross investment (gross fixed capital formation) in period t, and EC was obtained estimating equation (2).[9] Table 1 reports the unit root test for the lnM, $lnKB$, $lnID - lnEC$ and $lnX - lnEC$ series.

As can be seen in Table 1, all series are integrated of order one, except $lnKB$ for the cases of Chile and Mexico, and $lnID - lnEC$ for the case of Chile, which are stationary. So, we can use the Bound Test Approach cointegration methodology to estimate equation (1) for each country scrutinized.[10] Table 2 reports the results of our estimations.

According to our results shown in Table 1, Argentina's estimated gross capital stock and income elasticities of the demand for imports have increased from 1991 – the year of its trade liberalization – onwards. Brazil's estimated gross capital stock elasticity of the demand for imports also increased after the inception of trade liberalization in 1991, while its income elasticity of the demand for imports was not affected. By contrast, Chile's gross capital stock and income elasticities of the demand for imports (1.01 and 1.68, respectively, for the entire period) did not change as a result of the trade liberalization that started in 1976. Finally, Mexico's gross capital stock and income elasticities of the demand for imports have also increased since 1986, the year trade liberalization started.

Now let us estimate the natural growth rate (equation (9)) with ordinary least squares (OLS) for the four Latin American countries researched. The data sources used are the World Development Indicators database of the World Bank, the CEPAL-STAT database of the Economic Commission for Latin America and the Caribbean, the Penn World Table version 9.0 and Termómetro de la Economía Mexicana database of Mexico Máxico; and the chosen variables are g = the growth rate of GDP, σ = the GDP to EC ratio and u = the annual percentage variations of the rate of unemployment. Table 3 reports the unit root tests for the g, ec, σ and u series.

As can be seen in Table 3, all series are stationary. Table 4 contains the OLS estimation results for equation (9).

---

7.   Following Thirlwall (1979), we do not include the effect of the percentage variations of the real exchange rate on the growth rate of the demand for imports. Although it is true that some authors (Rodrik 2008) have argued that the real exchange level may be relevant for the determination of the long-run growth rate through its effect on the profitability of the tradable industries and/or exports, this phenomenon is however beyond the scope of the present paper. Moreover, a competitive exchange rate is not free from adverse consequences, so it is no panacea for economic stagnation.
8.   See the description of the determination of K in Appendix 1.
9.   See the description of the estimation of EC in Appendix 1.
10.   This approach is applicable regardless of whether the underlying regressors are purely I(0), purely I(1), mutually cointegrated or any combination of these characteristics. This is, indubitably, a considerable advantage given the low power of the unit root test and the relatively small size of our data for each country.

                      Journal compilation © 2019 Edward Elgar Publishing Ltd

Table 1   Unit root test for lnM, lnKB, lnID – lnEC, lnX – lnEC series: 1950–2017

Variable	ADF	PP	ADFBPT	Variable	ADF	PP	ADFBPT
Argentina				*Argentina*			
lnM	−3.69**	−3.11	–	d(lnM)	−7.03*	−7.02*	–
lnKB	−1.70	−1.47	–	d(lnKB)	−3.04**	−3.17**	–
lnID − lnEC	−2.08	−2.08	–	d(lnID − lnEC)	−7.40*	−7.38*	–
lnX − lnEC	−0.69	−0.48	–	d(lnX − lnEC)	−8.54*	−8.62*	–
Brazil				*Brazil*			
lnM	−2.85	−2.68	–	d(lnM)	−8.10*	−8.14*	–
lnKB	−0.85	−0.34	–	d(lnKB)	−1.53	−1.49	−4.52**[a] (1978)
lnID − lnEC	−3.06**	−3.02**	–	d(lnID − lnEC)	−9.04*	−9.11*	–
lnX − lnEC	0.17	0.27	–	d(lnX − lnEC)	–	–	–
Chile				*Chile*			
lnM	−2.11	−2.25	–	d(lnM)	−7.43*	−7.43*	–
lnKB	−1.64	−0.02	−5.70**[b] (1981)	d(lnKB)	–	–	–
lnID − lnEC	−1.38	−1.53	−6.73*[b] (1981)	d(lnID − lnEC)	–	–	–
lnX − lnEC	−0.45	−0.49	–	d(lnX − lnEC)	−7.92*	−7.93*	–
Mexico				*Mexico*			
lnM	−3.68**	−2.94	–	d(lnM)	−6.68*	−7.29*	–
lnKB	−1.34	−0.42	−4.58**[b] (1981)	d(lnKB)	–	–	–
lnID − lnEC	−0.61	−0.57	–	d(lnID − lnEC)	−6.96*	−6.95*	–
lnX − lnEC	0.75	0.75	–	d(lnX − lnEC)	−7.60*	−7.60*	–

Notes: * and ** are statistically significant at the 1 per cent and 5 per cent levels. $d(\cdot)$ stands for the first difference operator. ADFBPT is the Augmented Dickey Fuller unit root test considering one break point, break year between parentheses.
a. Test was done assuming an additive outlier break type.
b. Tests were done assuming an innovative outlier break type.
All tests were done using the EViews software version 10.0. Level tests for lnM and lnKB assume the existence of intercept and trend, whilst level tests for lnID − lnEC and lnX − lnEC were done assuming the existence of intercept. The number of lags used for the ADF and ADFBPT tests were chosen according to the Schwarz information criterion, whereas the number of Bandwidth used for the PP test were chosen according to the Newey–West criterion.
Sources: Authors' elaboration using data from the World Development Indicators database of the World Bank, the CEPALSTAT database of the Economic Commission for Latin America and the Caribbean and the World Penn Table version 9.0.

          Journal compilation © 2019 Edward Elgar Publishing Ltd

Table 2   Estimation of the import demand function

	Dependent variable: *lnM*			
	Long-run relationship			
Country	Argentina[a]	Brazil	Chile	Mexico
Period	1950–2017	1950–2017	1950–2017	1950–2017
Constant	1.96*	30.00*	–	−6.01*
	(0.43)	(0.54)		(0.90)
lnKB	0.60*	–	1.01*	1.20*
	(0.03)		(0.11)	(0.05)
lnID – lnEC	1.46*	3.18*	0.74*	2.56*
	(0.19)	(0.78)	(0.27)	(0.53)
lnX – lnEC	–	1.38*	0.94*	–
		(0.16)	(0.23)	
D9117	−8.00*	–	–	–
	(1.63)			
D7180	–	0.89*	–	–
		(0.15)		
lnKB·D9117	0.78*	0.01***	–	–
	(0.10)	(0.01)		
lnKB·D8617	–	–	–	0.18*
				(0.02)
(lnX – lnEC)·D9117	0.82*	–	–	–
	(0.12)			
(lnX – lnEC)·D8617	–	–	–	1.33*
				(0.11)
Model type	Restricted constant, no trend	Restricted constant, no trend	No constant, no trend	Restricted constant, no trend
ARDL model	(1, 0, 0, 0, 0)	(4, 4, 4, 2, 0)	(2, 2, 4, 2)	(4, 0, 0, 0)
F-bounds test	–	–	–	–
F-statistic	40.73*	3.72**	8.54*	14.66*
t-bounds test	–	–	–	–
t-statistic	–	–	−4.72*	–
	Adjustment coefficient			
v_{Mt-1}	−0.83*	−0.29*	−0.39*	−0.56*
	(0.05)	(0.06)	(0.06)	(0.06)
t-bounds test	–	–	–	–
t-statistic	–	–	−6.02*	–
Jarque-Bera test	1.67	0.39	0.80	4.35
LM test (*F*-statistic, 1 lag)	1.54	0.01	0.14	2.21
White test (*F*-statistic)[b]	1.88***	0.52	1.48	1.02

Notes: *, ** and *** are statistically significant at the 1 per cent, 5 per cent and 10 per cent level (standard errors in parentheses).
a. Standard errors adjusted by the Newey–West procedure.
b. White tests do not include cross terms.
All estimations were done using the EViews software version 10.0. We use some dummy and composed dummy variables to capture structural breaks; *DXXYY* stands for a dummy variable with value equal to 1 from *19XX(20XX)* to *19YY(20YY)* and 0 otherwise. ARDL model indicates the number of lags of the dependent and independent variables. A complete report of the estimation, including the fixed regressors used in each case, is available on request from the authors.
Sources: Authors' elaboration using data from the World Development Indicators database of the World Bank, the CEPALSTAT database of the Economic Commission for Latin America and the Caribbean and the Penn World Table version 9.0.

Table 3   Unit root test for g, ec·σ and u series

Variable	ADF	PP	ADFBPT
Argentina (1971–2017)			
g	−5.72*	−5.69*	–
ec·σ	−2.89***[a]	−2.92***[a]	–
u	−7.02*	−7.02*	–
Brazil (1973–2017)			
g	−4.56*	−4.48*	–
ec·σ	−1.97	−1.06	−4.96*[c]
			(1988)
u	−5.95*	−5.92*	–
Chile (1976–2017)			
g	−5.74*	−5.72*	–
ec·σ	−3.02**	−2.77***[b]	–
u	−7.60*	−7.63**	–
Mexico (1974–2017)			
g	−5.36*	−5.34*	–
ec·σ	−3.20**	−3.31**	–
u	−5.65*	−5.58*	–

Notes: *, ** and *** are statistically significant at the 1 per cent, 5 per cent and 10 per cent level.
a. 2009 is omitted.
b. 2013 is omitted. For the omitted years, see the notes for Table 4.
c. Test was done assuming an innovative outlier break type.
All tests were done using the EViews software version 10.0. ADFBPT is the Augmented Dickey Fuller unit root test considering one break point; break year between parentheses. All tests were done assuming the existence of intercept, except all the tests for the *u* series, which assumed neither intercept nor trend. The number of lags used for the ADF and ADFBPT tests were chosen in accordance with the Schwarz information criterion, whilst the number of Bandwidth used for the PP test were chosen according to the Newey–West criterion.
Sources: Authors' elaboration using data from the World Development Indicators database of the World Bank, the CEPALSTAT database of the Economic Commission for Latin America and the Caribbean, the World Penn Table version 9.0 and Termómetro de la Economía Mexicana database of Mexico Máxico.

With the results shown in Table 4, we obtain g_{nn} as $\theta_2 ec\sigma_{ave}$ for the countries under inspection. Also, the modified growth rate consistent with a constant position of the trade balance as a percentage of GDP (g_{tbm}) is obtained as:

$$g_{tbm} = \frac{-\alpha_1 kb + \psi ec + [\lambda\phi + (1-\phi)(1-\lambda) - \alpha_3]\bar{x}}{\alpha_2 - (1-\phi)\lambda} + (1-\lambda)\bar{x}, \qquad (10)$$

where $\bar{x}$ is the simple average of x.[11] Figure 3 (see pp. 456–457) shows the relations between g_{nn} and ec and between g_{tb} and ec.

As shown in Figure 3, we obtained positive relations between g_{tb} and ec and between g_{nn} and ec for the four countries and sub-periods scrutinized, except for the

11.   We preferred to use $\bar{x}$ in lieu of x because we are presenting the empirical relation between g_{tb} and ec. When x is used, this relation is shifted up or down according to the exhibited value of x, whereas when using $\bar{x}$ the relation is stable for the period under examination.

   Journal compilation © 2019 Edward Elgar Publishing Ltd

Table 4   Estimation of the output growth rate

Country Period	Dependent variable: g			
	Argentina 1971–2017	Brazil 1973–2017	Chile 1976–2017	Mexico 1974–2017
$ec\cdot\sigma$	0.64*	1.27*	1.76*	0.99*
	(0.20)	(0.15)	(0.14)	(0.11)
u	−0.04**	−0.06*	−0.07*	−0.09*
	(0.02)	(−3.28)	(0.02)	(−0.02)
$D91$	9.91*	–	–	–
	(3.40)	–	–	–
$D92$	10.71*	–	–	–
	(3.39)	–	–	–
$D8190$	–	−3.68*	–	–
	–	(1.18)	–	–
$D82$	–	–	−14.98*	–
	–	–	(3.11)	–
$D83$	–	–	−10.34*	–
	–	–	(2.62)	–
$D9906$	–	–	−4.26*	–
	–	–	(1.12)	–
$u\cdot D9617$	−0.37*	–	–	–
	(−0.07)	–	–	–
R^2	0.63	0.39	0.69	0.53
Jarque–Bera test	0.64	0.36	0.21	0.08
LM test (F-statistic, 1 lag)	0.26	1.08	2.37	1.04
White test (F-statistic)[a]	1.60	1.64	0.88	0.98

Notes: * and ** are statistically significant at the 1 per cent and 5 per cent level (standard errors in parentheses).
a. White tests include cross terms.
All estimations were done using the EViews software version 10.0. Our estimations are very similar to those reported in this table when the year 2009 is omitted for the case of Argentina and the year 2013 for the case of Chile. We use some dummy and composed dummy variables to capture structural breaks; *DXX* stands for a dummy variable with value equal to 1 in *19XX* and 0 otherwise; *DXXYY* stands for a dummy variable with value equal to 1 from *19XX(20XX)* to *19YY(20YY)* and 0 otherwise.
Sources: Authors' elaboration using data from the World Development Indicators database of the World Bank, the CEPALSTAT database of the Economic Commission for Latin America and the Caribbean, the Penn World Table version 9.0 and Termómetro de la Economía Mexicana database of Mexico Máxico.

(negative) relation between g_{tb} and ec in Argentina during sub-period 1975–1990. More specifically, we identified the features shown below, country-wise.

4.1   Argentina

In this case, two relevant sub-periods were found. The first one can be decomposed into two segments, 1971–1974 and 1991–2017. During this time span, the elasticity of g_{tb} vis-à-vis ec was greater than that of g_{nn} with respect to ec, implying a self-correcting scenario. During most of this sub-period the Argentinian economy tends to work below the equilibrium position and closer to g_{nn} than to g_{tb}, which means that Argentina was accumulating capital inflows.

So, at the end of the first segment, and after the Argentinian oil crisis of 1973, the import substitution growth strategy was replaced by an economic liberalization program, which mainly covered domestic issues and the Argentinian government implemented contractive policies to reduce both private and public investments and then to rein in capital inflows. Over the second sub-period, 1975–1990, g_{nn} and g_{tb} were positively and negatively related to ec, respectively,[12] featuring a self-aggravating system hand-in-hand with a strong reduction of g.

Given the bad performance of the Argentinian economy, an Open Trade Liberalization program was implemented during President Menem's administration (in 1991), paving the way for the beginning of the second segment of the first sub-period (1991–2017). In this second segment, g increased, but the economy started to accumulate capital inflows. Consequently, in 2016 president Macri implemented restrictive policies to halt g; the effect of such policies on the relations between g_{nn} and ec and between g_{tb} and ec are yet to be seen.

4.2   Brazil

In Brazil, the elasticity of g_{tb} vis-à-vis ec happened to be higher than that of g_{nn} with respect to ec during the three identified scenarios, which means that all of them are self-correcting scenarios. During the first sub-period (1973–1980), which belongs to the state-led industrialization period, the annual average of g_{nn} (8.51 per cent) was somewhat higher than that of g_{tb} (7.59 per cent), whilst the annual average of g fell in between (8.05 per cent). However, the annual average of the trade balance position was negative, −2.49 percentage points of GDP, which contributed to the foreign debt crisis of 1982.

The $ec - g_{nn}$ relationship shifted down through 1981–1990 (the lost decade), most likely as an outcome of the restrictive economic policies experienced. Consequently, the annual average of both g_{nn} and g were pretty similar, 1.67 per cent and 1.66 per cent respectively, whereas the annual average of g_{tb} was much higher (5.65 per cent).

The $ec - g_{nn}$ relationship shifted up and that of $ec - g_{tb}$ shifted down from (1991) the inception of trade liberalization onwards. These movements implied an increase of the equilibrium value of ec. In turn, the annual average of both g_{tb} and g were about the same, 2.47 per cent and 2.48 per cent respectively, and somewhat higher than the annual average of g_{nn}, 2.02 per cent. It is worth noting that the equilibrium value of g_{nn} and g_{tb} was equal to 0.25 per cent, which implies a depressive economy in comparison with the values exhibited during the first sub-period.

4.3   Chile

The first sub-period ran from 1976 to 1989, and was a self-correcting scenario. The annual averages of g_{nn} and g_{tb} were very similar, 7.05 per cent and 6.80 per cent, and the annual average of g was lower (4.67 per cent). Now, although the Chilean economy escaped fast from the external debt crisis of the early 1980s, our results suggest an aggressive restrictive economic policy was implemented in 1982 in order to reduce g and generate subsequent higher trade balance surpluses to meet international financial liabilities: during 1976–1981 the annual average of the trade balance position

12.   The negative relationship between g_{tb} and ec could have been the result of a strong decline of the elasticity of economic capacity with respect to gross investment, which implied that import substitution allowed by EC was lower than the imports required to generate EC (Vázquez-Muñoz 2018).

                          Journal compilation © 2019 Edward Elgar Publishing Ltd

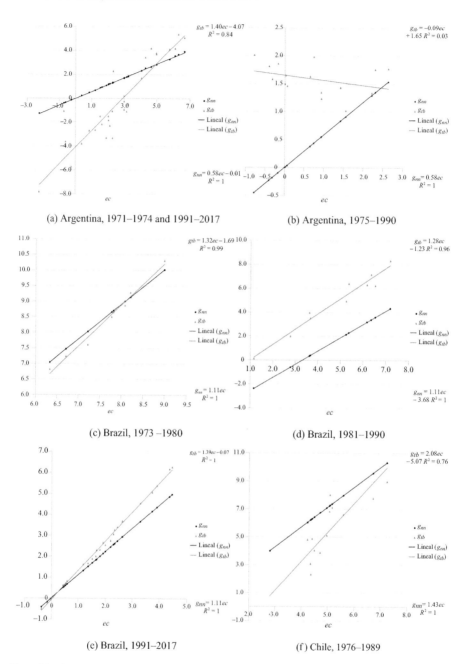

(a) Argentina, 1971–1974 and 1991–2017

(b) Argentina, 1975–1990

(c) Brazil, 1973–1980

(d) Brazil, 1981–1990

(e) Brazil, 1991–2017

(f) Chile, 1976–1989

Notes: Lineal conveys the OLS estimated relations between g_{tb} and ec and between g_{nn} and ec.
Sources: Authors' elaboration using data from the World Development Indicators database of the World Bank, the CEPALSTAT database of the Economic Commission for Latin America and the Caribbean and the Penn World Table version 9.0.

Figure 3   Relation between g_{nn} and ec and between g_{tb} and ec

Journal compilation © 2019 Edward Elgar Publishing Ltd

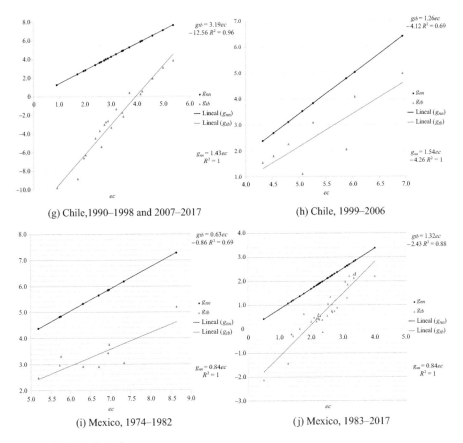

(g) Chile, 1990–1998 and 2007–2017

(h) Chile, 1999–2006

(i) Mexico, 1974–1982

(j) Mexico, 1983–2017

Figure 3   (continued)

was equal to 4.40 percentage points, whilst from 1983 to 1989 it was equal to 10.40 percentage points.

As regards the sub-periods 1990–1998 (a time of deepening of economic liberalization reforms) and 2007–2017 (beginning with leftist governments), the $ec - g_{tb}$ relation shifted down and its slope increased, implying a fall in the equilibrium value of ec. However, the Chilean economy worked far below the equilibrium value of ec; the annual average of g_{nn} and g were pretty similar, 4.46 per cent and 4.98 per cent respectively, but much higher than the annual average of g_{tb}, −1.02 per cent, which represents a decreasing trade balance surplus (decreasing capital outflows).

Finally, throughout the sub-period 1999–2006 the $ec - g_{nn}$ relation shifted down and the $ec - g_{tb}$ relation shifted up, and its slope decreased, resulting in a self-aggravating scenario where the annual average of g_{nn}, g_{tb} and g were 3.97 per cent, 3.29 per cent and 3.67 per cent respectively. In this sub-period, the restrictive economic policy allowed the Chilean economy to experience an annual average of *dxmy* equal to 13.38 percentage points, representing an accumulation of capital outflows that helped the country to cope with external financial fragility. Nonetheless, such an economic policy stand induced a reduction of g.

    Journal compilation © 2019 Edward Elgar Publishing Ltd

4.4   Mexico

It can be argued that Mexico experienced a self-aggravating scenario from 1974 through 1982. Throughout this sub-period the annual average of g (5.92 per cent) was higher than those of g_{nn} and g_{tb} (5.58 per cent and 4.08 per cent respectively). The Mexican economy experienced a high growth regime and increasing trade balance deficits (increasing capital inflows). While those trade deficits may have enhanced ec, they also generated an external financial fragility which led to the 1982 external debt crisis.

During the sub-period 1983–2017, the Mexican government followed IMF-type macroeconomic adjustment economic policies and, beginning in 1986, implemented a radical process of economic liberalization. As a consequence, the $ec - g_{tb}$ relation shifted down and its slope increased, resulting in a self-correcting scenario. However, as in the first sub-period, the annual average of g (2.29 per cent) was somewhat higher than that of g_{nn} (2.06 per cent) in this sub-period. The latter, in turn, was higher than the average of g_{tb} (0.82 per cent). Therefore, the Mexican economy evolved towards a self-correcting scenario involving lower equilibrium values of ec, g_{nn} and g_{tb}.

5   FINAL REMARKS

The main thrust of this article is as follows. We have argued that Thirlwall's (1979) principle that g_{tb} is the critical constraint on growth and bridged a theoretical gap in dynamic theory, a *lacuna* left by Harrod's extension of Keynes's (1936 [1964]) static short-run analysis of effective demand to the long-run setting. We have also attempted to draw together, from Thirlwall's perspective, the analyses of the interaction between economic capacity, the endogeneity of the natural growth rate and the external constraint on output expansion.

Our research led us to identify two possible scenarios, showing the theoretical relations between g_{nn} and g_{tb}, namely the self-correcting scenario where g_{tb} is more elastic than g_{nn} vis-à-vis ec, and the self-aggravating scenario where g_{nn} is more elastic than g_{tb} with respect to ec, that is, ec affects g_{tb} negatively. Moreover, if the economy's external financial fragility increases rapidly, both the self-correcting and the self-aggravating processes could be interrupted by restrictive economic policies. This Thirlwallian-driven narrative, as it were, also led us to empirically assess our central tenet (ec is a determinant of the relations between g_{tb}, g_w and g_{nn}) for the cases of Argentina, Brazil, Chile and Mexico. We found that, in all countries, the relationships between ec and g_{nn} and between ec and g_{tb} are positive, except for the case of Argentina where the relation between g_{tb} and ec was negative in the sub-period 1975–1990.

The main policy implication of the previous analysis can be summarized as follows: our model shows that in the self-correcting scenario the gap between g_{tb} and g_{nn} tends to reduce, albeit some degree of financial fragility is present. If the government tries to tackle financial fragility implementing conventional restrictive economic policies, the position will worsen as such policies will widen the aforementioned gap, shrink the growth rate of output and increase the unemployment. On the contrary, in the self-aggravating scenario the $g_{tb} - g_{nn}$ gap tends to expand, and so does financial fragility. In this case a restrictive economic policy will reduce both financial fragility and the $g_{tb} - g_{nn}$ gap. As g_{nn} is endogenous, the unemployment rate will not increase as a result of lower output growth.

       Journal compilation © 2019 Edward Elgar Publishing Ltd

By and large, most governments of developing economies adopt recessionary policies when faced with slow growth *cum* financial fragility; this policy stand only worsens the economic outlook. A wiser alternative policy would be to enhance capital accumulation with the aim of both easing financial fragility and reducing the balance-of-payments constraint to economic growth, as Thirlwall argued long ago.

REFERENCES

Barbosa-Filho, N. (2001), 'The balance of payments constraint: from balanced trade to sustainable debt', *Banca Nazionale del Lavoro Quarterly Review*, 54(219), 381–400.

Berleman, M. and J.E. Wesselhöft (2014), 'Estimating aggregate capital stocks using the perpetual inventory method: a survey of previous implementations and new empirical evidence for 103 countries', *Review of Economics*, 65(1), 1–34.

Boggio, L. and G. Seravalli (2002), 'Is the natural rate of growth exogenous? A comment', *Banca Nazionale del Lavoro Quarterly Review*, 55(221), 219–227.

Ciriaci, D. (2007), 'Tasso di crescita naturale e crescita cumulativa nelle regioni italiane', *Moneta e Credito*, LX(239), 287–310.

Dray, M. and A.P. Thirlwall (2011), 'The endogeneity of the natural rate of growth for a selection of Asian countries', *Journal of Post Keynesian Economics*, 33(3), 451–468.

Harrod, R.F. (1936), *The Trade Cycle: An Essay*, Oxford: Clarendon Press.

Harrod, R.F. (1939), 'An essay in dynamic theory', *The Economic Journal*, 49(193), 14–33.

Harrod, R.F. (1948), *Towards a Dynamic Economics*, London: Macmillan.

Keynes, J.M. (1936 [1964]), *The General Theory of Employment, Interest and Money*, New York: A Harvest Book/Harcourt.

Lanzafame, M. (2009), 'Is regional growth in Italy endogenous?', *Regional Studies*, 43(8), 1001–1013.

Lanzafame, M. (2010), 'The endogeneity of the natural rate of growth in the regions of Italy', *International Review of Applied Economics*, 24(5), 533–552.

Lanzafame, M. (2014), 'The balance of payments-constrained growth rate and the natural rate of growth: new empirical evidence', *Cambridge Journal of Economics*, 38(4), 817–838.

León-Ledesma M.A. (2006), 'Cycles, aggregate demand and growth', in P. Arestis, J.S.L. McCombie and R. Vickerman (eds), *Growth and Economic Development: Essays in Honour of A. P. Thirlwall*, Cheltenham, UK and Northampton, MA: Edward Elgar Publishing, pp. 82–95.

León-Ledesma, M.A. and A.P. Thirlwall (1998), 'The endogeneity of the Natural Rate of Growth', Discussion Paper No 9821, Department of Economics, University of Kent.

León-Ledesma, M.A. and A.P. Thirlwall (2000), 'Is the natural rate of growth exogenous?', *PSL Quarterly Review*, 53(215), 433–445.

León-Ledesma, M.A. and A.P. Thirlwall (2002), 'Is the natural rate of growth exogenous? A reply', *Banca Nazionale del Lavoro Quarterly Review*, 55(221), 229–232.

Lewis, A. (1954), 'Economic development with unlimited supplies of labour', *The Manchester School*, 22(2), 139–191.

Libânio, G.A. (2009), 'Aggregate demand and the endogeneity of the natural rate of growth: evidence from Latin American economies', *Cambridge Journal of Economics*, 33(5), 967–984.

McCombie, J.S.L. and A.P. Thirlwall (1997), 'Economic growth and the balance of payments constraint revisited', in P. Arestis, P. Palma and M. Sawyer (eds), *Markets, Unemployment and Economic Policy: Essays in Honour of G. Harcourt*, vol. 2, Cheltenham, UK and Lyme, NH: Edward Elgar Publishing, pp. 498–511.

Moreno-Brid, J.C. (1998/1999), 'On capital flows and the balance-of-payments-constrained growth model', *Journal of Post Keynesian Economics*, 21(2), 283–298.

Nell, K.S. and A.P. Thirlwall (2017), 'Why does the productivity of investment vary across countries?', *PSL Quarterly Review*, 70(282), 213–245.

Journal compilation © 2019 Edward Elgar Publishing Ltd

Oreiro, J.L., L. Nakabashi, G.J. Costa da Silva and G.J. Guimarães e Souza (2007), 'The economics of demand-led growth: theory and evidence for Brazil', *CEPAL Review*, (106), 151–168.

Perrotini, I. and E. Molerés (2012), 'On Harrod's natural rate of growth and the role of demand: an empirical assessment', *Panorama Económico*, VIII(15), 1–25.

Perrotini, I. and D. Tlatelpa (2003), 'Crecimiento endógeno y demanda en las economías de América del Norte', *Momento Económico*, (128), 10–15.

Perrotini, I. and J.A. Vázquez-Muñoz (2017), 'Endogenous growth and economic capacity: theory and empirical evidence for the NAFTA countries', *PSL Quarterly Review*, 70(282), 247–282.

Pesaran, M.H., Y. Shin and R.J. Smith (2001), 'Bound Testing Approaches to the analysis of level relationships', *Journal of Applied Econometrics*, 16(3), 289–326.

Rodrik, D. (2008), 'The real exchange rate and economic activity', *Brookings Papers on Economic Activity*, 39(2), 365–439.

Shaikh, A.M. (2016), *Capitalism*, New York: Oxford University Press.

Shaikh, A.M. and J. Moudud (2004), 'Measuring capacity utilization in OECD countries: a cointegration method', The Levy Economics Institute, Working Paper No 415.

Thirlwall, A.P. (1979), 'The balance of payments constraint as an explanation of the international growth rate differences', *Banca Nazionale del Lavoro Quarterly Review*, 32(128), 45–53.

Thirlwall, A.P. (2001), 'The relationship between the warranted growth rate, the natural rate, and the balance of payments equilibrium growth rate', *Journal of Post-Keynesian Economics*, 24(1), 81–88.

Thirlwall, A.P. and M.N. Hussain (1982), 'The balance of payments constraint, capital flows and growth rate differences between developing countries', *Oxford Economic Papers*, 34(3), 498–510.

Vázquez-Muñoz, J.A. (2018), 'La Acumulación de Capital como un determinante de la Tasa de Crecimiento de la Ley de Thirlwall', *Contaduría y Administración*, 63(3), 1232–1261.

Vogel, L. (2009), 'The endogeneity of the natural rate of growth: an empirical study for Latin-American countries', *International Review of Applied Economics*, 23(1), 41–53.

    Journal compilation © 2019 Edward Elgar Publishing Ltd

APPENDIX 1

A1.1 Determination of the net capital stock

Following Berleman and Wesselhöft (2014), we built the net capital stock using the growth rate of the net capital stock $(\hat{K})$:

$$\hat{K} = \frac{I_t}{K_{t-1}} - \delta_t, \tag{A1}$$

where I_t is gross investment in period t, K_{t-1} is the net capital stock in period $t-1$, and δ_t is the depreciation rate of capital in period t. Then, solving equation (A1) for K_{t-1} *we obtain:*

$$K_{t-1} = \frac{I_t}{\hat{K} + \delta_t}. \tag{A2}$$

Now, we assume that $\hat{K}$ is equal to the trend growth rate of gross investment $(\hat{I})$. Therefore, we can rewrite equation (A2) as:

$$K_{t-1} = \frac{I_t}{\hat{I} + \delta_t}. \tag{A2$'$}$$

Then, we have $\hat{I}$ through the OLS estimation of the following equation:

$$ln(I_t) = \beta_3 + \beta_4 t + v_{It}, \tag{A3}$$

where β_i are the parameters to be estimated, t is a trend variable and v_{It} is an error term; β_4 is the estimated value of $\hat{I}$. Finally, we can build the net capital stock series using the gross investment series, the depreciation rate series and $\hat{I}$ as follows:

$$K_t = K_{t-1} + I_t - \delta K_{t-1}. \tag{A4}$$

To estimate equation (A3) for the countries scrutinized, we obtained information from the World Development Indicators database of the World Bank, the CEPALSTAT database of the Economic Commission for Latin America and the Caribbean and the World Penn Table version 9.0. We used Gross Fixed Capital Formation, measured in constant local currency, as the gross investment series. The estimations of equation (A3) were not included due to space constraints, however they are available from the authors upon request. Once we estimated the trend growth rate of gross investment, we had the net capital stock series for each country in our sample using equation (A4).[13]

---

13. We used the depreciation rate series reported in the World Penn Table version 9.0 for each researched country.

  Journal compilation © 2019 Edward Elgar Publishing Ltd

A1.2   Estimation of the economic capacity series

Following Shaikh and Moudud (2004) and Shaikh (2016), we obtained the economic capacity series for each country estimating equation (A5) with the Bound Test Approach:

$$lnY_t = \gamma_0 + \gamma_1 lnK_t + v_{Yt}, \tag{A5}^{14}$$

where γ_i are the parameters to be estimated and v_{Yt} is an error term. GDP, measured in constant local currency, is the variable Y. The estimations of equation (A5) were not included due to space constraints; they are available from the authors upon request. Using the long-run relationship, we can estimate the economic capacity (EC) series for each scrutinized country.

14.   Following Shaikh (2016), we adjusted K with the ratio Gross Fixed Capital Formation price index to the GDP price index in order to eliminate any spurious relative price term from the cointegration relationship between output (Y) and the net stock of capital (K).

Review of Keynesian Economics, Vol. 7 No. 4, Winter 2019, pp. 37–59

Thirlwall's law and the terms of trade: a parsimonious extension of the balance-of-payments-constrained growth model*

Esteban Pérez Caldentey
Chief, Financing for Development Unit, Economic Development Division, Economic Commission for Latin America and the Caribbean, Santiago, Chile

Juan Carlos Moreno-Brid
Professor of Economics, UNAM, Mexico City, Mexico

This paper extends the balance-of-payments-constrained (BoPC) growth model and Thirlwall's law to include the terms of trade with and without capital flows. Without capital flows a positive (negative) change in the terms of trade by improving (worsening) export performance can ceteris paribus *augment (reduce) the rate of growth of an economy compatible with balance of payments' long-run equilibrium. With the inclusion of capital flows the BoPC dynamics become more complex. Assuming no changes in the real exchange rate and in the import elasticity of demand, an improvement in the terms of trade can increase the level of the external deficit compatible with BoPC growth. This results from the terms-of-trade effects on the purchasing of exports and on foreign-capital inflows. The positive effect of an improvement in the terms of trade may be partially offset by an appreciation of the real exchange rate and an increase in the import elasticity of demand, when the model is extended to allow for such interactions in the analysis.*

Keywords: *balance-of-payments constrained growth, Thirlwall's law, terms of trade, capital flows, income*

JEL codes: *F32, F41, F43, F63*

1 INTRODUCTION

One of the most important distinguishing features of Post-Keynesian economics is the role attributed to demand in the determination of economic performance both in the short and the long run and the importance of the external sector in setting limits or placing a restriction to economic growth. Thirlwall's law, enunciated by Anthony P. Thirlwall four decades ago (Thirlwall 1979), exemplifies this approach. It specifies the rate of growth that a given economy can achieve without running in balance-of-payments difficulties. More precisely, Thirlwall's law states that the rate of growth

---

* The opinions here expressed are the authors' own and may not coincide with the institutions with which they are affiliated. The authors wish to thank Carlos Julio Moreno (Universidad Santo Tomás, Bogotá, Colombia) for valuable research assistance. The authors are grateful to Martín Puchet, John McCombie, Anthony P. Thirlwall and an anonymous referee for very useful comments on an earlier version of this paper.

Journal compilation © 2019 Edward Elgar Publishing Ltd
The Lypiatts, 15 Lansdown Road, Cheltenham, Glos GL50 2JA, UK
and The William Pratt House, 9 Dewey Court, Northampton MA 01060-3815, USA

of a country, say country A, relative to that of the rest of the world is proportional to the ratio of the income elasticity of demand for A's exports by the rest of the world divided by A's income elasticity of demand for imports.

Thirlwall's law is derived from the balance-of-payments-constrained (BoPC) growth model which is based on several simplifying assumptions – including an infinite elasticity of supply, that the foreign and the domestic price-elasticity of import (export) demand have the same magnitude in absolute terms, that the price of exports is equal to the domestic price and that the import price equals the price of foreign goods that compete with exports that permit an improved analytical tractability of the external sector. This also allows Thirlwall's law and the BoPC growth model to provide important insights into the workings of economies in the real world such as that demand constraints can bite before supply constraints do, that income effects prevail over substitution effects, and that structural change can, through its effect on the income elasticities of imports and exports, alter the balance-of-payments equilibrium rate of growth.

In keeping with the simplicity and at the same time realism of this approach we provide a parsimonious extension of the BoPC growth model and of Thirlwall's law that consists in including the terms of trade in both formulations with and without capital flows. This responds to an observed stylized fact. Namely, since the 2000s, commodity prices – in particular, of energy and metals and minerals – have registered price-significant gains. The rates of growth of commodity indices of agriculture, energy and metals and minerals have resembled those of the 1970s, while prices have remained at an all-time high level. The inclusion of capital flows also responds to another stylized fact. Many economies, especially smaller ones, receive capital flows on a permanent basis. Moreover, in general, for commodity-producing and -exporting countries, movements in the terms of trade tend to be positively associated with movement in long-term capital flows (for example, foreign direct investment) so that the inclusion of both variables permit us to integrate into the analysis the real and monetary (financial) sides of the balance of payments.

The inclusion of the terms of trade (if they are significant) implies that the rates of growth compatible with balance-of-payments equilibrium should be calculated on the basis of income rather than gross domestic product (GDP). The inclusion of capital flows implies that the basic balance rather the current account is the correct measure of a country's external position.

In this paper, when capital flows are not taken into consideration, a positive (negative) change in the terms of trade by improving (worsening) export performance can *ceteris paribus* augment (reduce) the rate of growth of an economy compatible with balance of payments' long-run equilibrium. At the same time, a positive (negative) change in the terms of trade is associated with an appreciation (depreciation) of the real exchange rate which can have a negative effect on long-term growth. In so far as the real exchange rate is not a significant determinant of the long-term rate of growth (as is shown in most of the literature on BoPC growth models), Dutch Disease effects are ruled out and the terms of trade have a positive effect on the long-run trajectory of an economy.

When capital flows are combined with the terms of trade, the BoPC dynamics become more complex. We initially assume away changes in the real exchange rate and in the import elasticity of demand, and focus on the positive effect of an improvement in the terms of trade, that is, an increase in the level of the external deficit compatible with BoPC growth. This results, on the one hand, on a permanent effect directly provoked by the improvement of the terms of trade and its effect on the purchasing power of exports; and, on the other hand, on a temporary effect associated with the foreign-capital inflows induced by the terms-of-trade improvement. The positive effect of an improvement in the terms of trade may be partially offset by an appreciation of the real exchange rate and an increase in the import elasticity of demand, if the model is extended to allow for such interactions in the analysis.

The paper comprises seven sections. Following the introduction, Section 2 presents empirical evidence on commodity-price trends since the beginning of the 2000s. Section 3 presents the canonical balance-of-payments-constrained growth model. Section 4 presents the modified model to take into account the terms of trade. Section 5 provides a discussion of the theoretical and policy implications that follow from the inclusion of the terms of trade. Section 6 presents the modified model with capital flows and the terms of trade. Section 7 concludes.

2   THE EVOLUTION OF COMMODITY PRICES AND THE TERMS OF TRADE

The analysis of commodity prices in the period running from 1960 to 2018 shows, in the majority of cases, an upward trend beginning in the year 2000 which has continued for nearly two decades.[1] This is shown in Figure 1 for a sample of commodity prices for agriculture (Arabica coffee and soybean meal), energy (natural gas and crude oil), and minerals and metals (iron ore and copper).

With the exception of natural gas, the average prices for these commodities have trended upwards since the 2000s. During the periods 2000–2008 and 2010–2018, the price of Arabica coffee increased, on average, from US$2.1 to US$3.4 per kilogram and that of soybeans from US$249 to US$436 per metric ton. In the energy sector, the price of crude oil rose, on average, from US$45 to US$78 per barrel. Finally, in the minerals and metals sector the price of iron and of copper increased, on average, from US$59 to US$103 and from US$3563 to US$6844 per metric ton.

Also, the empirical evidence shows statistically significant cross-correlation coefficients among all commodity groups since 2000 (see Table 1). This adds to the evidence in support of the hypothesis of an upward and generalized trend movement in commodity prices.

1.   This is attributed to both real and financial factors. On the real side the emphasis has been placed, among other factors, on the role played by China in the world economy and as a major importer and consumer of raw materials. Currently China's economy is one the six largest economies in the world. China represents 8 percent of world GDP, 17 percent of world investment, 5 percent of world final consumption, and 10 percent of world exports (measured in constant 2005 dollars). Since the start of economic reforms in 1979 and until very recently, China's real GDP increased at an annual average rate of 10 percent, expanding its real GDP 14-fold. In terms of financial factors, the argument has been made that commodities have taken on an increasing role as financial assets, in the sense that prices respond to changes in expectations about future demand conditions rather than to actual supply-and-demand market conditions. Some of the manifestations of the growing role of commodities as financial assets include the growth in activity in commodity future markets including commodity derivatives, the strengthening of the co-movement among different commodity prices and between commodities and stock markets, and the use of commodities as collaterals for loans and credit. Erten and Ocampo (2012) argue that super-cycles of commodities tend to last about 30 to 40 years. Using data from the second half of the nineteenth century (1870) to 2008, both authors identify the presence of three super-cycles of similar-duration commodities (1894–1932; 1932–1971; 1971–1999). As the latest data show, the commodity cycle that started in early 2000 has lasted for nearly two decades.

                    Journal compilation © 2019 Edward Elgar Publishing Ltd

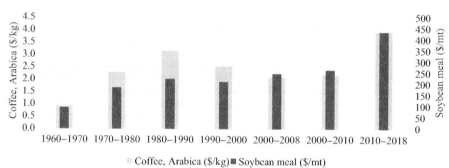

Average prices (US$) of commodities: Agriculture

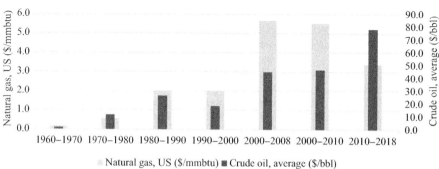

Average prices (US$) of commodities: Energy

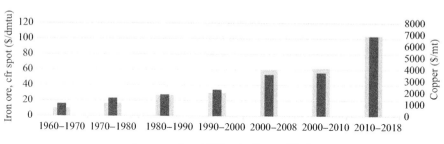

Average prices (US$) of commodities: Minerals and Metals

Note: Crude oil, average ($/bbl) dollars per barrel; natural gas, US ($/mmbtu) dollars per 1 million British thermal units (MMBtu); soybean meal ($/mt) dollars per metric ton; Coffee, Arabic ($/kg) dollars per 1 kilogram; iron ore, cfr spot ($/dmtu) dollars per dry metric tonne; copper ($/mt) dollars per metric ton.
Source: World Bank (2019).

Figure 1   Evolution of average commodity prices for agriculture, energy, and minerals and metals, US$, 1960–2018 (quarterly data)

Table 1 Simple correlation coefficients for selected commodity groups, 1960–2018 (quarterly data)

	1960–1970	1970–1980	1980–1990	1990–2000	2000–2010	2000–2008	2010–2018	2000–2018
Agriculture and energy	0.34**	0.44**	0.13	−0.06	0.55***	0.34**	0.62**	0.60**
Energy and metals and minerals	−0.10	0.60**	0.02	0.44**	0.61**	0.36**	0.74**	0.66**
Agriculture and metals and minerals	−0.02	0.67**	0.69**	0.30**	0.49**	0.25**	0.64**	0.58**

Note: The statistical significance of the correlation coefficient was determined on the basis of the formula $\rho = \frac{r\sqrt{n-2}}{\sqrt{1-r^2}}$, where r is the simple correlation coefficient and n the number of observations. ρ follows a student-t distribution. ** denotes significance at the 95 percent level of confidence.

Source: Author's own, on the basis of World Bank (2019).

Finally, a standard cycle analysis for the period 1960–2013 based on the identification of turning points of commodity prices[2] shows that the expansionary phase of the cycle for the commodity grouping including agriculture, energy, and metals and minerals was either more pronounced or tended to last longer. This can be seen by computing the amplitude and duration of the expansionary phase (from the trough to the peak) of the cycle as well as by obtaining the cumulative effect (see Table 2).[3]

The upward movement in commodity prices has translated into a continuing increase in the terms of trade for exporters of commodity products (petroleum, agriculture and minerals, and mining). Contrarily, the exporters of manufactured goods have witnessed a decline in the terms of trade (See Figure 2).

Finally, a simple correlation exercise between the evolution of the terms of trade and economic growth for the selected exporters of minerals and mining products and exporters of petroleum products for the period 2001–2017 shows, first, that 90 percent and 68 percent of the countries in each sample had a positive correlation coefficient; and, second, that the median correlation coefficient for each grouping reached 0.36 and 0.24 for the same period.

3   THE CANONICAL BALANCE-OF-PAYMENTS-CONSTRAINED GROWTH MODEL

In this section we set out the canonical BoPC growth model developed by A.P. Thirlwall and J. McCombie.[4] According to this approach, an economy faces a binding external

2.   The Classical cycle methodology here used views the cycle as a set of turning points of a time series representing the level of aggregate economic activity without consideration to a trend (Harding and Pagan 2001; 2002). The inflection points of the series are then used as a basis to analyse the cycle in terms of a series of indicators such as the duration, intensity of an expansion (trough-to-peak) and a contraction (peak-to-trough), and the degree of coincidence between two given time series. Central to this approach is the identification of the turning points of a series. The turning points of a series are usually identified using the Bry and Boschan (1971) algorithm developed originally for monthly data and adapted to deal with quarterly observation by Harding and Pagan (2002). The algorithm consists in identifying local maxima and minima for a given series following a logarithmic transformation using specific censoring rules (Bry and Boschan 1971; Male 2009). These include the specification of two quarters for a minimum duration for a single phase, and a minimum duration of five quarters for a complete cycle (Harding and Pagan 2002; 2005). The peak for a series y_t is found when y_t is greater than $y_{t\mp k}$ for $k = 1.2$. Similarly, the trough for a series y_t is found when y_t is less than $y_{t\mp k}$ for $k = 1.2$. The algorithm excludes the occurrence of two successive peaks or troughs.

3.   The duration (D) of an expansion is defined as the ratio of the total number of quarters of expansion to the total number of peaks in a series. That is, $D = \dfrac{\sum_{t=1}^{T} S_t}{\sum_{t=1}^{T-1}(1-S_{t+1})S_t}$, where S is a binary variable which takes a 1 during an expansion and a 0 during a contraction. The numerator in (1) $\left(\sum_{t=1}^{T} S_t\right)$ denotes the total duration of expansions and the denominator $\left(\sum_{t=1}^{T-1}(1-S_{t+1})S_t\right)$ measures the number of peaks in the series. For its part, the intensity or amplitude (A) of the expansion is measured as the ratio of the total change in aggregate economic activity to the total number of peaks. That is: $A = \dfrac{\sum_{t=1}^{T} S_t \Delta Y_t}{\sum_{t=1}^{T-1}(1-S_{t+1})S_t}$, where Y is a measure of economic activity (GDP in our cases) and the numerator $\left(\sum_{t=1}^{T} S_t \Delta Y_t\right)$ is the total change in economic activity. The cumulative effect is defined as the product of the amplitude of the expansion by its duration divided by two $\left(CM = \frac{A*D}{2}\right)$.

4.   See for example McCombie and Thirlwall (1994; 1999); Thirlwall (1979; 1982; 1997; 2011).

Table 2 *Turning points and cycle indicators for selected commodity groups (estimation period: 1960m1–2016m11)*

Agriculture					Energy					Metals and minerals				
Troughs	Peaks	Duration months	Amplitude (%)	Cumulative effect	Troughs	Peaks	Duration months	Amplitude (%)	Cumulative effect	Troughs	Peaks	Duration months	Amplitude (%)	Cumulative effect
1960m11	1964m1	39	14.4	281.0	1980m11	1986m7	69	46.6	1607.7	1962m9	1966m4	44	8.1	177.9
1965m8	1966m8	13	9.3	60.3	1987m7	1988m10	16	17.7	141.9	1967m4	1970m4	37	5.6	103.6
1968m8	1970M11	28	14.7	205.1	1990m10	1992m1	16	1.1	9.1	1971m1	1972m4	16	2.6	21.0
1971m11	1974m11	37	93.7	1733.0	1992m9	1994m3	19	13.5	128.1	1972m10	1974m4	19	68.9	654.1
1975m12	1977m4	17	46.0	390.7	1996m12	1998m12	25	16.0	200.0	1975m11	1980m2	52	49.8	1295.2
1977m10	1980m11	38	37.3	708.7	2000m11	2001m12	14	2.3	16.1	1982m6	1983m8	15	15.0	112.5
1982m10	1984m5	20	30.8	307.7	2008m7	2009m2	8	31.1	124.4	1985m11	1988m6	32	23.1	369.8
1986m6	1988m6	23	29.7	341.6	2011m4	2012m6	15	14.3	107.3	1990m2	1990m9	8	2.6	10.4
1991m7	1992m1	7	2.9	10.3	2013m9	2016m1	29	22.1	320.5	1991m12	1992m7	8	0.9	3.6
1992m10	1994m9	24	26.4	316.4	–	–	–	–	–	1993m11	1995m1	15	10.4	78.1
1995m9	1996m5	9	8.8	39.7	–	–	–	–	–	1996m10	1997m8	11	1.6	8.8
1999m7	2000m2	8	4.1	16.5	–	–	–	–	–	1999m3	2000m1	11	2.0	11.0
2001m10	2004m3	30	35.7	535.5	–	–	–	–	–	2001m10	2008m3	78	91.1	3551.7
2004m10	2008m6	45	70.4	1583.5	–	–	–	–	–	2008m12	2011m2	27	48.2	650.4
2008m12	2011m2	27	48.2	650.4	–	–	–	–	–	2012m8	2013m2	7	7.1	24.9
2011m12	2012m7	8	7.9	31.7	–	–	–	–	–	–	–	–	–	–

Source: Author's own, on the basis of World Bank (2019).

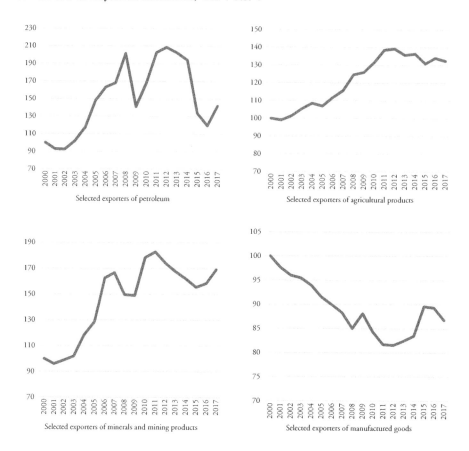

Note: The selected exporters of petroleum include Algeria, Angola, Azerbaijan, Brunei Darussalam, Chad, Colombia, Congo, Equatorial Guinea, Gabon, Iran, Iraq, Kazakhstan, Kuwait, Libya, Nigeria, Oman, Qatar, Russian Federation, Saudi Arabia, Trinidad and Tobago, Turkmenistan, and Venezuela. The selected producers of agricultural products include American Samoa, Argentina, Belize, Benin, Côte D'Ivoire, Cuba, Ecuador, Ethiopia, Falkland Islands (Malvinas), Fiji, Guatemala, Guinea-Bissau, Kenya, Malawi, Maldives, Paraguay, Republic of Moldova, Seychelles, Solomon Islands, Somalia, Uganda, Uruguay, and Zimbabwe. The selected producers of minerals and mining include Armenia, Botswana, Burkina Faso, Chile, Democratic Republic of Congo, Eritrea, Guinea, Guyana, Jamaica, Kyrgyzstan, Mali, Mauritania, Mongolia, Namibia, Peru, Sierra Leone, Suriname, Tajikistan, and Zambia. The selected producers of manufactured goods include Bangladesh, Belarus, China, Hong Kong, India, Malaysia, Mexico, Morocco, Pakistan, Philippines, Singapore, South Korea, Taiwan, Thailand, Turkey, Ukraine, and Vietnam.
Source: Authors' own, on the basis of UNCTAD (2019).

Figure 2   Terms of trade for selected exporters of petroleum, agricultural products, minerals and mining products, and manufactured goods, 2000–2017 (annual data)

constraint when its, say, performance in world trade and its interaction with international financial markets sets an upper limit to the rate of the economy at which the economy can expand without incurring a critical disequilibrium in its balance of payments. And this rate of growth is lower than the rate that internal conditions (such as the rate of both recorded and disguised unemployment and the degree of capacity

Journal compilation © 2019 Edward Elgar Publishing Ltd

utilization) would warrant.[5] This definition assumes that BoPC economies tend to grow at a rate lower than the one compatible with full employment and, more generally, full capacity utilization. One implication of this view is that the organization of the global financial architecture has a restrictive bias on world economic expansion, actually preventing countries subject to external constraints from realizing their growth potential.[6]

The external constraint presupposes that an economy is unlikely to be able to maintain a current-account deficit for a long period, except if they receive significant net inflows of foreign direct investment or official assistance flows on a permanent or long-term basis (McCombie and Thirlwall 1999). In the latter case, the relevant variable to assess the external constraint is the basic balance (the current account (CA) plus long-term financial flows (FF)). (See Section 4, below.)

Thus, according to a very simple model of the BoPC growth approach, countries have to keep their current account (or basic balance) in equilibrium in the long run. In other words:

$$CC - FF = 0 \Longleftrightarrow P_x X + FF = P_m ME, \tag{1}$$

where CA = current account; X and M = volume of exports and imports; E = nominal exchange rate; P_x and P_m = price of exports expressed in local currency and price of imports expressed in the foreign currency of the imports; and FF = financial flows in nominal terms.[7]

The specification of both equations follows the conventional approach known as the imperfect substitutes model. It is built upon the assumption that domestic and foreign goods are not perfect substitutes. And, by taking for granted an infinite elasticity of supply, the model claims that exports and imports are essentially demand-determined. It thus argues that the two main determinants of – say – imports are the importing country's income, the own price of imports, and the domestic price of locally produced tradable goods and services. Correspondingly, the main determinants of exports are the rest of the world's income and the price of export goods relative to the price of foreign-made goods that compete with them in the international market. In addition, monetary illusion is typically assumed away and a zero-homogeneity restriction is imposed to guarantee that the foreign and the domestic price-elasticity of import (export) demand have the same magnitude in absolute terms. Since the model is a two-goods model, it is generally assumed that the price of exports is equal to the domestic price (that is, $P_x = P_d$) and that the import price is equal to the price of foreign goods that compete with exports (that is, $P_m = P_f$).

Setting out from equation (1), the real growth rate of an economy can be expressed as a function of the real exchange rate [1], changes in long-term financial flows measured in real terms [2], and exogenous changes in the level of real external aggregate demand [3]. The real exchange rate (RER) is defined as the ratio of the price of the foreign good to the domestic good expressed in terms of the local currency

5.   See McCombie and Thirlwall (1999, p. 49).
6.   Keynes made a similar criticism of the international monetary system prior to Bretton Woods (and his 'clearing union' consisted precisely in replacing the contractionary bias with an expansionary character (Keynes 1980, p. 74: 'This transfer would substitute an expansionist, in place of a contractionist, pressure on world trade.'
7.   For the sake of simplicity, we assume away other components of the current account such as interest payments, remittances, and profit transfers.

                           Journal compilation © 2019 Edward Elgar Publishing Ltd

($RER = \frac{P_d}{P_f * e}$ in levels and ($\dot{p}_d - \dot{e} - \dot{p}_f$) in rates of change). Another way to put it is that it measures domestic costs in proportion to foreign costs expressed in the same currency.

$$\dot{y}_{bpc} = \underbrace{\frac{(1 + \theta\psi + \gamma)(\dot{p}_d - \dot{e} - \dot{p}_f)}{\xi}}_{[1]} + \underbrace{\frac{(1 - \theta)(\dot{f} - \dot{p}_d)}{\xi}}_{[2]} + \underbrace{\frac{\pi\dot{y}_{RM}}{\xi}}_{[3]}, \tag{2}$$

where the variables include $\dot{y}_{bpc}$ = rate of variation in the real growth of a country that is compatible with the external equilibrium as defined earlier; $\dot{p}_d$ = rate of variation of domestic prices (domestic inflation); $\dot{p}_f$ = rate of variation of external prices (imported inflation); $\dot{e}$ = rate of variation in the nominal exchange rate; $\dot{f}$ = rate of variation in real financial flows; and $\dot{y}_{RM}$ = rate of variation of real growth in the rest of the world.

The parameters comprise: ψ, γ = price elasticities of exports and imports, $\psi, \gamma < 0$; ξ, π = income elasticities of imports and exports, $\xi, \pi > 0$; θ and $(1 - \theta)$ = proportion of current-account debits financed from export earnings and financial flows, respectively.

According to (2), the real growth rate of an economy is positively related to external demand growth weighted by the import-and-export-elasticity ratio, to a depreciation of the real exchange rate, and to higher rates of growth in long-term financial flows.[8]

There are four ways that the external constraint on growth can be eased: (i) a permanent increase in the rate of growth in external demand; (ii) a permanent increase in the rate of growth in long-term financial flows; (iii) a permanent depreciation in the real exchange rate; and (iv) the implementation of policies for structural change in the countries of the periphery capable of reducing (epsilon) and/or increasing (pi). Equation (2) can be simplified to focus the analysis on certain issues connected with these four alternatives. For example, an assumption that changes over time in the real exchange rate tend to cancel out or amount to little variation in the long run results in the growth rate compatible with the balance-of-payments constraint being expressed with reference to financial flows and aggregate demand in the rest of the world.[9]

$$\dot{y}_{bpc} = \frac{(1 - \theta)(\dot{f} - \dot{p}_d)}{\xi} + \frac{\pi\dot{y}_{RM}}{\xi}. \tag{3}$$

In the case where the current account remains in balance over the long run (that is, where $\theta = 1$ and $(1 - \theta) = 0$), the growth rate compatible with the balance-of-payments constraint depends exclusively on the growth rate of the rest of the world and the income elasticities of exports and imports.

$$\dot{y}_{bpc} = \frac{\pi\dot{y}_{RM}}{\xi}. \tag{4}$$

8.   These make it possible to finance long-run growth to a greater degree than a permanent zero-current-account deficit would allow (McCombie and Thirlwall 1994).
9.   According to Thirlwall, the relative prices measured in a common currency (that is, the real exchange rates) do not vary too much in the long term (in other words, the Marshall–Lerner condition is fulfilled: Thirlwall 1979, p. 49). In fact, the hypothesis that relative prices expressed in a common currency do not vary too much in the long term is due to different types of factors: price changes which conform to variations in nominal exchange rates; the existence of highly competitive markets; the existence of oligopolistic market structures; the existence of wage-bargaining mechanisms at the national level (McCombie and Thirlwall 1994, p. 320; McCombie 2009; Davidson 1992).

     Journal compilation © 2019 Edward Elgar Publishing Ltd

This formulation came to be known as Thirlwall's law. According to it, the long-term growth of an economy compatible with balance-of-payments equilibrium depends on the ratio of its export and import income elasticities and on the rate of growth of the rest of the world.

4   THE CANONICAL BALANCE-OF-PAYMENTS-CONSTRAINED GROWTH MODEL AND THIRLWALL'S LAW WITH THE TERMS OF TRADE

In equation (3) the terms of trade have been assumed to have no influence on the BoPC growth rate of the economy. However, given their importance, a simple and straightforward extension of the analytical model can be put forward to explicitly consider the influence of the terms of trade. The terms of trade (TOT) are defined as the ratio of export prices (P_X) to import prices (P_M) expressed in domestic currency. That is,

$$TOT = \frac{P_X}{P_M * e}. \tag{5}$$

The terms of trade measure the rate of exchange of imports per unit of exports; that is, the volume of imports that can be obtained with one unit of exports. The terms of trade are presented in terms of indices for a given base year and, as a result, reflect the proportional change in the price of exports and imports. In a two-goods model, since the price of exports is equal to the domestic price (that is, $P_x = P_d$) and the import price equals the price of foreign goods that compete with exports (that is, $P_m = P_f$), the terms of trade coincide with the real exchange rate $(RER = \frac{P_d}{P_f * e} = TOT = \frac{P_X}{P_M * e})$.[10]

In order to differentiate between both variables, it is necessary to introduce (at least) a third good, a domestically produced good, and its price need not coincide with the price of the export good $(P_d \neq P_X)$. As a result, $RER = \frac{P_d}{P_f * e} \neq TOT = \frac{P_X}{P_M * e}$.

The distinction between the real exchange rate (RER) and the terms of trade (TOT) involves two important modifications to the canonical balance-of-payments-constrained growth model presented in equation (2). First, the terms of trade (TOT) must be included as an explanatory variable in the export and import functions.

$$X = f(RER, TOT, Y_{RW}) = b \left[\frac{P_d}{P_M * e} \right]^\Psi * \left(\frac{P_X}{P_M} \right)^\alpha * (Y_{RW})^\pi \tag{6}$$

$$M = f(RER, TOT, Y) = a \left[\frac{P_M * e}{P_d} \right]^\gamma * \left(\frac{P_M}{P_X} \right)^\beta * (Y)^\xi, \tag{7}$$

where, α, β = the export and import elasticities with respect to the terms of trade (TOT) and $\alpha > 0$ and $\beta < 0$.

10.   This is the reason why in some formulations (for example McCombie and Thirlwall 1999, p. 48) the first term of the BoPC growth equation (see above equation (2)) is said to refer to the terms-of-trade effect rather than the real exchange rate.

            Journal compilation © 2019 Edward Elgar Publishing Ltd

Equations (5) and (6) are used to obtain the rate of growth compatible with balance-of-payments equilibrium taking into account the terms of trade. That is,

$$\dot{y}_{bpc} = \underbrace{\frac{(\theta\psi + \gamma)(\dot{p}_d - \dot{e} - \dot{p}_f)}{\xi}}_{[1]} + \underbrace{\frac{(1-\theta)(\dot{f} - \dot{p}_d)}{\xi}}_{[2]} + \underbrace{\frac{\pi\dot{y}_{RM}}{\xi}}_{[3]}$$

$$+ \underbrace{\frac{\theta\dot{p}_x - \dot{p}_m - \dot{e}}{\xi} + \frac{(\alpha + \beta)(\dot{p}_x - \dot{p}_m - \dot{e})}{\xi}}_{[4]}. \tag{8}$$

In equation (8) the balance-of-payments-constrained rate of growth depends now on the real exchange rate [1], changes in long-term financial flows measured in real terms [2], and exogenous changes in the level of real external aggregate demand [3] and the terms of trade [4] captured by the term: $\frac{\theta\dot{p}_x - \dot{p}_m - \dot{e}}{\xi} + \frac{(\alpha + \beta)(\dot{p}_x - \dot{p}_m - \dot{e})}{\xi}$.

According to equation (7) a long-term deterioration (improvement) in the terms of trade brings about a reduction (increase) in the long-term rate of expansion of the economy consistent with balance-of-payments equilibrium. In addition, the effect of the terms of trade will also depend on the strength of the import and export elasticities with respect to the terms of trade. If $\alpha > \beta$, $(\alpha < \beta)$, in absolute terms, the overall effect of both elasticities will be positive (negative).

In the case where the current-account remains in balance over the long run (that is, where $\theta = 1$ and $(1 - \theta) = 0$) and the variation in the real exchange rate is equal to zero, equation (8) reduces to:

$$\dot{y}_{bpc} = \frac{\pi\dot{y}_{RM}}{\xi} + \frac{(\alpha + \beta + 1)\dot{tot}}{\xi}. \tag{9}$$

If, in addition, we postulate that the rate of growth of the rest of the world multiplied by the income elasticity of exports equals the rate of growth of exports (that is, $\pi\dot{y}_{RM} = \dot{x}$), equation (9) becomes:

$$\dot{y}_{bpc} = \frac{\dot{x}}{\xi} + \frac{(\alpha + \beta + 1)\dot{tot}}{\xi}. \tag{9a}$$

Accordingly, Thirlwall's law being modified by taking into account variations in the terms of trade implies that the long-run growth trajectory of an economy compatible with balance-of-payments equilibrium is determined by the rate of growth of exports, the rate of growth of the terms of trade, the income elasticity of imports, and the elasticities of imports and exports to the terms of trade.

The incorporation of the terms of trade in the canonical balance-of-payments-constrained growth model opens up important issues for consideration at the theorical level and also for policy analysis. The following section examines some of these implications, including: (i) the possibility of expanding the level of generality of the balance-of-payments-constrained growth model; (ii) getting the binding external constraint right; (iii) the relation between the terms of trade and the real exchange rate; and (iv) the interdependence between the terms of trade and the import and export income elasticities.

     Journal compilation © 2019 Edward Elgar Publishing Ltd

5   THE BALANCE-OF-PAYMENTS-CONSTRAINED GROWTH MODEL WITH THE TERMS OF TRADE: SOME IMPLICATIONS

5.1   A greater level of analytical generality

The inclusion of the terms of trade in the specification of the balance-of-payments-constrained growth model has important implications. For one thing, it makes the model more general. If the effect of the terms of trade is greater or less than one ($tot \lessgtr 1$), the rate of growth compatible with balance-of-payments equilibrium depends not only on the factors affecting the rate of growth of the rest of the world, and those determining the income elasticities (and price elasticities if these are statistically significant), but also those determining the international production and price of commodities which may depend on the economic conditions of particular countries (such as China for metals and Arab oil-producing countries for energy) and/or on the conditions and structure of financial markets and their *modus operandi*.[11] In this sense, financial markets not only play the role of reinforcing the balance-of-payments constraint as argued by McCombie and Thirlwall (1994) but can also have the opposite effect, as illustrated by their influence on the commodity boom that took place from the beginning of the 2000s until the global financial crisis (2008–2009), as well as during 2010–2011.[12]

5.2   Getting the binding external constraint right (in an extended version)

The inclusion of the terms of trade requires us to make the distinction between GDP and gross national income in the analysis of economic growth. A positive (negative) terms-of-trade effect (TOT) means that income is greater (smaller) than GDP and thus, when TOT effects are significant, the use of GDP to measure economic growth could underestimate or overestimate the rate of expansion of an economy compatible with balance-of-payments equilibrium. In this sense, the relevant variable for growth is gross national income rather than real GDP.

This can be easily seen by expressing gross national disposable income (NI_t) as gross domestic product (GDP_t) plus net factor payments to the rest of the world

---

11.   A number of studies find that commodity prices are determined in financial markets. See for example Gromping (2006) and Vernengo and Pérez Caldentey (2019). In the case of commodities markets, global banks have played an important role in three ways (Lane 2012). Global banks have become important commodity dealers in over-the-counter derivatives markets. At the global level, commodity trading revenues were estimated at US$2 billion in 2003, reaching a peak of over US$14 billion in 2008 and then experiencing a decline, being currently at US$4 billion (Meyer and Hume 2014). However, available data on commodity derivatives show values that are much higher, and these closely follow the commodity super-cycle. In 2003, the value of the notional amounts of commodity derivatives outstanding at the global level was estimated at US$1.6 trillion, increasing to US$14 trillion in June 2008. Currently the value of global commodity derivatives stands at US$2.1 trillion (BIS 2019). In addition, global banks have provided a significant share of lending to commodity dealers and, more importantly, in some cases have become highly interconnected with commodity dealers (commodity-trading firms). Finally, global banks have become involved in the physical trading of commodities by, in the same way as commodity-trading firms, holding physical inventories, making markets in commodities, and by providing shipping and commodity storage (Lane 2012).
12.   See McCombie and Thirlwall (1994, pp. 454–455).

$(NPRW_t)$, current transfers (CT_t), and the terms-of-trade effect(TTE_t), that is, $NI_t = GDP_t + NPRW_t + CT_c + TTE_t$.

The terms-of-trade effect equals the volume of goods and services exports (X_t) (or exports at constant prices) multiplied by the change in the trade price index:

$$TTE_t = X_t \frac{(P_x - P_m)}{P_m} = X_t\left(\frac{P_x}{P_m} - 1\right),$$

where P_x, P_m = unit price indices for exports and imports. Replacing TTE_t into the definition of national income gives $NI_t = GDP_t + NPRW_t + CT_c + X_t\left(\frac{P_x}{P_m} - 1\right)$. According to this expression, if other factors remain unchanged, an improvement in the terms of trade $(\Delta\frac{P_x}{P_m})$ translates into a rise in gross national disposable income (NI_t). From this expression, it is possible to decompose the difference between gross national disposable income (NI_t) and gross domestic product (GDP_t) into net factor payments to the rest of the world $(NPRW_t)$, current transfers (CT_t), and the terms-of-trade effect(TTE_t).

According to the above reasoning, in the presence of terms-of-trade (TOT) effects, GDP is an inaccurate proxy for the external constraint. If the terms-of-trade (TOT) effect is positive (negative), GDP underestimates (overestimates) the binding constraint, and, in this situation, there is more (less) space to undertake expansionary policies.

5.3   The relation between the terms of trade and the real exchange rate

In principle there is no reason to expect a systematic relation between the real exchange rate and the terms of trade, either in the long run or in the short run, given that the evolution of the RER is subject to a certain degree to the effects of the decisions of the monetary authorities and of the evolution of capital flows too. Figure 3 shows the absence of a significant relationship between both variables for a set of 94 countries for the period 2000–2017.

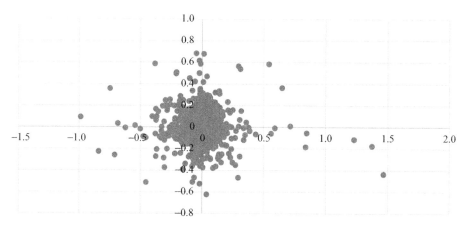

Source: World Bank (2019) and IMF (2019).

Figure 3   Scatter-plot of the rate of variation of the terms of trade and the real exchange rate, 2000–2017 (annual data)

                                    Journal compilation © 2019 Edward Elgar Publishing Ltd

However, one can identify instances where the real exchange rate and the terms of trade may be correlated for certain periods. The experience of many developing economies, in particular those of Latin American economies (the most recent being during the commodity boom of the 2000s), has tended to show a positive association between the improvement of the terms of trade and the appreciation of the exchange rate in real terms.

The implications may be important. If we postulate that the real exchange rate is not constant over time, then an improvement of the terms of trade (TOT) can have two opposing effects on the balance-of-payments-constrained growth of an economy. On the one hand, to the extent that such improvement is accompanied by an appreciation of the real exchange rate, it will tend to increase imports and reduce exports and thus to undermine the BoPC growth rate of output. On the other hand, such an improvement has a direct, favorable effect on the value of exports and thus on the rate of growth of output. The final net effect on the BoPC growth of output will depend on whether the magnitude of the terms-of-trade impact via the real exchange rate is greater than, equal to, or smaller than the magnitude of its direct effect on the unit value of exports.

5.4   The interdependence between the terms of trade and the income and export elasticities

Another important issue is to what extent can the income elasticities of exports and imports be taken as invariable in the long run in the presence of persistent improvements in the terms of trade? In this regard, is it the case that the long-term improvement in the terms of trade will, in the absence of industrial policies and exchange-rate policies, tend to shift the economic structure away from manufacturing, weaken the domestic backward and forward linkages, and deindustrialize and foster the reprimarization of an economy, thus raising the long-term income elasticity of imports, reducing the corresponding elasticity of exports, and eventually undermining the growth of an economy that is consistent with balance-of-payments equilibrium?

Latin America exemplifies this situation. Before the commodity boom, Latin American raw material and natural-based resource manufacturing exports represented 44 percent of the total in 2000–2001 at the beginning of the commodity boom. In 2008–2009, these exports represented 59 percent of the total. Concomitantly, the percentage of high- and medium-technology manufacturing exports declined from 44 percent to 33 percent of the total for the same periods.[13]

As Blecker and Setterfield (2019) and Cimoli and Porcile (2015) *inter alia* have stressed, the magnitude of the income elasticities of exports and imports reflect the productive structure (the supply side) of an economy and its capacity of produce key consumption and investment goods as well as intermediate inputs that may successfully compete in the domestic and world markets. The vast literature on the Dutch Disease and the so-called curse of natural resources provides valuable theoretical and empirical insights on how large improvements in the terms of trade in an economy, linked to a commodity boom, may weaken its manufacturing production and exports, as well as reduce the income elasticity of its exports and augment the income elasticity of its imports.

Also, as has been amply documented, this deindustrialization effect may be exacerbated if the surge in the terms of trade is accompanied by an appreciation of the real

---

13.   These estimations are based on ECLAC data which classify exports by technological intensity into high-, medium-, and low-technology manufactures, natural-based manufactures, and raw material (ECLAC 2019).

                                    Journal compilation © 2019 Edward Elgar Publishing Ltd

exchange rate. Market pressures towards the appreciation of the real exchange rate may spring from the inflow of foreign short- and long-term capital that tends to accompany many episodes of significant improvements in the terms of trade that are perceived to last during long periods of time. Given all these dynamics, when the commodity boom tends to wind down, the economy faces an even more binding balance-of-payments constraint on its long-term economic growth reflected in a lower ratio between its income elasticities of exports and imports *cum* capital flight.

It is somewhat paradoxical that the BoPC growth literature has not yet explicitly considered the influence of the terms of trade given its potentially strong interrelations with the foreign-capital movements, the real exchange rate, the productive structure and its non-price competitiveness, and, thus, the long-term growth potential of an economy.

To take into account the above-mentioned potential impacts of the evolution of the terms of trade on the rate of BoPC growth, it is useful to revise the canonical models of Thirlwall's law in order to allow for net changes in the capital account of the balance of payments. For this purpose, we proceed in the next section to consider an interesting analytical extension of the BoPC growth model put forward by one of the authors 20 years ago that explicitly focuses on long-term BoPC growth in the context of net foreign-capital inflows and the presence of persistent trade deficits in the context of sustainable trajectories of accumulation of foreign debt.

6   TERMS OF TRADE, CAPITAL FLOWS, AND THE BALANCE-OF-PAYMENTS CONSTRAINT ON ECONOMIC GROWTH

One of the first extensions of the BoPC growth model was introduced in order to capture the possibility of growth trajectories consistent with persistent, sustainable trade deficits. In its original formulation, the assumption of a long-term trade balance $(X = M)$ inherently implied that capital flows could not serve to finance persistent trade deficits.

However, there is ample empirical evidence of semi-industrialized nations that have been on long-term growth paths with persistent trade deficits but whose magnitudes do not expand significantly relative to GDP. The economic history of the developing world shows many examples of expanding economies with persistent trade deficits for long periods of time financed by foreign-capital inflows.

The two most well-known extensions, in this direction, of the BoPC growth model are McCombie and Thirlwall (1994) and Moreno-Brid (1998/1999), both of which put forward alternative stock–flow models in this tradition, allowing for long-term net capital inflows that guarantee a stable debt–income ratio.[14] In the latter case, the formulation assumes a long-term stable ratio of the trade balance as a proportion of GDP. In this sub-section, we take this model as a starting point to put forward an alternative of the BoPC growth model that not only allows for net capital flows, but also allows for the effects of the terms of trade (independently of the real exchange rate) on the long-term growth path of an economy.

The model of Moreno-Brid (1998/1999) consists essentially of the following four equations:

$$\dot{x} = \eta(\dot{p}_d - \dot{p}_f) + \pi\dot{z} \tag{10}$$

14.   See also McCombie and Thirlwall (2003).

                    Journal compilation © 2019 Edward Elgar Publishing Ltd

$$\dot{m} = \psi(\dot{p}_f - \dot{p}_d) + \xi\dot{y} \tag{11}$$

$$\dot{B} = 0 = (\mu\dot{m} - (\mu - 1)\dot{x} - \mu(\dot{p}_d - \dot{p}_f) - \dot{y}) \tag{12}$$

$$\mu = \frac{\dot{p}_f m}{(\dot{p}_f m - \dot{p}_d x)}. \tag{13}$$

Equations (10) and (11) are the conventional functions for exports and imports. Equation (12) specifies that the long-term balance-of-payments constraint is defined as a constant trade deficit as a proportion of GDP, where such a proportion is expressed as 'B.' Finally, to facilitate the algebraic expressions, identity (13) specifies that the proportion of imports relative to the trade deficit is defined as μ.

The solution of this model gives the following expression of $\dot{y}$, the long-term growth of GDP consistent with a trade deficit that is invariable as a proportion of GDP.

$$\dot{y} = \frac{[\mu(1 + \psi + \eta) - \eta](\dot{p}_d - \dot{p}_f)}{\xi\mu - 1} + (\mu - 1)\frac{\pi\dot{z}}{\xi\mu - 1}. \tag{14}$$

As the original model explains, it can be reasonably assumed that the numerator is different from zero.[15]

In addition, given that by construction,

$$\mu = \frac{1}{1 - \theta},$$

where θ is the initial ratio of the value of exports relative to imports (by assumption smaller than 1.0).

$$\theta = \frac{p_d X}{p_f m}.$$

Then equation (14) can also be expressed as:

$$\dot{y} = \frac{(1 + \psi + \theta\eta)(\dot{p}_d - \dot{p}_f)}{\xi - (1 - \theta)} + \theta\frac{\pi\dot{z}}{\xi - (1 - \theta)}. \tag{15}$$

Clearly, as equation (15) shows, in this extended model the BoPC growth rate $\dot{y}$ is influenced by the initial magnitude of the trade deficit, and thus implicitly too by the initial magnitude of the terms of trade. The original paper, in order to explore the stability properties, provided a graphical illustration of this extended model (see Figure 4).

Where line Q in Figure 4 represents the import demand function, (11) $\dot{m} = \psi(\dot{p}_f - \dot{p}_d) + \mu\dot{y}$. Line B is derived from equations (10) and (12), and represents all pairs of growth rates of GDP and of imports – given the terms of trade – that

---

15. As Moreno-Brid (1998/1999, p. 290) explained, 'the non-negativity [of the denominator] is met if the structure of the domestic economy is such that increase in real domestic income [that is not the result of a surge of exports] will unavoidably lead to a higher trade deficit.'

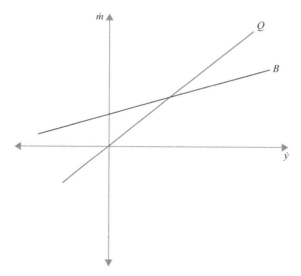

Figure 4   Graphical illustration of Thirlwall's model extended to include capital flows

satisfy the balance-of-payments constraint of maintaining a trade deficit as a constant proportion of GDP.

$$B = \{\dot{y}, \dot{m}\}/[0 = \dot{m} - \theta\pi y_{RM} - ((1 + \theta\eta)(\dot{p}_d - \dot{p}_f) - (1 - \theta)\dot{y}]\}. \qquad (16)$$

Which can also be expressed as

$$\dot{m} = \theta\pi\dot{y}_{RM} + (1 + \theta\eta)(\dot{p}_d - \dot{p}_f) + (1 - \theta)\dot{y}. \qquad (17)$$

The alternative we put forward below of this extended version of the BoPC growth model is built in the same spirit of the extension that we presented in the first section of this paper; that is, it is very parsimonious but not algebraically fully formally derived from the new long-term BoPC equilibrium condition defined as a stable trade deficit as a proportion of GDP.[16] However, we believe that it serves as an illustration of how the analytical scope of the BoPC growth model can be widened to cover the numerous cases of developing economies subject to significant shocks in their terms of trade and their induced effects on foreign-capital inflows.

A straightforward, simple way to extend the BoPC growth model is to start from its most synthetic expression given by equations (11) and (16), illustrated in Figure 5. Now, as long as we work with GDP and not with national income – which includes by definition a component that allows for the effect of a change in the terms of

16. The precise algebraic formulation of the revised model, to allow the impact of variations of the terms of trade, independently of those of the real exchange rate, forcefully requires us to take into account at least three different price indices, P_m, P_x, and P_y, and then work through the corresponding formulations but with the equilibrium condition expressed:

$$B = \frac{P_m M - P_x X}{P_y Y}.$$

    Journal compilation © 2019 Edward Elgar Publishing Ltd

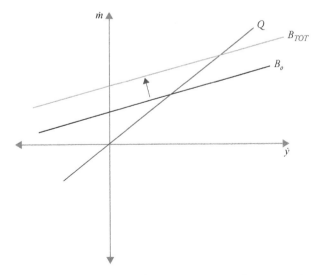

Figure 5   Impact of a once-and-for-all improvement in the terms of trade on B

trade – the import demand equation remains unaffected by any long-term improvement or deterioration of the terms of trade. However, this is not the same with equation (16). In it we introduce two modifications to take into account such effects. The first one, in a manner that is analogous to equations (6)–(9a) where we extended the canonical version of Thirlwall's law, defines a term 'tòt' – greater than, equal to, or smaller than 1.0, depending on whether we assume an improvement, no change, or a deterioration of the terms of trade – and we introduce it in a first approximation as an additional factor of exports or foreign demand. Note that if the import demand function would change as a result of variations in the terms of trade it would merely reinforce the changes in function B. Thus equation (17) is transformed to:

$$\dot{m} = t\dot{o}t + [\theta\pi\dot{y}_{RM} + (1 + \theta\eta)(\dot{p}_d - \dot{p}_f) + (1 - \theta)\dot{y}]. \tag{17a}$$

From here it follows that a permanent improvement of the terms of trade will shift line B upwards while maintaining unaltered line Q (the import demand) as well as the slope of line B (see Figure 4).

Another extension of the model is to consider the effects of changes in the terms of trade on the BoPC growth by allowing for a long-term shift in net foreign-capital inflows as a proportion of GDP. In other words, we now modify the assumption of long-term external equilibrium to allow for, say, a once-and-for-all increase (reduction) in the long-term magnitude of the trade deficit as a proportion of GDP associated with a long-term improvement in the terms of trade. By way of illustration, we may assume that a BoPC economy whose long-term trade deficit is 3 percent of GDP when subject to a significantly favorable and permanent shock in its terms of trade may witness an increase in its sustainable trade deficit to, say, 5 percent of GDP.

An immediate or simple way to incorporate this capital-flow-induced effect in the algebraic formulation of this revised BoPC growth model is to change the key assumption that $\frac{dB}{dt} = 0$, so that it may actually increase when subject to an increase in the terms of trade from its initial pre-shock proportion B_o to its final post-shock proportion B_{TOT}. We assume, for the sake of illustration, that $B_{TOT} - B_o = 0.02$, and that a gradual approximation to its new level (say, as a function of the time since the rise in the terms of trade) occurs. This can be expressed as:

$$B_t = B_o + B_{TOT} - \frac{0.02}{t}, \tag{18}$$

for all 't' after the increase in the terms of trade. Taking the rate of change of B, defined in equation (18), we obtain:

$$\dot{B} = \frac{0.02}{t^2}. \tag{19}$$

Now introducing the right-hand side of equation (19) into the right-hand side of equation (17a), to reflect this gradual, progressively slower shift of the trade deficit from its initial equilibrium B_o as a proportion of GDP to its new equilibrium B_{TOT}, we get this new expression:

$$\dot{m} = \frac{0.02}{t^2} + \{\dot{tot} + [\theta\pi\dot{y}_{RM} + (1+\theta\eta)(\dot{p}_d - \dot{p}_f) + (1-\theta)\dot{y}]\}. \tag{17b}$$

Thus, following this procedure, we see that the induced inflow of foreign capital will bring about an additional (though temporary) upward shift in line B, over and above the one directly caused by the improvement in the terms of trade.

As can be clearly illustrated by Figure 5, a persistent once-and-for-all positive improvement in the terms of trade will, *ceteris paribus*, alleviate the balance-of-payments constraint on the economy, and thus allow for a higher long-term rate of growth of GDP compatible with a stable trade deficit as a proportion of GDP. Such alleviation has two components: (i) a permanent one directly provoked by the improvement of the terms of trade and its effect on the purchasing of exports; and (ii) a temporary one associated with the foreign-capital inflows induced by the terms-of-trade improvement. This latter effect tends to weaken in time and eventually disappear as the magnitude of such induced capital inflows becomes progressively smaller relative to GDP.

So far in this analysis, we have only considered positive influences of an improvement in the terms of trade on the BoPC growth rate of the economy. This outcome rests on two key assumptions. The first is that the real exchange rate remains constant and especially that it does not appreciate! If this is not the case, then the intercept of the import demand function will augment, and the intercept of the B curve will decrease, somewhat undermining the positive effects of the BoPC growth rate brought about by the terms-of-trade improvement (see Figure 6, where lines B_o and Q depict the initial equilibrium growth paths of imports and GDP). Preventing a significant appreciation of the real exchange rate in the midst a most favorable improvement in the terms of trade and in the induced capital inflow that tends to accompany it is far from an easy task. This requires an empirical analysis to examine the relation between the evolution of the terms of trade and the real exchange rate for a number of selected countries.

A second obstacle that may arise as a consequence of a significant improvement in the terms of trade being perceived to be long-lasting, in particular when it is associated with a boom in the international price of its natural resources, is the increase in the income elasticity of its imports and the reduction of the income elasticity of its exports

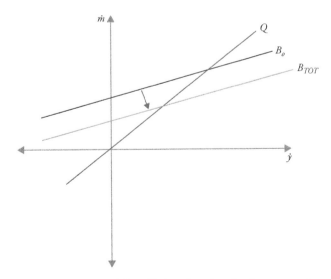

Figure 6   Impact of a once-and-for-all deterioration in the terms of trade on B

discussed previously. Such phenomena –sometimes referred to as premature deindustrialization or export reprimarization – has been a major concern, a major issue of analysis in the empirical literature of the 'Dutch Disease.'

When such changes in income elasticities occur, the balance-of-payments constraint can become drastic and acutely more binding when the natural resource boom ends. Indeed, as can be easily illustrated, the favorable impacts related to the increase in the purchasing power of exports and the inflow of foreign capital can be suddenly reversed. However, restoring the income elasticities of trade to the levels that prevailed before the natural resource boom may be extremely difficult, as they reflect deep changes in the economy's productive and export structures. To begin to revert these changes requires ambitious technology and innovations policies in particular to create or strengthen sophisticated industries, oriented to boost the local producers' competitiveness in the international and domestic markets. A far from easy task, particularly when such policies have been neglected during the boom years, as was the case for many developing economies in the period 2002–2008.

7   CONCLUSION

One of the major stylized facts of the past two decades has been the trend increase in the majority of commodity prices. This has translated into an improvement in the terms of trade for commodity-producing and -exporting countries, whereas manufacturing exporters and producers have witnessed a decline in the terms of trade. Yet, in spite of their importance and with a few exceptions (Gadea et al. 1999), the terms of trade have not been taken into account in a systematic way in open-economy macroeconomics, including in Post-Keynesian international economics.

In this paper we make a parsimonious inclusion of the terms of trade into the canonical BoPC growth model and into Thirlwall's law, one of the major contributions to Post-Keynesian economics of the past 40 years. Thirlwall's law incorporates some of the main insights of Keynes's *General Theory of Employment, Interest and Money* (1936) – such as that demand constraints bite before supply constraints do, that equilibrium with unemployment is a key feature of market economies, that income effects are more important than substitution effects, and that money is not neutral in the short and long run to an open economy.

The introduction of the terms of trade widens the application of the BoPC growth model and permits us to extract important insights on the impact of the terms of trade.

The impact of the terms of trade on the rate of growth of an economy compatible with balance-of-payments equilibrium depends on several factors: (i) changes in the real exchange rate; (ii) changes in capital flows; (iii) changes in the purchasing power of exports; and (iv) changes in the income elasticity of imports. The fact that these factors do vary in the same direction and may offset each other's impact on the BoPC rate of growth gives rise to rich balance-of-payments dynamics as well as opening the door to study and analysis of specific country source cases.

In addition, the analysis here presented has important implications for the macroeconomics of an open economy, and more specifically of a small open economy. An increase in the terms of trade means that income rather than GDP is the relevant variable for assessing the growth of an economy. Similarly, since increases in the terms of trade are accompanied by capital inflows, the relevant variable for gauging the external position of an economy is the basic balance rather than the current account. Finally, the paper points to the need to further analyse whether an improvement in the terms of trade can permanently soften the external constraint and whether increased capital flows will eventually lead to a hardening of the external constraint due to external debt-payment obligations.

REFERENCES

BIS (Bank for International Settlements) (2019), *OTC Commodity Derivatives Data*, Geneva: BIS.

Blecker, R. and M. Setterfield (2019), *Heterodox Macroeconomics: Models of Demand, Distribution and Growth*, Cheltenham, UK and Northampton, MA: Edward Elgar Publishing.

Bry, G. and C. Boschan (1971), *Cyclical Analysis of Time Series: Selected Procedures and Computer Programs*, New York: National Bureau of Economic Research.

Cimoli, M. and G. Porcile (2015), 'Productividad y cambio estructural: el estructuralismo y su diálogo con otras corrientes heterodoxas,' in A. Bárcena and A. Prado (eds), *Neo-estructuralismo y corrientes heterodoxas en América Latina y el Caribe a inicios del siglo XXI*, Santiago, Chile: ECLAC, pp. 225–242.

Davidson, P. (1992), *International Money and the Real World*, New York: St. Martin's Press.

ECLAC (2019), *Trade Statistics*, Santiago, Chile: ECLAC.

Erten, B. and J.A. Ocampo (2012), 'Super-cycles of commodity prices since the mid-nineteenth century,' DESA Working Paper, No 110 (ST/ESA/2012/DWP/110), New York: United Nations.

Gadea, D., M. Serrano Sanz, and M. Sabate (1999), 'Economic growth and the long run balance of payments constraint in Spain,' *Journal of International Trade and Economic Development*, 8(4), 389–417.

Gromping, U. (2006), 'Relative importance for linear regression in R: the package relaimpo,' *Journal of Statistical Software*, 17(1), 1–27.

Harding, D. and A. Pagan (2001), 'Extracting, analysing and using cyclical information,' Munich Personal RePEc Archive (MPRA) Working Paper, 15 August, available at: https://mpra.ub.uni-muenchen.de/15/.

Harding, D. and A. Pagan (2002), 'Dissecting the cycle: a methodological investigation,' *Journal of Monetary Economics*, 49, 365–381.

Harding, D. and A. Pagan (2005), 'A suggested framework for classifying the modes of cycle research,' *Journal of Applied Econometrics*, 20(2), 151–159.

IMF (2009), *World Economic Outlook*, Washington, DC: IMF.

IMF (2019), *International Financial Statistics, 2000–2019*, Washington, DC: IMF.

Keynes, J.M. (1936 [1964]), *The General Theory of Employment, Interest and Money*, New York: Harcourt Brace Jovanovic.

Keynes, J.M. (1980), *The Collected Writings of John Maynard Keynes, Volume XXV: Activities 1940–1944*, D. Moggridge (ed.), New York: Cambridge University Press.

Lane, T. (2012), 'Financing commodity markets: remarks,' Mimeo, BIS.

Male, R.L. (2009), *Developing Country Business Cycles: Characterizing the Cycle and Investigating the Output Persistence Problem*, PhD Thesis, University of York, Department of Economics and Related Studies.

McCombie, J. (2009), 'Economic growth and the balance of payments constraint: an introduction,' Cambridge, UK: Cambridge Centre for Economic and Public Policy, University of Cambridge.

McCombie J.S.L. and A.P. Thirlwall (1994), *Economic Growth and the Balance-of-Payments Constraint*, New York: St. Martin's Press.

McCombie J.S.L. and A.P. Thirlwall (1999), 'Growth in an international context: a post Keynesian view,' in J. Deprez and J.T. Harvey (eds), *Foundations of International Economics: Post Keynesian Perspectives*, New York: Routledge, pp. 35–90.

McCombie, J.S.L. and A.P. Thirlwall (2003), 'Capital flows, interest payments and the balance of payments constrained growth model: a theoretical and empirical analysis,' *Metroeconomica*, 54, 346–365.

Meyer, G. and N. Hume (2014), 'Wall Street banks count commodities trading profits,' *Financial Times*, 14 May.

Moreno-Brid, J.C. (1998/1999), 'On capital flows and the balance-of-payments-constrained growth model,' *Journal of Post Keynesian Economics*, 21(2), 283–298.

Thirlwall, A.P. (1979), 'The balance-of-payments constraint as an explanation of international growth rate differences,' *BNL Quarterly Review*, 32(128), 45–53.

Thirlwall, A.P. (1982), 'The Harrod trade multiplier and the importance of export-led growth,' *Pakistan Journal of Applied Economics*, 1(1), 1–21.

Thirlwall, A.P. (1997), 'Reflections on the concept of balance-of-payments-constrained growth,' *Journal of Post Keynesian Economics*, 19(3), 337–385.

Thirlwall, A.P. (2011), 'Balance of payments constrained growth models: history and overview,' *PSL Quarterly Review*, 64(259), 307–351.

UNCTAD (2019), *Commodity Statistics*, Geneva: UNCTAD.

Vernengo M. and E. Pérez Caldentey (2019), 'International rentiers, finance and income distribution: a Latin American perspective,' Draft Mimeo.

World Bank (2019), *Commodity Pink Sheet Data*, Washington, DC: World Bank.

Review of Keynesian Economics, Vol. 7 No. 4, Winter 2019, pp. 60–71

Thirlwall's law, external debt sustainability, and the balance-of-payments-constrained level and growth rates of output*

Gustavo Bhering, Franklin Serrano and Fabio Freitas
Universidade Federal do Rio de Janeiro (UFRJ), Rio de Janeiro, Brazil

Thirlwall's law, given by the ratio of the rate of growth of exports to the income elasticity of imports is a key result of balance-of-payments-constrained long-run growth models with balanced trade. Some authors have extended the analysis to incorporate long-run net capital flows. We provide a critical evaluation of these efforts and propose an alternative approach to deal with long-run external debt sustainability, based on two key features. First, we treat the external debt-to-exports ratio as the relevant indicator for the analysis of external debt sustainability. Second, we include an external credit constraint in the form of a maximum acceptable level of this ratio. The main results that emerge are that sustainable long-run capital flows can positively affect the long-run level of output, but not the rate of growth compatible with the balance-of-payments constraint, as exports must ultimately tend to grow at the same rate as imports. Therefore, Thirlwall's law still holds.

Keywords: *Thirlwall's law, debt sustainability, BoP constraint on growth, Harrod foreign-trade multiplier*

JEL codes: *F43, F32, O41*

1 INTRODUCTION

Thirlwall's law, which states that the long-run rate of growth of output consistent with the balance-of-payments (BoP) constraint is given by the ratio of the rate of growth of exports to the income elasticity of imports (Thirlwall 1979 [2004]), is regarded to this day as a benchmark in heterodox growth models. Thirlwall developed this rule in the context of a model with no persistent capital flows that was very similar to what Kaldor had previously worked with (Kaldor 1970 [1978]; 1971 [1978]). Since the appearance of this rule, some authors, including Thirlwall himself, aimed to inquire about the impact of long-run net capital flows on the BoP-constrained rate of growth.

From a general point of view, we can identify two strands within this literature: (i) models that include net capital flows as an exogenous variable; and (ii) models that include capital flows with a debt sustainability condition depicted by the stability of the proportion between the current-account deficit (or external debt) and GDP.

In this paper, we provide a critical evaluation of these models, with special attention to the last type of model, which deals with debt sustainability. The first type of model has the problem of including capital flows as exogenous and, thus, not discussing the conditions

*   The authors would like to thank (with the usual caveats) the editors of this symposium, as well as Robert Blecker for his very useful comments.

Journal compilation © 2019 Edward Elgar Publishing Ltd
The Lypiatts, 15 Lansdown Road, Cheltenham, Glos GL50 2JA, UK
and The William Pratt House, 9 Dewey Court, Northampton MA 01060-3815, USA

and possible limits to the long-run sustainability of these external capital flows. The second type of model is explicitly concerned with external debt sustainability but has some serious theoretical shortcomings. As we will show, by focusing on the ratio of the current account (or external debt) to GDP, these models implicitly consider domestic output as the measure of the capacity to pay for external liabilities. This is very unrealistic, as it leaves aside the crucial currency mismatch between the currency issued by a country and the currency in which its external liabilities are denominated and must be paid, which is a key feature of the very idea of a balance-of-payments constraint. Moreover, this leads to an implausible sustainability condition and also makes these models unable to determine the long-run *level* of aggregate output compatible with the BoP constraint.

In order to overcome these limitations, we propose an alternative framework to analyse long-run external debt sustainability. Our approach has two key features. First, we treat the debt-to-exports ratio as the relevant sustainability indicator because exports (and not GDP) are the source of cash flow in international currency used to pay external liabilities. Second, we include an external credit constraint in the form of a maximum acceptable level of this indicator. The main results that emerge are that sustainable (unsustainable) long-run capital flows can positively (negatively) affect the long-run level of output, but not the rate of growth compatible with the BoP constraint, as exports must ultimately tend to grow at the same rate as imports. Therefore, Thirlwall's law still holds.

We proceed as follows. In Section 2 we present a simplified version of the basic balanced trade model that uses Harrod's foreign-trade multiplier for the level of output and Thirlwall's law for the determination of long-run BoP-constrained rate of growth. In Section 3 we present our alternative framework to analyse long-run net capital flows and external debt, which will be compared and contrasted with the literature in the following two sections. In Section 4 we discuss the exogenous long-run net capital flows models. In Section 5 we deal with the models that discuss debt sustainability using the current-account-to-GDP ratio. In Section 6 we present some brief final remarks.

2   HARROD'S FOREIGN-TRADE MULTIPLIER AND THIRLWALL'S LAW: THE KALDOR–THIRLWALL APPROACH

Before we discuss how capital flows are treated in Kaldor–Thirlwall models of BoP-constrained growth, it is important to briefly describe the models that do not consider capital flows in order to allow us to compare them. These simplified models are depicted in Kaldor (1970 [1978]) and Thirlwall (1979 [2004]). The main idea behind these models is that, in the long run, imports are driven by the level of activity. In this sense, both the country's GDP and its rate of growth are constrained by the availability of foreign exchange which is determined solely by aggregate exports. Thus, if we combine the condition that exports must be equal to imports, $X = M$, and define imports as a function of output given by $M = mY$,[1] we are able to determine the level of output compatible with the external constraint through Harrod's foreign-trade multiplier:

$$Y_{BP} = \frac{X}{m}, \tag{1}$$

1.   Usually, imports are treated through a multiplicative non-linear function of output and real exchange rate. Here, for the sake of simplicity, we already assume that the real exchange rate is given and we opt for this linear specification of imports as induced by the level of output throughout the whole paper.

                    Journal compilation © 2019 Edward Elgar Publishing Ltd

where X is total exports, M is total imports, m is the marginal propensity to import, Y_{BP} is the level of output that meets the external constraint, and $1/m$ is Harrod's foreign-trade multiplier. Here, we consider that relative prices are given in the long run, as well as the nominal exchange rates, so that the real exchange rates are also given. All variables are measured in 'dollars' and there is no inflation.

The 'dynamic' version of Harrod's foreign-trade multiplier became known as Thirlwall's law, which extends the result of equation (1) to the rate of growth of output constrained by the external account. The rate of growth of Y_{BP} can be written as:

$$g_{BP} = \frac{g_X}{\pi}, \tag{2}$$

where g_{BP} is the rate of growth of Y_{BP}, g_X is the rate of growth of exports and π is the income elasticity of imports. Here, an income elasticity of imports greater (lower) than one means that the marginal propensity to import is increasing (decreasing) as the economy grows. Thirlwall's law became the benchmark rule for the BoP-constrained models, both at a theoretical and empirical level (Thirlwall 2011; Setterfield 2011; Blecker 2016).

These models have two important limitations. The first, which will not be discussed in this paper, is that within the Kaldor–Thirlwall literature, both the level of long-run output and the rate of growth compatible with the BoP constraint are treated as the *direct determinants* of the actual or effective values of these variables. Here we treat the long-run levels and rates of growth of output determined by these models only as proper external *constraints* and as such these constraints may or may not be binding in the long run.[2] In this simplified model of balanced trade, two hypotheses are made for an always binding BoP constraint (Kaldor 1970 [1978]; Thirlwall 1982). The first is that the overall domestic marginal propensity to spend is equal to one and the second is that there are no autonomous components in aggregate demand other than exports.

The second limitation is that, of course, the idea that trade will always tend to balance and that there are no capital flows in the long run is very unrealistic. Later, as we shall see in Sections 4 and 5, Kaldor–Thirlwall literature moved forward, incorporating long-run capital flows and discussing how long-run net capital flows would modify the BoP-constrained rate of growth of output as given by Thirlwall's law in the case of balanced trade.

3   A FRAMEWORK TO ANALYSE CAPITAL FLOWS AND EXTERNAL DEBT

In order to simplify our exposition, we consider here long-run net capital flows on the BoP account as consisting only of the flow of new external debt to finance the current-account deficit. Since Thirlwall's original model did not allow for long-run capital flows, the constraint was set as the need to pay for imports with export revenues. Here, since long-run capital flows are possible, the constraint is that a country cannot lose international reserves indefinitely. We can write the equation for the BoP as:

$$BoP = X - M - R + F, \tag{3}$$

2.   For a discussion on the problems of considering the BoP constraint as always binding, see Freitas (2003).

Journal compilation © 2019 Edward Elgar Publishing Ltd

where R is the net income sent abroad and F is the net financial inflows in the capital account. Here, we assume that the net income sent abroad corresponds exclusively to the payment of external debt services in the form of interest. The result of BoP measures the variation of international reserves in a given period. As a long-run condition, let us assume that a country cannot lose its reserves indefinitely. That is, in the long run, it is not possible to lose reserves continuously, but there is no insurmountable problem in accumulating them. Thus, the result of the BoP must be such that $BoP \geq 0$. For the boundary condition, $BoP = 0$, we have:

$$F = M - X + R. \tag{4}$$

That is, net capital flows must be enough to pay for the current-account deficit. These flows of new external debt can be rewritten as the variation of the stock of external debt since new debt always corresponds to the need to finance the current-account deficit. Thus, in our simplified analysis, changes in net external liabilities are due to the current-account deficit (deficit in the trade balance plus factor service payment). In formal terms, we can write:

$$D - D_{-1} = M - X + R, \tag{5}$$

where D is the stock of external debt (or net external liability) in period t. The variables without subscript refer to period t and subscript -1 corresponds to $t - 1$. We assume that the net financial inflows F is equal to the change in the stock of external debt $D - D_{-1}$, which allows us to establish a relationship between the current-account deficit and the change in the stock of external debt by passing from equation (4) to equation (5). Also, we must add one more equation to the system in order to consider interest payments as a function on the past stock of external debt:

$$R = rD_{-1}. \tag{6}$$

That is, we will consider that the net income sent abroad is the payment of an average net cost of the liability, r, and on the value of the accumulated stock of external debt. Within this context, it is necessary to evaluate the impact of capital flows on output and growth with regard to both the conditions of debt sustainability and possible limits on the size of the external debt.

Since the external constraint basically means a scarcity of foreign currency which is not issued by the country, there is a *currency mismatch* (unless we are dealing with the USA in the current floating dollar standard). Due to the currency mismatch, the ability to repay the external debt should reflect the ability to obtain foreign currency. Thus, the macroeconomic variable that represents the ultimate direct inflow of foreign exchange earnings are *exports* (Medeiros and Serrano 2006). Therefore, we think that the adequate indicator for measuring the capacity to repay external debt is the ratio of external debt to exports. It follows that a satisfactory analysis of the impact of capital flows on long-run output should be based on the sustainability and possible limits of the size of the external debt-to-exports ratio. Starting from equations (5) and (6), we are able to determine the level of the debt-to-exports ratio in period t:

$$d = \frac{M}{X} - 1 + \frac{1 + r}{1 + g_X} d_{-1}, \tag{7}$$

where d is the debt-to-exports ratio and g_X is the growth rate of exports.

                    Journal compilation © 2019 Edward Elgar Publishing Ltd

Let us look at the sustainability conditions that would prevent the debt-to-exports ratio from growing indefinitely. From the difference equation in (7), we have two conditions for d not to explode in the long run. First, if there is a given external account primary deficit (relative to exports) of any size, the cost of external debt given by the interest rate on external debt r has to be lower than the rate of growth of exports. If the rate of interest is greater than the rate of growth of exports, a country will not be able to generate enough foreign-currency revenue to pay for the increase in external debt stemming from interest payments alone, which leads to the explosion of the ratio of external debt relative to exports in the long run. Hence the first condition for external debt sustainability is that $r < g_X$.

Second, even if the condition that $r < g_X$ is met, the ratio between imports and exports cannot grow in the long run, or else a trade deficit would always grow faster than exports, creating debt at a higher pace than exports revenue. In other words, in the long run, *imports should not grow faster than exports*.[3] This is precisely the same long-run constraint imposed by Thirlwall's law in the simplified model with zero net capital flows. As we can see, even if we include capital flows and external debt, the fact that external debt cannot grow indefinitely as a proportion of exports leads to the same constraint on the relation between the rate of growth, but not the levels, of imports and exports.

However, although necessary, these two conditions are not sufficient to describe the limits to external debt and the country's creditworthiness. If we imposed only that external debt cannot grow relative to exports continuously in the long run, we could arrive at the unrealistic conclusion that a country with a low level of indebtedness measured by the ratio d is as much constrained by the BoP as a country with a very high level of indebtness, provided that they both maintain a somewhat stable, or at least not explosive, path for d.

It is more realistic to assume that credit constraints will appear if the level of indebtedness given by the ratio d is sufficiently high. The assumption that we shall make here is that there is a foreign credit constraint, a given limit to the level of this indicator, above which international financial institutions interrupt the financing of the current-account deficit. As this indicator measures a country's ability to pay, beyond a definite given level that we shall call d_{Max}, banks will no longer finance external deficits. Inserting this in (7), we can find the maximum ratio of imports to exports for which the level of indebtedness is at its limit level determined by credit constraint conditions:[4]

$$\frac{M}{X} = 1 + d_{Max}\left(\frac{g_X - r}{1 + g_X}\right), \tag{8}$$

where d_{Max} is the maximum value of d and is an exogenous parameter, given by the limits to external debt financing set by international financial institutions. Thus, when we have the possibility of external debt ($d_{Max} > 0$), there is no need for balanced trade. Balanced trade would imply $M/X = 1$. It follows that from equation (8), for $r \neq g_X$ and $d_{Max} \neq 0$, we have $M/X \neq 1$. To simplify, let us consider:

$$d_{Max}\left(\frac{g_X - r}{1 + g_X}\right) = b, \tag{9}$$

3.   Lourenço (2015) draws attention to the condition that is generally implicit in analyses of the sustainability of external debt that the growth rate of imports should not be higher than that of exports.

4.   Here we simply calculate the level of d when it is stable at its maximum level. We make $d = d_{-1} = d_{Max}$.

                              Journal compilation © 2019 Edward Elgar Publishing Ltd

where b is the ratio between the capacity to import and exports (hence equal to 1 if $X = M$). Assuming, as in Section 2, that imports are induced by the level of output, $M = mY$, we get:

$$Y_{BP} = \frac{X(1 + b)}{m}. \tag{10}$$

In this model, b represents the debt-financing conditions and their limits, namely the ceiling imposed by international creditors and the relationship between the cost of liabilities and the rate of growth of exports. In fact, the model in Section 2 would be a particular case, in which $b = 0$, that is, $d_{Max} = 0$, since it would not be possible to maintain permanent capital flows and, thus, no long-run external debt.

Furthermore, the long-run output allowed by the BoP constraint with capital flows may be larger or smaller than the balanced trade output depending on the sign of b. More specifically, the sign of b will be determined by the relationship between the average cost of liabilities and the rate of growth of exports. When $r < g_X$, we have $b > 0$. and when $r > g_X$. we have $b < 0$. For a permanent positive growth rate of d, the debt at some point will achieve its upper bound. Hence, for $b < 0$, the presence of external debt further constrains output relative to the simplified model in Section 2. This means that if a country has a stock of net external liabilities, a change in the average cost of liabilities that makes it larger than the rate of growth of exports renders foreign debt unsustainable and further constrains output, as the country has to generate current-account surplus to meet the limits to its foreign debt and will do so by limiting imports through lower output. Alternatively, for a lower cost of liabilities relative to the rate of growth of exports, the possibility of external debt has a positive impact on the levels of long-run BoP-constrained output.

The main conclusion we draw from this framework relative to the model of balanced trade in Section 2 is that capital flows will in general have an impact (positive or negative depending on the relation between the rate of growth of exports and the interest rate and thus on the sign of b) on the long-run level of output that balances the BoP. In the BoP-constrained rate of growth of output, for given levels of d_{Max}, the interest rate and the growth rate of exports, b will be constant over time, and thus Y_{BP} will necessarily grow at a rate equal to the ratio between the rate of growth of exports and the income elasticity of imports. Thus, in the longer run, the BoP-constrained rate of growth remains the same: Thirlwall's law. A result easily understood once we consider that while the level of imports may be (if $b > 0$) permanently higher than exports, those imports cannot grow permanently at a faster rate than exports without making the current account and external debt relative to exports grow without limit.

4   EXOGENOUS NET CAPITAL FLOWS IN KALDOR–THIRLWALL MODELS

In this section, we discuss the Kaldor–Thirlwall models that consider long-run capital flows as an exogenous variable following Thirlwall and Hussain (1982 [2004]) and McCombie and Thirlwall (2004). These models aim at further developing upon the balanced trade model we discussed in Section 2 to include long-run net capital flows and the possibility of a long-run current-account deficit. Here, net capital flows are considered as being exogenous. From equation (4) in the previous section, we can arrive at the long-run level of output compatible with the BoP constraint given by the no-change-in-external-reserves condition for a given F and R as:

$$Y_{BP} = \frac{X + F - R}{m}. \tag{11}$$

Capital flows will have a positive impact on the long-run level of output compatible with the BoP constraint if $F > R$, that is, if new capital inflows are greater than the amount of interest payments in previously acquired debt. In this case, long-run output is larger than that of a balanced trade model following Harrod's foreign-trade multiplier. But depending on the external financing conditions, capital flows may have a positive or negative impact on long-run output, since interest payments can also be larger than the capital flows ($F < R$). In the balanced trade model, we argued that two hypotheses had to be made in order to assume that the BoP is always binding. This is hardly realistic in the case of balanced trade and requires even more implausible assumptions when there are capital flows. Indeed, assuming that the domestic marginal propensity to spend is equal to one is not enough to determine the conditions under which the BoP constraint is always binding.[5] Now there must also be some other autonomous components of demand besides exports (for example, government spending) in order to allow for actual output to be compatible with the BoP constraint. This is implausible for two reasons. First, because there is no endogenous market mechanism that would make this other supposedly 'autonomous' demand have the exact value required to make the economy hit the level of BoP-constrained output (so it is in practice induced by it). Second, this level of 'autonomous' demand may well have to be equal to zero (if $F = R$) or even negative, in the case that $F > R$ and the BoP-constrained level of output with capital flows is lower than the one with balanced trade.

However, the model we find in Thirlwall and Hussain (1982 [2004]), for instance, does not directly address this issue of the impact of capital flows on the determination of the long-run *level* of BoP-constrained output.[6] Instead, these models evaluate only the possible impact of capital flows on the long-run BoP-constrained *rate of growth*. Starting from our constraint on the BoP given by equation (11), we derive the long-run rate of growth compatible with the BoP constraint as:

$$g_{BP} = \frac{\alpha_1 g_X + \alpha_2 g_F - (1 - \alpha_1 - \alpha_2) g_R}{\pi}, \tag{12}$$

where the αs correspond to each component's weight (X, F, and R) in the total sum $X + F - R$. Now, the rate of growth will be greater or lower than Thirlwall's law

---

5.   Thirlwall (1982) argues that the presence of any autonomous component of demand other than exports would entail a trade deficit, which is true only when the domestic marginal propensity to spend is equal to one. Thirlwall does not make clear what changes for the determination of the long-run level of output regarding the two hypotheses discussed in Section 2 when he moves from the model of balanced trade to the capital-flows model. However, since Thirlwall discussed that other autonomous components of demand would yield a deficit in his 1982 paper and also since he never abandoned the idea of a domestic marginal propensity to spend equal to one in any later works, we must assume that the domestic marginal propensity to spend is equal to one and there is some autonomous component of demand other than exports in this model.

6.   Differently from the models with balanced trade, as in Kaldor (1970 [1978]) and in Thirlwall (1982), there is no equation determining the equilibrium level of output in these models with capital flows nor a discussion on how these variables would affect it.

depending on the rates of growth of F (new net capital flows) and R and their respective relative weights. But note that if the BoP-constrained rate of growth is greater than that indicated by Thirlwall's law, then the rate of growth of imports, which is a function of the growth of the BoP-constrained level of output, will then be necessarily faster than the rate of growth of exports. Conversely, if g_{BP} in equation (12) is lower than that indicated by Thirlwall's law, exports would necessarily be growing faster than the rate of growth of imports. Of course, it is not realistic to assume that the weights in (12) are exogenous parameters in the long run, since they increase or decrease over time according to differences in rates of growth of the different components of this sum. Nor is it at all reasonable to assume that the rate of growth of interest payments bears no connection in the long run to the rate of growth of net capital flows.

Following the framework we presented in Section 3, if output grows faster than Thirlwall's law, the external debt-to-exports ratio will be growing continuously in the long run. This seems to be very unrealistic, since it is likely that a credit constraint will appear at high levels of debt relative to exports. In the simplified trade-balanced model, there was an implicit hypothesis on the limit to the level of debt, where d_{Max} would be zero. Here, the exogenous net capital flows removes any limit to the current-account deficit, since this limit cannot be realistically defined by a maximum absolute value of net capital flows, but by some connection between the creation of debt via current-account deficits and credit constraints. As we saw in Section 3, once we impose this limit to the debt-to-exports ratio, we return to Thirlwall's law as the relevant long-run constraint on growth. Thus, if we consider that there is a limit to external debt, it is not reasonable to determine the long-run constraint on growth through equation (12) based on the weighted sum of exports, net capital flows and interest payments, because if this sum yields a long-run rate of growth greater than Thirlwall's law, there is certainly a long-run unsustainable path for the debt-to-exports ratio.

To overcome these limitations, it is necessary to introduce the analysis of the debt sustainability conditions of external debt. This is precisely the route taken in the Kaldor–Thirlwall literature, where exogenous capital flows gave place to some condition of external debt sustainability.

5   DEBT SUSTAINABILITY IN KALDOR–THIRLWALL MODELS

In the Kaldor–Thirlwall approach, the external debt sustainability conditions are generally treated through an indicator of external debt sustainability given by the ratio between the current-account deficit and domestic output (McCombie and Thirlwall 1997; Moreno-Brid 1998; 2003; Barbosa-Filho 2001 [2004]). These authors establish that as a long-run constraint, external debt relative to GDP cannot grow indefinitely,[7] so the rate of growth of net capital flows which pay for the current-account deficit must be equal to the rate of growth of domestic output. Again, as in the model of the previous section above, these models do not treat the impact of this proportionality between capital flows and domestic output on the determination of long-run level of aggregate output constrained by the BoP, only the extent to which it affects the BoP-constrained growth rates and may make this rate of growth different from Thirlwall's law.

---

7.   Barbosa-Filho (2001 [2004]) refers to this as a 'non-Ponzi' condition.

As Moreno-Brid (1998) shows, the stability of the proportion between current-account deficit and GDP will imply the stability of the stock of external debt relative to GDP as well, which makes the conditions for the former equal the conditions for the latter. Because of this equivalence, in this section we will proceed by using the ratio of external debt relative to GDP as our indicator of debt sustainability in order to compare this model with the framework we presented in Section 3 using the debt-to-exports ratio.

First, we have to look to the general conditions that determine debt sustainability in the long run within these models and then proceed to evaluate the implications of these conditions on the determination of long-run levels and rates of growth of BoP-constrained output. Thus, we start by writing an expression analogous to (7) but relative to GDP instead of exports. Assuming $f = D/Y$, we have:

$$f = m - \frac{X}{Y} + \frac{1+r}{1+g}f_{-1}. \tag{13}$$

The first general condition for debt sustainability in equation (13) is that $r < g$, which means that output (giving the impression that, somehow, domestic growth generates capacity to pay foreign debt in this model) must grow faster than the growth of interest payments, or else debt relative to GDP will always grow indefinitely. It is important to note that this condition must always hold for debt to be sustainable in these terms. Thus, for the rest of our argument, we assume that $r < g$.

Second, the stability of f also depends on the relation between trade deficit and output. Here we have two possibilities. The first is that output grows at a rate lower than or equal to the rate of growth determined by Thirlwall's law. In this case, there is no unsustainable debt, since any rate of growth of output within these limits makes the ratio f above fall indefinitely. The second possibility, which is more relevant to this model, is when output grows faster than Thirlwall's law, thus creating a growing trade deficit relative to output, as exports grow at an exogenous rate. In this case, we must evaluate whether the presence of external debt and a current-account deficit can in fact allow for a greater long-run rate of growth compared to Thirlwall's law. Hence we need to look closer at the behavior of the ratio of trade deficit relative to GDP when imports grow faster than exports.

If imports grow faster than exports, the level of imports will tend to dominate the level of exports and tend to determine the total value of the trade deficit. This means that this value of the trade deficit relative to GDP will tend to be determined solely by the ratio of imports relative to output, which in our imports function is m. In terms of equation (13) the sum $m - X/Y$ will tend to m. If $r < g$, the equilibrium value for the ratio f will be:

$$f^* = m\frac{1+g}{g-r}. \tag{14}$$

Thus, when imports grow faster than exports, the stability of f depends on the behavior of the marginal propensity to import and, hence, on the income elasticity of imports. If the income elasticity of imports is lower than one, output grows faster than imports, m falls and then the debt-to-output ratio falls indefinitely since debt created by imports always grows at a slower pace than output, for any rate of growth of output. If the income elasticity of imports is equal to one, imports grow as fast as output, m is constant and the ratio between debt and GDP is stable, and it is stable for any long-run rate of growth of output. Finally, if the income elasticity of imports is greater than one, imports grow faster than output, m grows over time and any creation of debt will be unsustainable, because debt will grow according to imports, and output is never able to catch up. In this case, a country would eventually have to maintain a balanced trade with zero deficit, as in Harrod's foreign-trade multiplier, where output is constrained by Thirlwall's law.

Barbosa-Filho (2001 [2004]) arrives at this same result analysing a model without interest payments, that the stability of the model with unbalanced trade and given long-run exchange rates requires that the income elasticity of imports is equal to one. According to him, 'the only way to have stable and unbalanced trade in the long run is to impose the auxiliary assumption that the income elasticity of home imports equals one' (ibid., p. 131). However, in this case, the ratio f is stable here for any rate of growth of output, which means that, in the same way as the case in which income elasticity of imports is lower than one, there is simply no BoP constraint on long-run growth.

Hence, in this model, there is no BoP constraint on growth provided that imports do not grow faster than output (income elasticity of imports less than or equal to one). Note that the additional condition of the rate of growth of output being greater than the rate of interest on external debt is very easy to meet by policy-makers simply increasing the rate of growth of domestic demand. This only shows how inadequate it is to assume that the external-debt-to-domestic-output ratio is the relevant condition for debt sustainability.

Moreover, despite the problems with the BoP-constrained rate of growth of output described above, the long-run level of output compatible with the BoP is *indeterminate* in this model. As we argued at the beginning of this section, when the stock of external debt is proportional to GDP, the current-account deficit is also proportional to GDP. This allows us to go back to equation (11) for the level of long-run output with exogenous capital flows and make the term $F - R$ proportional to output as well. If we make $F - R = jY$, we are able to arrive at the BoP-constrained level of long-run output in this model, defined by:

$$Y_{BP} = \frac{X}{m-j}.$$ (15)

The parameter j is the difference between capital flows and interest payments relative to output. If we go back to the BoP accounts, we know that this sum is equal to the trade deficit. Hence, we can rewrite the expression for j as $j = m - X/Y$. If we substitute this expression for j in equation (15), we end up with the relation $Y_{BP} = Y$, which simply states that any level of actual output determines the BoP-constrained level of output. When there is external debt, since in this approach GDP is implicitly assumed to be the measure for the capacity to pay foreign liabilities, output is what is supposedly constrained by the BoP and at the same time what alleviates this same constraint. This is the ultimate reason why output is indeterminate, because debt can be sustainable for any level of output.

This sustainability condition is unusual and unrealistic, as debt is sustainable for any growth rate, even if exports grow much more slowly than imports, as long as imports do not grow faster than output. This problem and the indeterminacy of the BoP-constrained level of output are both founded on the fundamental problem of implicitly treating domestic output (instead of exports) as an indicator of external debt repayment capacity. The local government can easily take measures to inject new purchasing power in the economy increasing (private or public) autonomous demand in order to provide (demand-led) output growth. However, this injection of purchasing power is not denominated in foreign currency and therefore does not mean a greater availability of foreign exchange to pay for imports.

6   FINAL REMARKS

In a 1983 paper, while commenting on the condition for long-run growth (Thirlwall's law), Thirlwall argued that '[t]he only assumptions needed to produce this result are that in the long run trade must be balanced on current account (*or that there is a constant ratio of capital inflows to export earning*) and that the real terms of trade … remains constant' (Thirlwall 1983, p. 250, emphasis added).[8] After developing our framework independently, we interpret this passage as Thirlwall suggesting that Thirlwall's law would also be valid in a model with capital flows, if the ratio between capital flows and exports tend to be constant (which would also imply a stable debt-to-export ratio). However this, as we have seen in Section 4, was not the route taken by Thirlwall himself in the exogenous capital-flow models in which it is assumed that imports may grow permanently faster than exports and so can the capital flows (and external debt) to exports ratio. And the literature that tried to further develop the BoP-constrained model including debt sustainability conditions (as well as the recent review of these models by Blecker and Setterfield 2019) also did not follow Thirlwall's suggestion in his 1983 paper when it considered, as we argued in Section 5 above, quite unrealistically, a constant ratio of capital inflows relative to domestic output, instead of exports, as the relevant condition for debt sustainability.

In line with Thirlwall's (1983) remark, we have shown that, using the more relevant debt-to-exports ratio and postulating the existence of credit constraints for high levels of this indicator, including capital flows in the BoP constraint will affect the levels but not the BoP-constrained rates of growth, as the latter will still be determined by Thirlwall's law.

REFERENCES

Barbosa-Filho, N.H. (2001 [2004]), 'The balance of payments constraint: from balanced trade to sustainable debt,' in J.S.L. McCombie and A.P. Thirlwall (eds), *Essays on Balance of Payments Constrained Growth: Theory and Evidence*, London: Routledge, pp. 126–140.

Blecker, R.A. (2016), 'The debate over "Thirlwall's Law": balance-of-payments-constrained growth reconsidered,' *European Journal of Economics and Economic Policies: Intervention*, 13(3), 275–290.

Blecker, R.A. and M. Setterfield (2019), *Heterodox Macroeconomics: Models of Demand, Distribution and Growth*, Cheltenham, UK and Northampton, MA: Edward Elgar Publishing, forthcoming.

Boianovsky, M. and R. Solis (2014), 'The origins and development of the Latin American structuralist approach to the balance of payments, 1944–1964,' *Review of Political Economy*, 26(1), 23–59.

Freitas, F. (2003), 'Uma análise crítica do modelo kaldoriano de crescimento liderado pelas exportações,' *Encontro Nacional de Economia*, 31, Porto Seguro/BA.

8.   Quoted in Boianovsky and Solis (2014). These authors also draw attention to the fact that Thirlwall (1983) admits that Raul Prebisch anticipated this law in the 1950s.

Kaldor, N. (1970 [1978]), 'The case for regional policies,' in N. Kaldor, *Further Essays on Economic Theory*, New York: Holmes and Meier, pp. 139–154.

Kaldor, N. (1971 [1978]), 'Conflicts in national economic objectives,' in N. Kaldor, *Further Essays on Economic Theory*, New York: Holmes and Meier, pp. 155–175.

Lourenço, A. (2015), 'Modelos Heterodoxos de Crescimento em Economias Abertas: uma Extensão dos Modelos de Kaldor-Thirlwall,' *Revista de Economia Contemporânea*, 19(3), 475–502.

McCombie, J.S.L. and A.P. Thirlwall (1997), 'Economic growth and the balance-of-payments constraint revisited,' in P. Arestis, G. Palma, and M. Sawyer (eds), *Markets, Unemployment and Economic Policy: Essays in Honour of Geoff Harcourt*, vol. 2, London: Routledge, pp. 498–511.

McCombie, J.S.L. and A.P. Thirlwall (eds) (2004), *Essays on Balance of Payments Constrained Growth: Theory and Evidence*, London: Routledge.

Medeiros, C. and F. Serrano (2006), 'Capital flows to emerging markets under the flexible dollar standard: a critical view based on the Brazilian experience,' in M. Vernengo (ed.), *Monetary Integration and Dollarization: No Panacea*, Cheltenham, UK and Northampton, MA: Edward Elgar Publishing, pp. 218–242.

Moreno-Brid, J.C. (1998), 'On capital flows and the balance-of-payments-contrained growth model,' *Journal of Post Keynesian Economics*, 21(2), 283–298.

Moreno-Brid, J.C. (2003), 'Capital flows, interest payments and the balance-of-payments constrained growth model: a theoretical and empirical analysis,' *Metroeconomica*, 54(2–3), 346–365.

Setterfield, M. (2011), 'The remarkable durability of Thirlwall's Law,' *PSL Quarterly Review*, 64(259), 393–427.

Thirlwall, A.P. (1979 [2004]), 'The balance of payments constraint as an explanation of international growth rate differences,' in J.S.L. McCombie and A.P. Thirlwall (eds), *Essays on Balance of Payments Constrained Growth: Theory and Evidence*, London: Routledge, pp. 21–27.

Thirlwall, A.P. (1982), 'The Harrod trade multiplier and the importance of export-led growth,' *Pakistan Journal of Applied Economics*, 1(1), 1–21.

Thirlwall, A.P. (1983), 'Foreign trade elasticities in centre–periphery models of growth and development,' *Banca Nazionale del Lavoro Quarterly Review*, 36, 249–261.

Thirlwall, A.P. (2011), 'Balance of payments constrained growth models: history and overview,' *PSL Quarterly Review*, 64(259), 307–351.

Thirlwall, A.P. and M.N. Hussain (1982 [2004]), 'The balance of payments constraint, capital flows and growth rate differences between developing countries,' in J.S.L. McCombie and A.P. Thirlwall (eds), *Essays on Balance of Payments Constrained Growth: Theory and Evidence*, London: Routledge, pp. 28–39.

   Journal compilation © 2019 Edward Elgar Publishing Ltd

Review of Keynesian Economics, Vol. 7 No. 4, Winter 2019, pp. 72–90

Growth transitions and the balance-of-payments constraint

Excellent Mhlongo and Kevin S. Nell*
College of Business and Economics, School of Economics, University of Johannesburg, South Africa

This paper re-evaluates the recent criticisms of 'Thirlwall's law' against the literature on growth transitions. The unpredictable nature of growth transitions in developing economies suggests that the evidence derived from single-regime regression models, on which critics have based most of their arguments, is only suggestive about the long-run causes of growth. A rigorous test of Thirlwall's law requires a more in-depth analysis of turning points in a developing country's growth performance, and whether the growth law accurately predicts the sustainability of growth transitions. These arguments are illustrated with an application to South Africa over the period 1960–2017. The results show that it is misleading to evaluate Thirlwall's law across a single regime. Once regime shifts are controlled for, the growth law accurately predicts South Africa's growth performance during 1977–2003, and sheds light on the sustainable and unsustainable nature of growth transitions across the sub-periods 1960–1976 and 2004–2017, respectively. Since the literature on growth transitions identifies a competitive exchange rate as an initiating source of growth, rather than an individual long-run determinant, the omission of the level of the real exchange rate from the original growth law should not be regarded as a major weakness.

Keywords: *balance-of-payments-constrained growth, growth transitions, multiple regimes, South Africa*

JEL codes: *E12, F43, O11, O24, O25*

1 INTRODUCTION

The main objective of this paper is to draw an explicit link between the literature on growth transitions and the balance-of-payments-constrained (BoPC) growth model, as originally developed by Thirlwall (1979). Pritchett's (2000) influential study shows that, in contrast to industrialised and East Asian countries, most developing economies exhibit shifts in growth rates that lead to distinct patterns, and that these patterns remain unexplained in cross-country and panel growth regressions. Motivated by Pritchett and earlier work by Easterly et al. (1993), several subsequent studies, such as Hausmann et al. (2005), Jerzmanowski (2006), Jones and Olken (2008) and Kerekes (2012), have attempted to identify the key determinants of growth transitions. A common finding of these studies is that there is a distinct difference between factors that initiate growth transitions and those that sustain them.

---

* Corresponding author: Email: knell@uj.ac.za.

Journal compilation © 2019 Edward Elgar Publishing Ltd
The Lypiatts, 15 Lansdown Road, Cheltenham, Glos GL50 2JA, UK
and The William Pratt House, 9 Dewey Court, Northampton MA 01060-3815, USA

Growth accelerations of 3.5 per cent per annum sustained for at least eight years are a common feature of most developing economies (Hausmann et al. 2005). However, most of these growth accelerations tend to fizzle out and do not match the long-run growth transitions sustained over many decades in several Asian economies.

How do the recent criticisms of Thirlwall's (1979) original BoPC growth model hold up when they are evaluated against the literature on growth transitions? A critique of the BoPC model is that it excludes the *level* of the real exchange rate as a determinant of long-run growth, and that exports are primarily constrained from the supply side rather than world demand, as predicted by 'Thirlwall's law' (Blecker 2016; Razmi 2016).

Razmi (2016) provides an empirical test of Thirlwall's law vis-à-vis his own alternative model for a sample of 167 countries over the period 1950–2011. Thirlwall's law predicts that there should be a strong positive correlation between domestic income growth and world income growth. The evidence obtained from Razmi's (2016) generalised method of moments (GMM) panel data estimates indicates that world income growth is a statistically insignificant determinant of output growth, whereas the growth rate of physical capital accumulation is positive and significant. As far as the exchange rate is concerned, both the level of the real exchange rate (proxied by an undervaluation index) and the growth rate of the real terms of trade are statistically significant and contain theory-consistent signs. Overall, the GMM estimates seem to support Razmi's (2016) alternative model, in which foreign demand is infinitely elastic and export growth responds to physical capital accumulation through a one-off change in the level of the real exchange rate.

How compatible is Razmi's (2016) empirical evidence with the existing literature on growth transitions mentioned above? The unstable and unpredictable nature of growth patterns in developing countries implies that panel data estimates are only suggestive of what determines *long-run* growth. In fact, the results obtained from Razmi's panel data estimates do not necessarily disprove the relevance of Thirlwall's law. Favourable real terms-of-trade shocks, an undervalued real exchange rate and a faster rate of physical capital accumulation would generate *unsustainable* growth transitions if an economy's long-run growth rate is ultimately determined by Thirlwall's law (x/π). All these variables might be significant determinants of growth in a regression model that averages growth into a single regime, but because conventional panel data regressions do not distinguish between variables that initiate and sustain a growth transition, the regression results are uninformative about the long-run determinants of growth. This is precisely the message of the literature on growth transitions (Pritchett 2000; Hausmann et al. 2005), and consistent with empirical evidence which shows that exchange-rate-induced surges in output growth, investment and exports eventually fizzle out (Hausmann et al. 2005; Berg et al. 2012; Freund and Pierola 2012; Libman et al. 2019). Something else is required to sustain growth (Rodrik 2005; 2006; 2018).

A rigorous test of Thirlwall's law would therefore require a more in-depth and detailed analysis of turning points in a typical developing country's growth performance and whether growth transitions are unsustainable because they are initiated through forces that fall outside the domain of the simple growth rule. To illustrate these arguments empirically, this paper re-examines the relevance of Thirlwall's law in South Africa over the period 1960–2017. The country-specific application in this paper provides an interesting comparison with Razmi (2016) who, in addition to his panel data estimates, also presents time-series estimates for a handful of individual countries over the period 1950–2011, including South Africa. Razmi's (2016) regression results for South Africa are broadly consistent with the panel data evidence insofar as the exchange-rate variables are statistically significant, and the magnitude of the physical capital accumulation coefficient is much larger than the estimate on world income.

The results in this paper show that it is misleading to evaluate Thirlwall's growth law across a single regime in South Africa. Although Thirlwall's growth law under-predicts South Africa's actual growth performance over the full sample period 1960–2017, it provides some explanation of why growth spurts have historically been volatile and unsustainable. The original growth law accurately predicts South Africa's actual growth performance over the period 1977–2003. Outside this regime, the economy has relied heavily on capital inflows to lift the balance-of-payments con-straint on demand growth. Although long-term capital inflows were a characteristic feature over the period 1960–1976 of faster output growth, inflows during the period 2004–2017 were more volatile and short-term in nature. In fact, the evidence in this paper shows that the economy's actual growth rate is converging back to the predicted rate of the BoPC growth model during 2004–2017. Moreover, surges in physical capi-tal accumulation and output growth have generally coincided with foreign-capital inflows and a deteriorating current-account deficit ratio, rather than improved export performance. Although a competitive exchange rate could well play an important role in initiating a growth transition in South Africa, the relevance of Thirlwall's law suggests that growth will eventually fizzle out if it is not complemented with trade and industrial policies that improve the structural demand characteristics of export goods in foreign markets.

2   THE SUSTAINABILITY OF GROWTH TRANSITIONS

The focus of this paper is on Thirlwall's (1979) original growth law and whether it remains relevant in the context of a typical developing country with multiple growth regimes. Several studies have analysed the importance of structural change and how it affects the predictive ability of the BoPC growth model (see for example Cimoli et al. 2010; Nell 2013; Tharnpanich and McCombie 2013; Bagnai et al. 2016). The underlying hypothesis in this paper is that long-run growth in a developing econ-omy is pinned down by the simple version of the law. The long-run growth rate, however, is not always directly observable when growth shifts are triggered by real terms-of-trade shocks and capital flows that may be unsustainable over the long run.

As a basic reference point, it is useful to begin with the extended BoPC growth model of Thirlwall and Hussain (1982) which includes capital inflows and real terms-of-trade effects. Since the full derivation of the model is well known, we only report the final equation of the extended version:

$$y^{SA^{***}} = \frac{\left(1 + \left(\frac{E}{R}\right)\eta + \psi\right)(p_{dt} - p_{ft} - e_t) + \left(\frac{E}{R}\right)\varepsilon z_t + \left(\frac{C}{R}\right)(c_t - p_{dt})}{\pi}, \tag{1}$$

where $y^{SA^{***}}$ is the BoPC growth rate of South Africa; η (< 0) and ψ (< 0) are the price elasticities of demand for exports and imports, respectively; p_{dt} is the growth rate of the domestic price of exports at time t; e_t is the rate of change of the nominal exchange rate measured in units of domestic currency per foreign currency ($e_t > 0$ denotes a depreciating exchange rate); p_{ft} is the growth rate of the foreign price of imports; ε (> 0) is the income elasticity of demand for exports; z_t is world income growth;

                    Journal compilation © 2019 Edward Elgar Publishing Ltd

$c_t - p_{dt}$ is the growth rate of real capital inflows, assuming that the economy is in an initial current-account deficit position; E/R and C/R are the proportions of the import bill financed by export earnings and net capital inflows, respectively; and $\pi \, (> 0)$ is the income elasticity of demand for imports.

The BoPC growth literature often assumes that the real terms of trade (or real exchange rate) cannot continuously depreciate or appreciate (Thirlwall 2011). It is therefore plausible to assume that in the long run the rate of change of the real terms of trade is zero $(p_{dt} - p_{ft} - e_t = 0)$.[1] It is further assumed that a deteriorating current-account deficit reflects a growing foreign-debt burden. Since an economy cannot borrow indefinitely in foreign markets, the long-run restrictions $E/R = 1$ and $C/R = 0$ apply to equation (1). With these restrictions imposed, equation (1) gives the original BoPC growth model developed by Thirlwall (1979):

$$y^{SA^*} = \frac{x_t}{\pi}. \tag{2}$$

Perraton (2003) dubs equation (2) the 'weak' version of Thirlwall's law because an empirical fit of the model does not explicitly support the assumption that the growth rate of the real terms of trade is zero; it could still be contained in the growth rate of real exports, x_t. Hence, the 'strong' version of the law is specified as follows:

$$y^{SA^*} = \frac{\varepsilon z_t}{\pi}. \tag{2'}$$

Equations (1)–(2′) can be used to explain why growth transitions in developing countries are typically volatile and unsustainable. An investment-led strategy may generate faster growth over a period of time, but if it does not change the structural parameters of equation (2′) in a favourable way, the current-account deficit in equation (1) will deteriorate over time and lead to a slowdown in income growth to preserve equilibrium on the current account.

It is useful to pause for a moment and go back to Razmi's (2016) panel data evidence. Consistent with Razmi's (2016) evidence, the growth rate of the physical capital stock may well be a significant determinant of income growth over a specific sample period. The key question, however, is whether faster growth in the capital stock generates a deteriorating current-account deficit over time, or whether, consistent with Razmi's (2016) model, it raises export growth from the supply side to preserve current-account equilibrium. Libman et al. (2019) examine investment surges over eight-year windows and show that the trade balance (exports minus imports) to GDP ratio typically becomes negative during the acceleration period, and eventually recovers to its original level of around zero after a decade. However, the net effect on income growth is unclear, because the recovery is partly due to a rise in exports and a fall in imports. The decrease in imports implies a slowdown in income growth. Moreover, long-run equilibrium on the trade balance would require a surplus in the post-acceleration phase, which may entail a further slowdown in income growth to curtail imports.

Real terms-of-trade shocks in equation (1) are another source of instability in a country's growth performance (Easterly et al. 1993). More recently, growth

---

1.   Blecker (2016), in his critical review of the theoretical and empirical literature, argues in favour of this proposition of BoPC growth models.

   Journal compilation © 2019 Edward Elgar Publishing Ltd

accelerations in many sub-Saharan Africa (SSA) countries since 2000 have been attributed to favourable terms-of-trade shocks, rather than growth-inducing structural change and rapid industrialisation (McMillan et al. 2014; de Vries et al. 2015; Bagnai et al. 2016; Diao et al. 2017; Rodrik 2018). However, history tells us that primary commodity booms tend to fizzle out and that sustained growth transitions are usually accompanied by rapid industrialisation (Bagnai et al. 2016; Rodrik 2018).

Relating these insights to the BoPC growth model, it can be seen from equation (1) that a positive terms-of-trade shock $(p_{dt} - p_{ft} - e_t > 0)$ will initiate a growth transition, assuming $|\frac{\dot{E}}{R}\eta + \psi| < 1$. Because the terms of trade cannot rise forever, long-run growth is determined by world income growth and the relative income elasticities in equation (2'). Again, a statistically significant real terms-of-trade effect in growth regressions (Razmi 2016) may simply pick up unsustainable growth transitions.

One of the main criticisms that have been levelled against the simple version of the BoPC growth model in equation (2') is that it omits any *level* effect of the real exchange rate on growth. Blecker (2016) and Razmi (2016) point out that this specification is inconsistent with existing empirical studies, most notably Rodrik (2008a), which show that an undervalued real exchange rate impacts positively on long-run growth (also see Rapetti et al. 2012). Razmi's (2016) model assumes, in contrast to equation (2'), that export demand is infinitely elastic in world markets, so that export growth is boosted from the supply side through a faster rate of capital accumulation induced by an undervalued real exchange rate. Missio et al. (2017), on the other hand, develop a model in which the income elasticities of demand for exports and imports in equation (2') are endogenous to movements in the level of the real exchange rate. In their model, an undervalued real exchange rate lifts the balance-of-payments constraint on growth.

It is important to acknowledge, however, that Rodrik (2005; 2006; 2018) identifies the real exchange rate as a key *initiating* source of growth, while institutional reforms, investment in education and complementary industrial policies that ensure an ongoing process of diversification into new tradables are required to sustain growth in the long run. Rapetti (2013), on the other hand, emphasises the importance of supportive demand and wage management policies to ensure that the growth-inducing effect of an exchange-rate depreciation is sustained, while the model of Razmi et al. (2012) outlines additional prerequisites.

The fact that growth accelerations in many developing countries have eventually petered out suggests that the conditions necessary to sustain growth are absent, which brings us back to the long-run growth prediction of the simple version of the BoPC growth model in equation (2'). It is, therefore, a misnomer to regard econometric evidence of a statistically significant link between output growth and the real exchange rate as evidence against the *long-run* growth prediction of the BoPC model. As the experience of East Asian countries and China suggests, complementary industrial and trade policies may well be required to raise the income elasticity of demand for exports and reduce the income elasticity of demand for imports in equation (2') (Gouvea and Lima 2010; Bresser-Pereira and Rugitsky 2018).

Another criticism against the BoPC growth literature relates to the near-identity argument implied by the weak and strong versions of the law in equations (2) and (2') (see Blecker 2016; Razmi 2016). To illustrate the near-identity argument, consider the import demand function with zero growth in the real terms of trade:

$$m_t = \pi y_t^{SA}, \tag{3}$$

                   Journal compilation © 2019 Edward Elgar Publishing Ltd

where m_t is the growth rate of the volume of imports at time t; π is the income elasticity of demand for imports; and y_t^{SA} is South Africa's domestic income growth rate. Substituting (3) into equation (2) gives:

$$\frac{y_t^{SA^*}}{y_t^{SA}} = \frac{x_t}{m_t}. \tag{4}$$

Equation (4) shows that a statistical test of whether the actual growth rate is equal to the BoPC growth rate ($y^{SA^*} = y_t^{SA}$) in equation (2) is equivalent to testing whether $x_t = m_t$. It follows that empirical evidence in favour of equation (4) does not unambiguously support the causal mechanism that underlies Thirlwall's BoPC growth law, which states that domestic income growth is exogenously determined by world demand. Razmi's (2016) model, in which export demand is infinitely elastic in world markets, also predicts that exports and imports grow at the same rate in the long run.

To distinguish Thirlwall's growth law from alternative models, it is necessary to show that world income growth is a significant determinant of domestic income growth, as implied by equation (2'). In this context, it is instructive to follow the generalised version of the balance-of-payments model developed by Nell (2003) and specify South Africa's BoPC growth rate as a function of world income growth disaggregated according to its different (potential) trading partners:

$$y^{SA^*} = \beta_1 y_t^{OECD} + \beta_2 y_t^{RSADC}, \tag{5}$$

where y_t^{OECD} is the real income growth rate of countries belonging to the Organisation for Economic Co-operation and Development (OECD) at time t; y_t^{RSADC} is the real income growth rate of the rest of the Southern African Development Community (RSADC); and β_1 (> 0) and β_2 (> 0) are reduced form parameters.

If, in a regression analysis, OECD growth and/or RSADC growth are significant determinants of South Africa's growth rate in equation (5), it will show that the demand for exports is not infinitely elastic in foreign markets but constrained by world income growth. Although the focus in this paper is on the empirical relevance of the simple version of the BoPC growth law in equation (2), the fitted results of the generalised model in Nell (2003) are useful to complement the main findings.

3   THE RELEVANCE OF THE BoPC GROWTH MODEL IN SOUTH AFRICA: SOME DESCRIPTIVE EVIDENCE

The discussion thus far has stressed that an empirical test of the BoPC growth model across a single regime may lead to misleading inferences if an economy's actual growth performance is characterised by multiple regimes. Accordingly, this paper draws on Nell and De Mello (2019), who use the Bai and Perron (1998; 2003) procedure to identify structural break points endogenously in South Africa's historical growth performance. Four potential break points are identified: 1976, 1985, 1994 and 2003, where the break dates represent the last date of the previous growth regime. Nell and De Mello (2019, p. 274) further argue that 1985 and 1994 do not represent 'real' turning points in South Africa's long-run growth performance. Following the economic sanctions and debt moratorium imposed by Western nations in 1985, South Africa grew at a negative rate of -1.22 per cent per annum (in per-capita terms) over the period 1985–1993. The democratic elections in 1994 and South

Africa's readmission into the global economy led to a 'growth revival' from 1994 until 2003. Faster growth over the period 1994–2003, however, was more indicative of a recovery phase after the recessionary conditions that prevailed during the period 1985–1993, rather than a long-run growth transition.

Figure 1 plots the natural logarithm (*ln*) of South Africa's real gross domestic product (GDP) series over the period 1960–2017, together with a subdivision of the growth regimes 1960–1976, 1977–2003 and 2004–2017 identified above. All the data in this paper are annual and sourced from the South African Reserve Bank (SARB). Although data on real GDP are available from 1946 onwards, the real terms-of-trade series only starts in 1960, which restricts the sample period from 1960 until 2017.

Table 1 reports the average growth rates across regimes in Figure 1, together with the current-account-to-GDP ratio, the growth rate of the real terms of trade (the price of exports relative to the price of imports in domestic currency, excluding gold), and the growth rates of real imports and exports of goods and services. To evaluate the sustainability of South Africa's improved growth performance during 2004–2017 in a later section, Table 1 also includes an additional regime over the period 2008–2017.

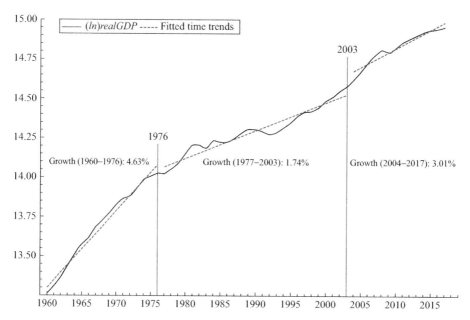

Notes:
1. The fitted time trends are obtained by regressing (*ln*)*realGDP* on an intercept term and a time trend. The slopes of the fitted time trends proxy the average growth rates reported in the figure, which are calculated as log differences. For example, the average growth rate over the period 1960–1976 is calculated as: [(*ln*)*realGDP*$_{1976}$ − (*ln*)*realGDP*$_{1959}$]/17.
2. The average growth rate over the period 1977–2003 excludes the years 1980 and 1981, when a surge in the price of gold generated rapid (outlying) growth (Nell and De Mello 2019). The average growth rate over the period 2004–2017 excludes outlying growth of −1.55 per cent in 2009, following the global financial crisis in 2008.
Source: SARB (see Appendix 1).

Figure 1   South Africa's different growth regimes, 1960–2017

   Journal compilation © 2019 Edward Elgar Publishing Ltd

Table 1   Summary statistics across different growth regimes

Growth regime	Average real GDP growth (%)	Average growth of imports (%)	Average growth of exports (%)	Average current account ratio (%)	Average growth of real terms of trade (%)
1960–1976	4.63	5.17	2.79	−1.95	−1.44
1977–2003	1.74	2.44	2.85	0.62	−0.69
2004–2017	3.01	6.62	3.84	−3.90	1.91
2008–2017	2.10	3.96	2.69	−3.88	1.64

Notes:
1. The growth rates of the variables are calculated as log differences.
2. All the average growth rates (except the real terms of trade) during 2004–2017 and 2008–2017 exclude outlying (negative) growth in 2009, following the global financial crisis in 2008.
Source: SARB (see Appendix 1).

Table 1 shows that South Africa's average real GDP growth rate of 4.63 per cent during its fastest-growing regime (FGR) (1960–1976) coincides with an average current-account deficit ratio of −1.95 per cent, an excess of import growth over export growth of 2.38 percentage points, and negative growth in the real terms-of-trade of −1.44 per cent. From these summary statistics, it can be inferred that the extended version of the BoPC growth model in equation (1) may be more relevant in this regime than the simple version in equations (2)–(2′), because the former incorporates the growth-inducing effects of real terms-of-trade movements and capital inflows.

The growth narrative in Nell and De Mello (2019) suggests that long-term capital inflows in the form of foreign direct investment (FDI) played a key role in financing the current-account deficit ratio in the post-World War II period until 1976. However, this regime came to an end when the Soweto uprising in 1976 triggered a disinvestment campaign by foreign investors and long-term capital flight.

The period 1977–2003 represents South Africa's slowest-growing regime (SGR), with an average real GDP growth rate of 1.74 per cent (excluding outlying growth in 1980–1981, as explained in the note of Figure 1). In contrast to South Africa's FGR, Table 1 shows that the current-account ratio, real terms-of-trade growth and excess of import growth over export growth are all 'close' to zero during the SGR. The descriptive statistics in Table 1, therefore, suggest that Thirlwall's original growth law in equations (2)–(2′) could be the relevant model during the SGR regime.

Looking at the last regime over the period 2004–2017, Figure 1 and Table 1 show that South Africa's growth performance improved relative to the SGR, with an average real GDP growth rate of 3.01 per cent per annum (excluding outlying growth of −1.55 per cent in 2009, following the global financial crisis in 2008). Table 1 indicates that the improvement in South Africa's growth performance during 2004–2017 relative to the SGR coincides with a large current-account deficit ratio of −3.90 per cent, an excess of import growth over export growth of 2.78 percentage points, and positive growth of 1.91 per cent in the real terms of trade. In contrast to South Africa's FGR, the current-account deficit ratio during this regime was primarily financed through short-term capital inflows, such as of portfolio investment and 'other' inflows, rather than long-term FDI (Rangasamy 2014; Nell and De Mello 2019). The descriptive statistics suggest that the extended BoPC growth model in equation (1) may again become more relevant during this regime.

From the evidence in Table 1, it is apparent that the simple version of the BoPC growth model may not accurately predict the average growth rate in each regime, other than the period 1977–2003. Nevertheless, the main message of this paper is that the relevance of Thirlwall's original law should not only be evaluated in terms of its empirical fit, but also whether growth transitions initiated through capital inflows and/or real terms-of-trade movements are sustainable. To complement the descriptive evidence in Table 1, the focus in the next sections is on an empirical fit of Thirlwall's original growth law in equation (2), as well as a more detailed analysis on the sustainability of South Africa's growth transitions over the period 1960–2017.

4   IMPORT DEMAND FUNCTION

An empirical fit of Thirlwall's growth law in equation (2) requires an accurate estimate of the income elasticity of demand for imports in the following log-level import demand specification:

$$ln(M)_t = \beta_0 + \psi ln(MRP)_t + \pi ln(Y)_t + \varepsilon_t, \tag{6}$$

where M_t is South Africa's real imports of goods and services at time t; β_0 is an intercept term; MRP_t is the price of imports relative to the price of exports (excluding gold) measured in South African rand; Y_t is aggregate real GDP, which represents domestic income; and ε_t is an error term. Consistent with equation (1), it is hypothesised that the price elasticity of demand for imports is negative ($\psi < 0$) and the income elasticity is positive ($\pi > 0$). Appendix 1 provides a detailed description of all the variables and data sources.

To estimate the traditional import demand function in equation (6), this study employs the autoregressive distributed lag (ARDL) bounds-testing procedure of Pesaran et al. (2001). The solved long-run solution of the parsimonious ARDL model (2, 0, 2) over the period 1960–2017 is given by (t-statistics in parentheses):[2]

$$ln(M)_t = \underset{(-4.82)}{-1.00}\ ln(MRP)_t + \underset{(21.10)}{1.67}\ ln(Y)_t + \hat{\varepsilon}_t, \tag{7}$$

where $\hat{\varepsilon}_t$ is the equilibrium error-correction term. The F-statistic (5.37) of the bounds-testing procedure exceeds the I(1) critical value of 4.85, so the null hypothesis of no long-run relationship can be rejected at the 5 per cent significance level.[3]

The relative price and income elasticities in equation (7) contain theory-consistent signs and are significant at the 1 per cent significance level. A comparison with other import demand studies for South Africa shows that the magnitudes of the elasticity estimates in equation (7) are almost identical to those reported in Narayan and Narayan (2010) over the period 1960–2005, and comparable with the estimates in Arize and Nippani (2010) over the sample period 1973–2005.[4]

2.   The Schwarz (1978) Bayesian (SB) criterion is used to select the parsimonious specification from a general unrestricted ARDL model of order three.
3.   Due to a word-count restriction, we do not report all the details of the bounds-testing procedure. These results are available on request.
4.   Narayan and Narayan (2010) report relative price and income elasticities of −1.00 and 1.65, respectively. These estimates are comparable with Arize and Nippani's (2010) relative price elasticity of −0.78 and income elasticity of 1.85.

                           Journal compilation © 2019 Edward Elgar Publishing Ltd

The error-correction model representation of the underlying ARDL specification over the period 1960–2017 is reported below (*t*-statistics in parentheses and *p*-values in curly brackets):

$$\Delta ln(M)_t = \underset{(-4.46)}{-3.37} + \underset{(3.19)}{0.24\Delta ln(M)_{t-1}} - \underset{(-2.71)}{0.36\ \Delta ln(MRP)_t} + \underset{(18.03)}{4.78\ \Delta ln(Y)_t}$$

$$- \underset{(-2.91)}{1.26\ \Delta ln(Y)_{t-1}} + \underset{(3.32)}{0.09D_t} + \underset{(5.69)}{0.14Dcom_t} - \underset{(-4.39)}{0.21\hat{\varepsilon}_{t-1}}$$

(8)

Adjusted $R^2 = 0.87$

LM test (serial correlation): $F[2,45] = 1.41\{0.25\}$ Standard error $[\hat{\sigma}] = 0.03$
Functional form: $F[1,46] = 0.21\{0.64\}$ ARCH test: $F[2,45] = 0.30\{0.74\}$
Normality: $\chi^2\ [2] = 0.03\{0.98\}$ Chow test: $F[26, 11] = 0.84\ \{0.66\}$
Heteroscedasticity: $F[1,53] = 2.62\{0.11\}$ (sample split in 1991)

LM is the Lagrange multiplier test for second-order serial correlation and ARCH is a test for autoregressive conditional heteroscedasticity (Pesaran and Pesaran 1997). The dummy variables D_t and $Dcom_t$ are defined in Appendix 1. The error-correction model fits the data well (adjusted $R^2 = 0.87$), passes the required diagnostic tests, and all the variables are statistically significant at the 1 per cent level.[5] The estimate on the error-correction term ($\hat{\varepsilon}_{t-1}$) shows that 21 per cent of any disequilibrium between actual and equilibrium import demand is being made up during the course of a year.

The cointegration and diagnostic tests suggest that South Africa's import demand function is well specified over the period 1960–2017. This contention is further supported by a wide range of stability tests, which show that the error-correction model is constant and structurally stable (not reported here, but available on request).

5 FITTING THE BoPC GROWTH MODEL

Table 2 fits the simple version of the BoPC growth model in equation (2) over the full sample period 1960–2017 and across the different regimes identified in Table 1. The long-run income elasticity of demand for imports ($\hat{\pi} = 1.67$) in equation (7) is used to fit the BoPC growth model in column (2). McCombie's (1989) test is applied to assess whether the difference between the actual and predicted growth rate in column (3) is statistically significant. The test requires the calculation of an implied income elasticity of demand for imports, π', which is the hypothetical elasticity that would make the actual growth rate equal to the predicted growth rate. Under the null hypothesis, the implied elasticity is equal to the estimated elasticity: $\pi' = (\hat{\pi} = 1.67)$ If the null is not rejected based on a Wald test, then the actual and predicted growth rates are not statistically different from each other. Table 3 reports the results of McCombie's (1989) test across the different growth regimes.

5.   The null hypotheses of the diagnostic tests are the following: no residual serial correlation; no functional form misspecification; homoscedasticity; normal errors; no ARCH effects; and structural stability (Chow test) based on a sample split in 1991. The error-correction model passes all the diagnostic tests at conventional significance levels.

Table 2   Fitting the BoPC growth model across different regimes

Growth regime	(1) Actual average growth rate (%) (y_t^{SA})	(2) Predicted average growth rate (%) $(y^{SA^*} = x_t/\hat{\pi})$	(3) Difference: (1)–(2)	(4) Average growth of exports (%) (x_t)	(5) Income elasticity of demand for imports $(\hat{\pi})$
1960–2017	3.03	1.83	1.20	3.06	1.67
1960–1976	4.63	1.67	2.96	2.79	1.67
1977–2003	1.74	1.70	0.04	2.85	1.67
2004–2017	3.01	2.30	0.71	3.84	1.67
2008–2017	2.10	1.61	0.49	2.69	1.67

Table 3   McCombie's (1989) test

Growth regime	Estimated income elasticity of imports $(\hat{\pi})$	Hypothetical income elasticity of imports (π')	Wald test $(\chi^2(1))$	Wald test (p-value)
1960–2017	1.67	1.00	71.74	0.00
1960–1976	1.67	0.60	182.88	0.00
1977–2003	1.67	1.64	0.14	0.70
2004–2017	1.67	1.27	25.59	0.00
2008–2017	1.67	1.28	24.33	0.00

Consider the predictive ability of the BoPC growth model over the full sample period from 1960 to 2017 in Table 2. The difference between the actual and predicted growth rate of 1.2 percentage points in column (3) is statistically significant at the 1 per cent level based on McCombie's (1989) test in Table 3. Thus, the BoPC growth model under-predicts during the period 1960–2017.

What happens when the sample period is split into different regimes? In South Africa's FGR over the period 1960–1976, the difference between the actual and predicted growth rate of 2.96 percentage points in column (3) of Table 2 is statistically significant in Table 3. The under-prediction of the BoPC growth model during this regime may partly be attributed to capital inflows. Recall from Table 1 that South Africa's average real GDP growth rate of 4.63 per cent from 1960 to 1976 coincides with an average current-account deficit ratio of −1.95 per cent. During this regime, the South African economy benefited from substantial long-term capital inflows (FDI), which financed faster import growth of 5.17 per cent relative to export growth of 2.79 per cent (see Nell and De Mello 2019). Table 1 further shows that the real terms of trade (the price of exports relative to the price of imports) grew at a negative rate of −1.44 per cent over the period 1960–1976, thus refuting the zero restriction imposed by the simple version of the BoPC growth model in equation (2). However, without knowing the magnitudes of the price elasticities in the extended BoPC model (equation (1)) *a priori*, the growth effect of the real terms of trade is indeterminate.

In South Africa's SGR (1977–2003), the difference between the actual and predicted growth rate is only 0.04 percentage points in column (3) of Table 2. In this case, McCombie's (1989) test in Table 3 cannot reject the null at any conventional

                    Journal compilation © 2019 Edward Elgar Publishing Ltd

significance level. Thus, in the SGR, the simple version of the BoPC growth model accurately predicts South Africa's growth rate. The descriptive statistics in Table 1 support this proposition. Recall that the average growth rates of imports and exports closely match each other at 2.44 per cent and 2.85 per cent, respectively, while the current-account ratio is 'close' to its equilibrium value of zero at 0.62 per cent. Moreover, the growth rate of the real terms of trade (−0.69 per cent) is less pronounced in the SGR relative to the other regimes.

To counter the criticism that Thirlwall's original growth law in equation (2) is a near identity (Razmi 2016), as implied by equation (4), it is necessary to show that world income growth is a significant determinant of South Africa's domestic income growth rate. Consider the empirical fit of the generalised version of the BoPC growth model in equation (5). Nell (2003) shows that OECD growth is a significant determinant of South Africa's income growth rate over the period 1981–1998, with a difference between the actual and predicted growth rate of only 0.12 percentage points. These results complement the empirical fit of Thirlwall's original growth law in Table 2 over the SGR (1977–2003) and verify that South Africa's growth rate is constrained by world income growth.

Looking at the period 2004–2017, when South Africa's average growth rate of 3.01 per cent shows a marked improvement relative to the SGR, the difference between the actual and predicted growth rate in column (3) of Table 2 is 0.71 percentage points. Although McCombie's (1989) test in Table 3 shows that the difference is statistically significant, the under-prediction is small relative to the 2.96 percentage-point difference in the FGR (1960–1976). The descriptive statistics in Table 1 suggest that capital inflows and movements in the real terms of trade may account for the under-prediction in this regime. The growth rate of the real terms of trade is positive (1.91 per cent) and the excess of import growth over export growth is 2.78 percentage points.

5.1   The sustainability of South Africa's growth transitions

The preceding discussion shows that Thirlwall's growth law in equation (2) accurately predicts South Africa's growth rate over the period 1977–2003. Outside this regime, the growth law under-predicts. The SGR (1977–2003), therefore, serves as a useful reference point to evaluate the sustainability of South Africa's growth transitions outside this regime.

Because the simple version of the growth law assumes zero growth in the real terms of trade over the long run, negative growth of −1.44 per cent during 1960–1976 and positive growth of 1.91 per cent during 2004–2017 may partly explain why the actual and predicted growth rates are statistically different. However, this argument assumes that movements in the real terms of trade generate growth effects because the weighted price elasticities in equation (1) are of the right magnitude. In South Africa's case, however, this assumption may not necessarily hold. Narayan and Narayan (2010) find an insignificant long-run relative price effect in South Africa's export demand function over the period 1960–2005, while the magnitude of the real effective exchange-rate elasticity of 0.26 in Rangasamy and Brick (2007) during 1990Q1–2006Q4 is relatively small and becomes insignificant in their alternative export demand specification. From equation (1), it can be seen that the real terms-of-trade effect drops out if it is assumed that the relative price effect in the export demand function is zero ($\eta = 0$), together with the fact that the estimated relative price elasticity in equation (7) is unity ($\hat{\psi} = -1.00$). The simplified equation can be written as:

$$y^{SA^{**}} = \frac{\left(\frac{E}{R}\right)x_t + \left(\frac{C}{R}\right)(c_t - p_{dt})}{\pi}. \tag{9}$$

Equation (9) implies that the under-prediction of the BoPC growth model outside the 1977–2003 regime can be attributed to real capital inflows.

Consider the empirical fit of equation (9) over the sub-periods 1960–1976 and 2004–2017. Although capital inflows played a key role during 1960–1976, the current-account ratio shows a surplus during the first four years (1960–1963) of this regime. Since the economy experienced a short period of capital outflows during 1960–1963, it is not possible to calculate the growth rate of capital inflows for each year during the FGR regime (1960–1976). Instead, we focus our analysis on the period 2004–2017 when the current account recorded a deficit in each year, including 2003. In this regime, the growth rate of net capital inflows can be calculated for each year.

Table 4 shows that the difference between South Africa's actual growth rate and the predicted growth rate of equation (9) is −0.20 percentage points over the period 2004–2017. Using McCombie's (1989) procedure, the Wald test (p-value = 0.17) cannot reject the null that the actual growth rate is equal to the predicted growth rate of the extended model with capital inflows. The good fit of the extended model downplays the role of relative price changes.[6]

At the same time, however, the results do not imply that the economy can rely on an indefinite inflow of capital to lift the balance-of-payments constraint on demand growth (see Moreno-Brid 1998; Barbosa-Filho 2001). In this context, it is important to highlight that the real GDP growth rate of 3.01 per cent during 2004–2017 is inflated by a short period of 'super-fast' growth from 2004 to 2007, when growth surged to an average

Table 4   Fitting the BoPC growth model with capital inflows, 2004–2017

Growth regime	(1) Actual average growth rate (%) (y_t^{SA})	(2) Predicted average growth rate (%) ($y^{SA^{**}}$)	(3) Difference: (1)–(2)	(4) Export volume effect (%) $\left[\left(\frac{E}{R}\right)x_t\right]/\hat{\pi}$	(5) Real capital flows effect (%) $\left[\left(\frac{C}{R}\right)(c_t - p_{dt})\right]/\hat{\pi}$
2004–2017	3.01	3.21	−0.20	2.02	1.19

Notes:
1. The weights in columns (4) and (5) are E/R = 0.88 and C/R = 0.12, respectively; x_t = 3.84 per cent; $\hat{\pi}$ = 1.67; and the growth rate of real capital inflows, $c_t - p_{dt}$ (the growth of net capital inflows minus the domestic inflation rate, as measured by the GDP deflator), is equal to 16.52 per cent.
2. All the growth rates exclude outlying (negative) growth in 2009, following the global financial crisis in 2008.

6.   The significant relative price effect on income reported in Razmi (2016) is ambiguous. He finds that the log levels of export and import prices are significant determinants of the log level of income in South Africa over the period 1950–2011. However, the price variables are included separately in the income equation. A more appropriate specification, consistent with the BoPC growth model, would be to estimate the relative price effect as a log *ratio* rather than separate level effects. For more on this critique, see Nell (2013, pp. 126–127).

annual rate of 5.06 per cent (see Nell and De Mello 2019). During the period of super-fast growth, the current-account deficit ratio deteriorated at a rapid rate, with an excess of import growth over export growth of more than 6 percentage points.

A comparison of the results across the 2004–2017 and 2008–2017 regimes in Table 2 shows that the difference between the actual and predicted growth rate has shrunk from 0.71 to 0.49 percentage points. The convergence of South Africa's actual growth rate to the rate predicted by the simple version of the BoPC model implies that the growth rate of real capital inflows is slowing down over time. Consistent with the prediction of the BoPC growth model, the brunt of the adjustment has fallen on income growth to realign import growth with export growth and preserve current-account solvency. This is evident in a precipitous slowdown in income growth from an average rate of 5.06 per cent during 2004–2007 to 2.01 per cent over the period 2008–2017. Over the same sub-periods the excess of import growth over export growth dropped from 6 percentage points to 1.27 percentage points.

South Africa's experience with capital inflows differs markedly across the 1960–1976 and 2004–2017 regimes. FDI inflows during 1960–1976 seem to have played a prominent role in lifting the balance-of-payments constraint on growth over a more long-term basis (Nell and De Mello 2019). Because the real terms-of-trade data used in this paper only start in 1960, our FGR sample period is restricted, as opposed to Nell and De Mello (2019) who emphasise the growth-inducing effect of FDI over a longer period from 1952 to 1976. In contrast to the long-term nature of capital inflows in the post-World War II period until 1976, short-term inflows, such as portfolio investment and other inflows (inclusive of foreign borrowing), appear to have dominated since 2004 (Rangasamy 2014; Nell and De Mello 2019). However, as witnessed by South Africa's actual experience over the period 2004–2017, excessive reliance on short-term capital inflows can be highly disruptive and is not a source of sustained growth.

To summarise, South Africa's growth accelerations outside the BoPC regime (1977–2003) have generally coincided with surges in investment (see Nell and De Mello 2019) and a deteriorating current-account deficit ratio, rather than faster export growth. The results imply that South Africa's recent growth surge in the post-2003 period is unsustainable, and that the economy's long-run growth rate is converging back to the rate predicted by Thirlwall's law. The analysis further shows that it is uninformative to evaluate Thirlwall's growth law across a single regime *à la* Razmi (2016). Once regime changes are controlled for, the growth law provides valuable information on the sustainability of South Africa's different growth transitions.

6   CONCLUSION

This paper has re-evaluated some of the recent criticisms of Thirlwall's (1979) law against the literature on growth transitions. The actual growth experience of most developing countries is characterised by multiple regimes of growth accelerations and decelerations, rather than sustained growth, as has been the case in most advanced countries and several Asian economies. It follows that an empirical test of Thirlwall's law across a single regime is uninformative, because it is not possible to distinguish between sources of growth that initiate and sustain a growth transition. Real terms-of-trade movements and a faster rate of physical capital accumulation may initiate a growth acceleration, but because growth is not triggered by the variables and parameters that constitute Thirlwall's law, the growth transition will eventually fizzle out. A rigorous test of Thirlwall's law in a typical developing country would therefore require a more detailed and in-depth analysis of turning points in an economy's growth performance, and whether growth accelerations tend to dissipate over time because they are initiated through factors that fall outside the domain of the simple growth rule.

The empirical application shows that Thirlwall's growth law under-predicts South Africa's actual growth rate over the period 1960–2017. The under-prediction across the full sample period, however, is largely the result of volatile and unsustainable growth transitions that mask the true long-run determinants of growth in South Africa. The split of the sample period into different growth regimes reveals that the BoPC growth rule accurately predicts South Africa's actual growth rate during the period 1977–2003. The analysis further shows that the close fit of the model is not the result of an identity, as some of the critics have argued (Blecker 2016; Razmi 2016), but rather because the BoPC model accurately predicts the data-generating process. The results of the generalised version of the BoPC growth model in Nell (2003), over roughly the same period, show that OECD growth is a significant determinant of domestic income growth in South Africa, thus supporting the causal mechanism that underlies Thirlwall's original law.

Outside the 1977–2003 regime the South African economy has relied heavily on capital inflows to lift the balance-of-payments constraint on demand growth. The analysis in this paper during the 1960–1976 regime, together with the narrative in Nell and De Mello (2019) over a longer sample period, suggests that long-term capital inflows in the form of FDI have played an important role in lifting the balance-of-payments constraint on demand growth in the post-World War II period until 1976.

In contrast, during the 2004–2017 regime capital inflows were more volatile and short-term in nature. The results demonstrate that the difference between the actual and predicted growth rate of the BoPC growth model is only 0.71 percentage points during this regime, and that the difference is statistically insignificant when the model is augmented with capital inflows (assuming zero terms-of-trade effects). The results further indicate that the difference between the actual and predicted growth rate of the simple version of the BoPC model is contracting over time, which emphasises the unsustainable nature of capital inflows during the 2004–2017 regime. In the absence of long-term capital inflows, South Africa's long-run growth rate is converging back to the rate predicted by Thirlwall's simple growth law.

To summarise, consistent with Razmi's (2016) single-regime regression results, Thirlwall's law is also rejected when it is considered over the full sample period for South Africa. However, an analysis of this nature is uninformative in the presence of multiple regimes. Once regime changes are controlled for, it is shown that the growth law provides key information on the sustainability of South Africa's growth transitions.

Finally, it was argued that econometric evidence of a statistically significant link between output growth and the *level* of the real exchange rate does not necessarily imply that there exists a *long-run* relationship in the true sense of the word. Panel data and time-series evidence across a single regime is uninformative about the sustainability of different growth determinants when the actual growth performance of economies is characterised by multiple regimes. The literature on growth transitions identifies a competitive exchange rate as a key *initiating* source of growth, but other complementary measures are required to sustain growth. In the specific case of South Africa, it would be advisable to follow a two-pronged strategy. A competitive exchange rate could help to shift resources into the tradable sector and raise the exports of existing manufactures from the supply side (Edwards and Alves 2006; Rodrik 2008b; Razmi 2016; Iyke 2017). However, the relevance of Thirlwall's law in South Africa suggests that growth will eventually fizzle out if it is not complemented with additional policy measures that improve the structural demand characteristics of export goods in foreign markets and/or reduce the income elasticity of demand for imports.

ACKNOWLEDGEMENTS

We are grateful to Maria De Mello and an anonymous referee for valuable comments on an earlier draft of the paper.

REFERENCES

Arize, A.C. and S. Nippani (2010), 'Import demand behavior in Africa: some new evidence', *Quarterly Review of Economics and Finance*, 50(3), 254–263.

Bagnai, A., A. Rieber and T.A.-D. Tran (2016), 'Sub-Saharan Africa's growth, South–South trade and the generalised balance-of-payments constraint', *Cambridge Journal of Economics*, 40(3), 797–820.

Bai, J. and P. Perron (1998), 'Estimating and testing linear models with multiple structural changes', *Econometrica*, 66(1), 47–78.

Bai, J. and P. Perron (2003), 'Computation and analysis of multiple structural change models', *Journal of Applied Econometrics*, 18(1), 1–22.

Barbosa-Filho, N.H. (2001), 'The balance-of-payments constraint: from balanced trade to sustainable debt', *Banca Nazionale del Lavoro Quarterly Review*, 54(219), 381–400.

Berg, A., J.D. Ostry and J. Zettelmeyer (2012), 'What makes growth sustained?', *Journal of Development Economics*, 98(2), 149–166.

Blecker, R.A. (2016), 'The debate over "Thirlwall's Law": balance-of-payments-constrained growth reconsidered', *European Journal of Economics and Economic Policies: Intervention*, 13(3), 275–290.

Bresser-Pereira, L.C. and F. Rugitsky (2018), 'Industrial policy and exchange rate scepticism', *Cambridge Journal of Economics*, 42(3), 617–632.

Cimoli, M., G. Porcile and S. Rovira (2010), 'Structural change and the BOP-constraint: why did Latin America fail to converge?', *Cambridge Journal of Economics*, 34(2), 389–411.

De Vries, G., M. Timmer and K. de Vries (2015), 'Structural transformation in Africa: static gains, dynamic losses', *Journal of Development Studies*, 51(6), 674–688.

Diao, X., M. McMillan and D. Rodrik (2017), 'The recent growth boom in developing economies: a structural change perspective', NBER Working Papers, No 23132.

Easterly, W., M. Kremer., L. Pritchett and L.H. Summers (1993), 'Good policy or good luck? Country growth performance and temporary shocks', *Journal of Monetary Economics*, 32(3), 459–483.

Edwards, L. (2005), 'Has South Africa liberalised its trade?', *South African Journal of Economics*, 73(4), 754–775.

Edwards, L. and P. Alves (2006), 'South Africa's export performance: determinants of export supply', *South African Journal of Economics*, 74(3), 473–500.

Freund, C. and M.D. Pierola (2012), 'Export surges', *Journal of Development Economics*, 97(2), 387–395.

Gouvea, R.R. and G.T. Lima (2010), 'Structural change, balance-of-payments constraint, and economic growth: evidence from the multisectoral Thirlwall's Law', *Journal of Post Keynesian Economics*, 33(1), 169–204.

Hausmann, R., L. Pritchett and D. Rodrik (2005), 'Growth accelerations', *Journal of Economic Growth*, 10(4), 303–329.

Iyke, B.N. (2017), 'Exchange rate undervaluation and sectoral performance of the South African economy', *Journal of Economic Studies*, 44(4), 636–649.

Jerzmanowski, M. (2006), 'Empirics of hills, plateaus, mountains and plains: a Markov-switching approach to growth', *Journal of Development Economics*, 81(2), 357–385.

Jones, B.F. and B.A. Olken (2008), 'The anatomy of start–stop growth', *Review of Economics and Statistics*, 90(3), 582–587.

Kerekes, M. (2012), 'Growth miracles and failures in a Markov switching classification model of growth', *Journal of Development Economics*, 98(2), 167–177.

Libman, E., J.A. Montecino and A. Razmi (2019), 'Sustained investment surges', *Oxford Economic Papers*, doi: 10.1093/oep/gpy071.

McCombie, J.S.L. (1989), '"Thirlwall's Law" and balance of payments constrained growth: a comment on the debate', *Applied Economics*, 21(5), 611–629.

McMillan, M., D. Rodrik and Í. Verduzco-Gallo (2014), 'Globalization, structural change, and productivity growth, with an update on Africa', *World Development*, 63(C), 11–32.

Missio, F., R.A. Araujo and F.G. Jayme (2017), 'Endogenous elasticities and the impact of the real exchange rate on structural economic dynamics', *Structural Change and Economic Dynamics*, 42(C), 67–75.

Moreno-Brid, J.C. (1998), 'On capital flows and the balance-of-payments-constrained growth model', *Journal of Post Keynesian Economics*, 21(2), 283–298.

Narayan, S. and P.K. Narayan (2010), 'Estimating import and export demand elasticities for Mauritius and South Africa', *Australian Economic Papers*, 48(3), 241–252.

Nell, K.S. (2003), 'A "generalised" version of the balance-of-payments growth model: an application to neighbouring regions', *International Review of Applied Economics*, 17(3), 249–267.

Nell, K.S. (2013), 'An alternative explanation of India's growth transition: a demand-side hypothesis', *Cambridge Journal of Economics*, 37(1), 113–141.

Nell, K.S. and M.M. De Mello (2019), 'The interdependence between the saving rate and technology across regimes: evidence from South Africa', *Empirical Economics*, 56(1), 269–300.

Perraton, J. (2003), 'Balance of payments constrained growth and developing countries: an examination of Thirlwall's hypothesis', *International Review of Applied Economics*, 17(1), 1–22.

Pesaran, M.H. and B. Pesaran (1997), *Working with Microfit 4.0: Interactive Econometric Analysis*, New York: Oxford University Press.

Pesaran, M.H., Y. Shin and R.J. Smith (2001), 'Bounds testing approaches to analysis of level relationships', *Journal of Applied Econometrics*, 16(3), 289–326.

Pritchett, L. (2000), 'Understanding patterns of economic growth: searching for hills among plateaus, mountains, and plains', *World Bank Economic Review*, 14(2), 221–250.

Rangasamy, L. (2014), 'Capital flows: the South African experience', *South African Journal of Economics*, 82(4), 551–566.

Rangasamy, L. and K. Brick (2007), 'The implications of OECD growth for South African exports', *South African Journal of Economics*, 75(4), 644–658.

Rapetti, M. (2013), 'Macroeconomic policy coordination in a competitive real exchange rate strategy for development', *Journal of Globalization and Development*, 3(2), 1–31.

Rapetti, M., P. Skott and A. Razmi (2012), 'The real exchange rate and economic growth: are developing countries different?', *International Review of Applied Economics*, 26(6), 735–753.

Razmi, A. (2016), 'Correctly analysing the balance-of-payments constraint on growth', *Cambridge Journal of Economics*, 40(6), 1581–1608.

Razmi, A., M. Rapetti and P. Skott (2012), 'The real exchange rate and economic development', *Structural Change and Economic Dynamics*, 23(2), 151–169.

Rodrik, D. (2005), 'Growth strategies', in P. Aghion and S.N. Durlauf (eds), *Handbook of Economic Growth*, Amsterdam: North-Holland, pp. 967–1014.

Rodrik, D. (2006), 'Goodbye Washington consensus, hello Washington confusion? A review of the World Bank's economic growth in the 1990s: learning from a decade of reform', *Journal of Economic Literature*, 44(4), 973–987.

Rodrik, D. (2008a), 'The real exchange rate and economic growth', *Brookings Papers on Economic Activity*, 39(2), 365–439.

Rodrik, D. (2008b), 'Understanding South Africa's economic puzzles', *The Economics of Transition*, 16(4), 769–797.

Rodrik, D. (2018), 'An African growth miracle?', *Journal of African Economies*, 27(1), 10–27.

Schwarz, G. (1978), 'Estimating the dimensions of a model', *Annals of Statistics*, 6(2), 461–464.

Tharnpanich, N. and J.S.L. McCombie (2013), 'Balance-of-payments constrained growth, structural change, and the Thai economy', *Journal of Post Keynesian Economics*, 35(4), 569–598.

Thirlwall, A.P. (1979), 'The balance of payments constraint as an explanation of international growth rate differences', *Banca Nazionale del Lavoro Quarterly Review*, 32(128), 45–53.

Thirlwall, A.P. (2011), 'Balance of payments constrained growth models: history and overview', *PSL Quarterly Review*, 64(259), 307–351.

Thirlwall, A.P. and M.N. Hussain (1982), 'The balance of payments constraint, capital flows and growth rate differences between developing countries', *Oxford Economic Papers*, 34(3), 498–510.

APPENDIX 1

Table A1   Variable definitions and data sources

Variable	Description	Source/Calculation
$ln(Y)_t$	Natural logarithm of real GDP (constant 2010 prices).	South African Reserve Bank (SARB)
y_t^{SA}	Domestic income growth rate.	$ln(Y)_t - ln(Y)_{t-1}$
$ln(MRP)_t$	The price of imports relative to the price of exports in domestic currency, excluding gold.	SARB
$ln(M)_t$	Natural logarithm of real imports of goods and services (constant 2010 prices).	SARB
m_t	Growth rate of real imports.	$ln(M)_t - ln(M)_{t-1}$
$ln(M)_t$	Natural logarithm of real exports of goods and services (constant 2010 prices).	SARB
x_t	Growth rate of real exports.	$ln(X)_t - ln(X)_{t-1}$
$c_t - p_{dt}$	Growth rate of real capital inflows = growth of total net capital inflows (c_t), measured by the current-account deficit, minus the domestic inflation rate (p_{dt}), measured by the GDP deflator.	SARB Calculated as log differences.
Current-account ratio	Current account as a percentage of GDP. A negative (−) ratio denotes a deficit.	SARB
Real terms-of-trade growth rate	The price of exports relative to the price of imports in domestic currency, excluding gold.	SARB Calculated as log differences.
Dummy: D_t	Equals 1 in 1997 and 1998; zero otherwise.	Captures a sharp rise in import demand due to a surge in domestic inflation.
Dummy: $Dcom_t$	Equals −1 in 1966 and 1 during 1991–1992; zero otherwise.	A combined dummy with equal magnitudes and opposite signs. The negative effect on import demand in 1966 is a pure outlying observation, whereas the positive effect during 1991–1992 captures the effect of trade liberalisation measures (see Edwards 2005).

Note: The data cover the period 1960–2017.

Review of Keynesian Economics, Vol. 7 No. 4, Winter 2019, pp. 91–110

New Structuralism and the balance-of-payments constraint

Gabriel Porcile
Economic Commission for Latin America and the Caribbean, Santiago, Chile and Universidade Federal do Paraná (UFPR), Curitiba, Brazil

Giuliano Toshiro Yajima
PhD candidate, University of Rome, 'La Sapienza,' Italy

Structuralists and Post-Keynesians share the perspective that in the long run economic growth is shaped by the income elasticity of exports and imports, and that such elasticities are a positive function of the degree of diversification and technological intensity of the pattern of specialization. Since the mid 1970s, New Structuralists began to stress the role of two sets of variables in driving the pattern of specialization: a stable and competitive real exchange rate, and the relative intensity of innovation and diffusion of technology in the center and periphery. In this paper we modify the balance-of-payments-constrained growth model to include these two sets of variables. The model provides a mechanism that ensures the validity of the original Thirlwall perspective, namely that adjustment to the balance-of-payments-constrained equilibrium takes place through changes in the rate of growth of aggregate demand rather than through changes in relative prices. In addition, it shows that a macroeconomic policy aimed at sustaining a competitive real exchange rate is a necessary complement to an active industrial policy for fostering international convergence.

Keywords: *balance-of-payments-constrained growth models, technological innovation, structural change*

JEL codes: *F43, O40, O41*

1 MOTIVATION

This paper discusses the balance-of-payments-constrained (BoPC) growth model from the perspective of the Structuralist tradition. The central tenet of Structuralism is that the dynamics of innovation and the diffusion of technology create different production structures and learning dynamics that tend to reproduce or even amplify initial asymmetries in technological and productive capabilities (the technology gap and the pattern of specialization, respectively). If market forces are left alone, the result is a center–periphery dynamic that carries crucial implications for growth and income distribution. Such a dynamic can be observed across regions within a country and across countries at an international level.

Since the mid 1970s, new debates emerged in Latin America expanding the original Structuralist ideas on economic development. These new theoretical insights gave rise to what would be labeled 'New Structuralism' in the late 1980s (Rodríguez 2006, ch. 11), which benefitted from the cross-fertilization between the 'old' Structuralism and advances in the theory of technological change, structural change, inflation, and the

Journal compilation © 2019 Edward Elgar Publishing Ltd
The Lypiatts, 15 Lansdown Road, Cheltenham, Glos GL50 2JA, UK
and The William Pratt House, 9 Dewey Court, Northampton MA 01060-3815, USA

importance of the real exchange rate for economic growth. The New Structuralism began as a response to increasing difficulties faced by the Latin American countries to sustain its industrialization process, along with the macroeconomic instability that haunted the region in the late 1970s and 1980s. Initially, it sought to understand the specific challenges faced by the region in this period (Fajnzylber 1990; Sunkel 1991). Gradually, New Structuralist ideas became part of a broader intellectual tradition discussing the specific problems faced by open economies in an international system marked by strong technological and financial asymmetries (Ffrench-Davis and Ocampo 2001). In this process, New Structuralists benefitted from both new theoretical insights and empirical evidence.

In the theoretical realm, there are strong connections between the New Structuralism, the Schumpeterian, and the Keynesian schools of thought on growth and distribution. The key link between New Structuralism and the Keynesian traditions is the assertion (shared by the original center–periphery model and the Keynesian growth models for open economies) that the external constraint limits the ability of the periphery to raise its rate of growth and converge in income per capita with the developed economies (Rodríguez 2006; Cimoli et al. 2013). The external constraint is expressed in the ratio between the income elasticity of exports and the income elasticity of imports (Thirlwall's law in its simplest version – see Dixon and Thirlwall 1975). In turn, the key link between the New Structuralist tradition and the Schumpeterian tradition is the claim that the income elasticity ratio is rooted in different patterns of specialization in center and periphery, which vary in response to the co-evolution of structural and technological change (Verspagen 1993; Amable and Verspagen 1995; Faberberg and Verspagen 2002).

Empirical studies were also important as sources of inspiration for revisiting Structuralist ideas. In particular, the comparison between the industrialization path and policies in Latin America and the Asian economies was critical for understanding the role played in convergence by two sets of policy variables: industrial and technological policies that encourage economic diversification towards more technology-intensive sectors; and macroeconomic policies sustaining a stable and competitive real exchange rate, with its implications for managing the capital account and devising macroprudential policies (Ocampo et al. 2009). Important policy lessons came from Asia that had to be absorbed by Structuralists studying Latin America.

The paper is organized in six sections. Section 2 briefly reviews the empirical literature on the impact of the technology gap and the real exchange rate (RER) on structural change and growth. Section 3 presents the basic equations and the short-run equilibrium in a Thirlwall–Dutt model based on Dutt (2002). This model is modified and expanded to explore New Structuralist ideas in Section 4, based on the empirical evidence of Section 2. Section 5 focuses on comparative dynamics in the medium run and in the long run. In the medium run, the technology gap is given, but the RER and the investment rates may vary. In the long run, the technology gap varies. Section 6 concludes.

2   TECHNOLOGY, EXPORT DIVERSIFICATION, AND THE RER: A REVIEW OF THE EMPIRICAL EVIDENCE

The idea that there is a positive association between technological capabilities and the degree of diversification and sophistication of exports finds extensive empirical support in the literature. For a comprehensive review of the technology-specialization link, see Fagerberg et al. (2001), Fagerberg and Verspagen (2002), Cimoli and Katz (2003),

Felipe et al. (2012), and Bogliacino and Pianta (2016). On the other hand, the role of the RER in fostering changes in the pattern of specialization has been less consensual at both the empirical and the theoretical levels. We will focus mainly on reviewing the empirical contributions, while the theoretical aspects of this relationship are explored in the following sections. We will argue that the literature tends to support the idea that the RER can have a significant impact on the pattern of specialization. This result is important for the New Structuralist view of the determinants of growth and will be used extensively in our modified Thirlwall–Dutt Model presented below.

The pioneer work is Baldwin (1988), who suggests that the RER may produce 'hysteresis in trade,' that is, there is a permanent effect on exports of a temporary change in the RER. By running a structural break regression of the log of the real exchange rate on the log of import prices for the US in the period 1967–1987, he observes that large and persisting appreciations of the RER in the 1980s lowered the pass-through from RER to import prices. He gives as an explanation the fact that foreign competitors have to pay the sunk costs required to access the US domestic market. As those costs cannot be recovered, once these firms enter the US market they prefer to squeeze their profit margins by applying a lower pass-through rather than to exit the market. The decline of the pass-through in import prices following a period of appreciation is also confirmed for Japan by Otani et al. (2003; 2006).

McMillan and Rodrick (2011) and Diao et al. (2017) define structural change as the residual from the decomposition of productivity growth in a 'within' and a 'structural' component. Using the ten-sector database of the Groningen Growth and Development Center (GGDC), they reported a positive and statistically significant effect on the structural component in a panel of 39 countries covering the 1950–2015 period. Mbaye (2013), in a panel of 72 countries over the period 1970–2008, observes that depreciation has a higher impact on the growth of total factor productivity than on capital accumulation. This result is by and large explained by a 'pure composition effect' – that is, production reallocation from the non-tradables to the tradables sectors. Rodrick (2008) argues that currency undervaluation helps to overcome market and institutional failures that compromise the expansion of the tradable sector. His econometric exercise identifies a larger effect of depreciation on countries that present below-average institutional quality, signaling the possibility of using devaluation as a second-best policy for structural change in developing economies.

Another stream of literature addresses structural change in terms of an increase in the extensive margin, that is, the diversification of exported products. Freund and Pierola (2008; 2012) argue that a large depreciation of the RER allows developing countries to open up new lines of exports, and hence they can benefit more from an undervalued currency. A similar argument is put forward by Elbadawi et al. (2012), who provide evidence that overvaluations had a negative impact on export diversification for 83 sub-Saharan countries in the period 1970–2004. Colacelli (2010) and Goya (2014; 2018) find out that the impact of the RER on export diversification happens mainly through the variety channel (the increase in the number of different products exported), rather than through the concentration channel. They observe that not only the level of the RER, but also RER volatility, affects export diversification, especially in the case of diversification towards more sophisticated goods. The effect of a higher RER may also be driven by processes of import substitution.[1]

1.   Moreira et al. (2017) has shown that in Latin America for the period 2008–2014 a 1 percent increase in the RER led to a reduction in import penetration on average by 0.41 percent to 0.69 percent.

Caglayan and Demir (2019) take into account differences in both skill content and the direction of trade in assessing the impact of the RER on exports. They provide evidence of the RER positively affecting medium- and low-skill manufactures, while high-skill ones and primary goods are less responsive. Cimoli et al. (2013), working with a panel of 111 countries for the period 1961–2008, find out that the RER has a significant impact on the technological intensity of exports after controlling for the level of GDP per capita. At variance with the previous results, Agosin et al. (2012), working with a data set of 79 countries, do not find an effect of the RER level, although they identify a negative impact of RER volatility on export diversification.[2]

Within the Post-Keyensian tradition, and in particular in the framework of Thirwall's law, the price and income elasticities of exports and imports are considered to depend on the country's pattern of specialization. Gouvêa and Lima (2010) show empirical evidence of how elasticities vary as a result of changes in export patterns, although they do not discuss to what extent such changes respond to the RER. Bresser-Pereira et al. (2014) and Bresser-Pereira (2016) have suggested that the ratio between the income elasticities of exports and imports may vary as a result of the RER and hysteresis effects. Bresser-Pereira et al. (2014) argue that this ratio varies as a function of the difference between the observed and the industrial equilibrium RER.[3] Marconi et al. (2015) have tested this hypothesis for a panel of 65 countries between 1995 and 2012, finding a positive association between this distance and the income elasticity ratio, a result that is robust to the introduction of several control variables (such as the share of manufacturing in GDP, the current-account balance as a percentage of GDP, and the growth rate of the export of manufactured goods). The importance of the RER for growth and the income elasticities ratio is confirmed by Missio et al. (2015) for a broad sample of 103 countries between 1978 and 2007 and by Nassif et al. (2015; 2018) working with Brazilian data during the period 1980–2010. Gala (2008) highlights the differences in the management of the RER between East Asian and Latin American economies to explain the contrasting growth performance of the two regions since the 1990s. According to Razmi et al. (2012), the channel through which an undervalued RER can stimulate output growth is to be found in the investment demand that stimulates, in particular, the tradable sector. Libman et al. (2019) demonstrate in a panel of 184 countries for 1950–2014 that episodes of sustained capital accumulation lead to a shift from agriculture to manufacturing sectors and cause the trade balance to follow a U-shaped pattern – following an initial deterioration due to increased imports and then recovering afterwards as the export sector gains competitiveness. A combination of a competitive RER with active industrial policies has been observed in most of the successful cases of catching up and convergence (Cimoli et al. 2019).

Some Post-Keynesian scholars contend that the development effects of the exchange rate should be qualified in some cases. Razmi and Blecker (2008) observe that RER devaluations in developing countries do help to increase their growth rate, but at the expense of growth in other countries at a similar level of development. Ibarra and Blecker (2015), in their estimate of the BoPC rate of growth of Mexico, find small effects of the RER on exports due to the high share of imported intermediate inputs in

---

2.   For the New Structuralists, the RER should be both competitive and stable. See, on this point, Ffrench-Davis and Ocampo (2001), Ocampo et al. (2009), Ffrench-Davis (2012) and Guzmán et al. (2018).

3.   The industrial equilibrium RER is defined by Bresser-Pereira (2016) as the one that makes competitive those industrial firms that are using state-of-the-art technology.

the total cost of Mexican exporters. Although these authors do not dismiss the hypothesis of a developmental channel for a competitive RER level, they show that its effects may be limited in certain cases which are relevant for developing economies. Moreover, Ribeiro et al. (2019), in a panel of 54 countries for 1990–2010, challenge the idea that the RER directly affects growth, arguing instead that when the level of techno-logical capabilities and the labor income share are added as controls, exchange-rate misalignment ceases to be statistically significant. This poses the question of the relative efficacy of different policies to change the pattern of specialization and spur long-run growth, and how these policies interact. Storm and Naastepad (2015) show that the fast export recovery of Germany after the global financial crisis was due mainly to its non-price competitiveness – owing to its active industrial policy – rather than to wage moderation. This is in line with the evidence provided by Schumpeterian empirical analysis which holds that innovation, R&D, and patenting are key variables in sustaining export growth. Evidence from China and Korea sug-gests that RER and industrial and technological policies have worked together in the successful cases of catching up (Lee 2013).

All in all, a competitive RER may contribute to export diversification and hyster-esis phenomena may be at work, making diversification a persistent, rather than a temporary, outcome. As the export structure varies – driven by the extensive margin – so does the ratio between the income elasticities of exports and imports. This effect may be small in some cases, especially when exports are intensive in imported inputs. Moreover, the historical experience of Asia and Latin America suggests that – in the successful cases of convergence – managing the RER to upgrade the export structure has gone hand-in-hand with active industrial and technological policies (Ocampo et al. 2009; Cimoli et al. 2013).

3 A MODIFIED DUTT–THIRLWALL MODEL: BASIC EQUATIONS AND SHORT-RUN EQUILIBRIUM

This section takes as a point of departure the model set forth by Dutt (2002) and proposes three modifications to this model. The first modification is to relate the dynamics of the RER to mark-up pricing; the second modification is to include the determinants of the pattern of specialization in the model, based on the literature reviewed in the previous section; the third modification is to make changes in capitalists' expectations a function of the trade balance. These modifications allow us to suggest a Robinsonian interpreta-tion of the adjustment mechanism to external disequilibrium – through changes in investment decisions (see Robinson 1966 [1973]) rather than through changes in the terms of trade. We argue that these modifications are consistent with the insights of Thirlwall's law and the Structuralist tradition.

Prices in the center and periphery are set based on a mark-up rule as stated in equations (1) and (2), respectively:

$$P_N = (1+f)W_N b_N \tag{1}$$

$$P_S = (1+z)W_S b_S, \tag{2}$$

where the subscripts N and S represent North and South, or center and periphery, respectively; P_S is the price of the good produced in the periphery; P_N is the price of the good produced in the center; f is the mark-up in the center; z is the mark-up

 Journal compilation © 2019 Edward Elgar Publishing Ltd

in the periphery; W_N and W_S are nominal wages; and b_N and b_S are labor coefficients (labor per unit of output). Define the profit share as $\sigma = (PY - WL)/PY$, then, using the price equation (2) and the technical coefficient of labor in the periphery, $b_S = L_S/Y_S$, it is possible to find the profit share in the periphery:

$$\sigma_S = 1 - \frac{WL}{PY} = \frac{z}{(1+z)}. \tag{3}$$

The static condition for equilibrium in the trade balance is:

$$P_S X = P_N EM. \tag{4}$$

There are no capital flows in the model nor remittances of factor payments. Hence external equilibrium implies equilibrium in the trade balance. In equation (4), E is the nominal exchange rate (price of the foreign currency in units of the domestic currency), which will be assumed constant and equal to 1. Define the real exchange rate as $q = P_N/P_S$. Exports from the periphery are represented by the following equations:

$$X_S = \theta_S q^{\mu_N} Y_N^{\varepsilon_{N(q,G)}} \tag{5}$$

$$\theta_S = \frac{\alpha_0[1 + (1 - s_N)f]}{1 + f}. \tag{6}$$

Equation (6) assumes that the center only imports (and the periphery only exports) consumption goods. This assumption matches the idea that the technological capabilities of the periphery lag behind those of the center, limiting the set of goods it can produce. From this assumption it follows that θ_S is the share of goods imported from the periphery in the consumption of the center. In turn, f is the mark-up in the center, s_N the savings rate of the capitalists in the center (it is assumed that workers do not save), $\sigma_N = f/(1+f)$ is the profit share in total income, $\omega_N = 1/(1+f)$ is the wage share, α_0 is a constant, μ_N is the price elasticity of imports, and $\varepsilon_N(q,G)$ is the income elasticity of imports of the center. Based on the review of the literature in Section 2, we claim that the income elasticity of imports (exports) of the center (periphery) is a function of the technological gap G and the RER in the periphery. The lower the technology gap (the higher the technological capabilities of the periphery as compared to those of the center) and the higher the RER, the more diversified and the more technology-intensive the pattern of specialization of the periphery will be.

The demand of imports from the periphery (which equals exports from the center) is:

$$X_N = \theta_N q^{-\mu_S} Y_S^{\varepsilon_S}. \tag{7}$$

In the periphery, workers only consume domestic goods, while capitalists save and invest all their profits in both domestic and foreign goods:

$$\theta_N = \beta_0 \sigma_S. \tag{8}$$

As shown in equation (3), $\sigma_S = z/(1+z)$ is the profit share in total income in the periphery, β_0 is a constant, and θ_N is the share of imported foreign capital goods in total investment in the periphery. The wage share is $\omega_S = 1/(1+z)$.

    Journal compilation © 2019 Edward Elgar Publishing Ltd

In equations (6) and (9), θ_S and θ_N are constants. By using equations (5) and (7) and log-differentiating equation (4) with respect to time, it is possible to find the dynamic condition for external equilibrium:

$$g_S^* = \left(\frac{\varepsilon_{N(q,G)}}{\varepsilon_S}\right) g_N + \frac{(\mu_N + \mu_S - 1)}{\varepsilon_S}\hat{q}, \tag{9}$$

where $\hat{q} = \widehat{P_N} - \widehat{P_S}$ and $g_{i=N,S}$ represents the proportional rate of growth ($g \equiv \dot{Y}/Y$). The rate of growth of the center is an exogenous constant g_N for the periphery (the periphery is a small country). Marshall–Lerner holds and hence $\mu_N + \mu_S > 1$. While equation (9) gives the rate of growth of the periphery consistent with the external constraint (g_S^*), the effective rate of growth depends on the capitalists' decisions over capital accumulation. At variance with Dutt's model, capitalists in the South follow a conventional Kaleckian investment function (Badhuri and Marglin 1990):

$$g_S = \gamma_0 + \gamma_1 u + \gamma_2 \sigma_S. \tag{10}$$

In equation (10), u is the rate of utilization of the stock of capital in the periphery ($Y/\overline{Y}$), where $\overline{Y} = vK$ is the income of the periphery when the capital stock is used at full capacity and v is capital productivity. The parameter γ_0 represents the animal spirit (driven by expectations about future growth in the periphery), γ_1 is the response to changes in the degree of capital utilization (which reflects the desire of the capitalists of keeping a certain level of unused capacity to respond to competitive threats under imperfect competition), and γ_2 gives the response of investment to the profit share in total income. All parameters are positive. Recall that capitalists save all profits, which implies $g_S = (I/K) = (S/K) = \sigma_S(Y/K) = \sigma_S uv$. To save notation, normalize $v = 1$. The short-run equilibrium is given by:

$$u^* = \frac{\gamma_0 + \gamma_2 \sigma_S}{\sigma_S - \gamma_1}. \tag{11}$$

For having a stable equilibrium, the following condition must be verified: ($\sigma_S > \gamma_1$). This condition implies that an increase in the rate of capital utilization has a stronger impact on savings than on investment decisions. The 'leak' of aggregate demand from savings is higher than the addition to aggregate demand coming from new investments. This condition prevents growth from taking an explosive path. Plugging (11) into (10) gives the effective rate of capital accumulation:

$$g_S = \gamma_0 + \gamma_1 \left(\frac{\gamma_0 + \gamma_2 \sigma_S}{\sigma_S - \gamma_1}\right) + \gamma_2 \sigma_S. \tag{12}$$

The economic growth regime is profit-led (wage-led) if a rise in σ_S increases (reduces) g_S. Taking the derivative with respect to the profit share in equation (12) renders:

$$\frac{\partial g_S}{\partial \sigma_S} = \gamma_1 \frac{-\gamma_1 \gamma_2 - \gamma_0}{(\sigma_S - \gamma_1)^2} + \gamma_2. \tag{13}$$

The signal of this derivative, positive or negative, defines whether the growth regime is profit-led or wage-led, respectively. The effects of a worsening of income distribution (a rise in σ_S) are twofold: (i) to reduce the rate of capital utilization (aggregate demand falls because income is concentrated in the hands of the class that saves more), thereby reducing incentives to invest; and (ii) to increase the profit share, thereby increasing incentives to invest. The higher γ_2 as compared to γ_1, the more likely it is that the second effect prevails and the more likely it is to have a profit-led economy.

From equations (4), (5), and (7) it is possible to find the RER that ensures external equilibrium:

$$q = \left[\frac{\theta_N}{\theta_S} \frac{(Y_S)^{\varepsilon_S}}{(Y_N)^{\varepsilon_{N(q,G)}}} \right]^{1/(\mu_S+\mu_N-1)}. \tag{14}$$

This is the static condition for equilibrium in the trade balance. In the following sections we will allow the RER and investments to vary in the medium run, and the technology gap to vary in the long run.

4   THE DYNAMIC SYSTEM: THE RER, ANIMAL SPIRITS, AND THE TECHNOLOGY GAP

The dynamic condition of equilibrium in the trade balance stated in equation (9) can be rearranged as follows:

$$\hat{q} = [1/(\mu_S + \mu_N - 1)](\varepsilon_S g_S - \varepsilon_{N(q,G)} g_N). \tag{15}$$

In the medium run the technology gap is constant, but the RER varies. Based on Blecker (2011) and Lima and Porcile (2013), we assume a variable mark-up. Firms set a target for the profit share in total income and adjust the mark-up to attain this target:

$$\hat{z} = \vartheta \left(\sigma_S^f - \sigma_S(z) \right) = \vartheta \left(\frac{z^f}{(1+z^f)} - \frac{z}{(1+z)} \right). \tag{16}$$

In equation (16), z^f is the mark-up aimed at by firms. The parameter ϑ is the speed of adjustment of the observed profit share to the profit share desired by the capitalists. If the observed profit share is lower than the desired profit share, they will raise their mark-ups to attain the desired profit share. The value of z^f depends on the monopoly power of the firms, and hence on the degree of openness of the economy, regulations, price elasticity, and barriers to entry in the different markets for the goods produced in the periphery. It also depends on the power of labor unions to transform productivity growth into higher real wages. All these factors shaping the monopoly power of the firm and labor bargaining power will be considered exogenous to the model.

The assumption that capitalists can define and attain a desired mark-up represented by z^f involves at least two crude simplifications. First, all firms are equal and command the same market power. Second, all firms respond identically to changes in

Journal compilation © 2019 Edward Elgar Publishing Ltd

unitary costs of production. Alternatively, z^f may be seen as an aggregate indicator of power relations between capitalists and workers, reflected in the institutions of the labor market and the institutions of the goods markets. This indicator will remain stable as long as these institutions and their underlying power relations are not significantly altered.

To keep the model tractable, we assume that wages increase hand-in-hand with labor productivity,[4] and therefore $\widehat{w}_s = -\widehat{b}_s$. Using this result in the price equation (2) gives $\widehat{P}_s = -\hat{z}$ (see also Lima and Porcile 2013). Recalling that $\hat{q} = \widehat{P_N} - \widehat{P_S}$ and setting (with no loss of generality) $\widehat{P_N} = 0$, then $\hat{q} = -\widehat{P}_s = -\hat{z}$. The rise in prices makes domestic inflation overcome international inflation; as a result, domestic goods become more expensive than foreign goods as compared with the initial situation, bringing the RER down. Equation (16) produces an equilibrium value for the RER which decreases monotonically with the mark-up z^f and the desired profit share σ_S^f aimed at by the firms. In equilibrium, when $z = z^f$, firms do not have the motive to change the mark-up and (with the assumption that $\widehat{w}_s = -\widehat{b}_s$), both domestic inflation and foreign inflation are equal to zero.

If the RER is determined in the labor market, which variable is doing the heavy lifting to lead the economy to its external equilibrium (zero net exports)? If relative prices no longer do the trick, it is necessary to specify a mechanism that ensures that the equality $\varepsilon_N g_N = \varepsilon_S g_S$ holds (for a comparison between the adjustment process in the modified model and the one suggested in Dutt (2002), see Appendix 1 at the end of the paper). We suggest a Robinsonian twist in the canonical Kaleckian investment function as the key adjustment mechanism. Joan Robinson argued that the role of an external surplus (deficit) is to boost (depress) the animal spirits of the capitalists. A surplus in the trade balance is a signal that growth will continue without being threatened by an external crisis, a sharp depreciation of the currency, or a sudden stop in foreign credit. In the words of Joan Robinson (1966 [1973], pp. 7–8):

> [T]he most important benefit of a surplus on income account, which affects the whole economy, is that, provided that there are energetic enterprises and thrifty capitalists to take advantage of it, it permits home investments to go full steam while a deficit country is nervously pulling on the brake for fear of excessive imports.

To formalize this idea, we make the animal spirits (represented by γ_0, the 'autonomous'[5] component of the investment function) a monotonically increasing function of the trade balance. The animal spirits diminish with a trade deficit and are stirred by a trade surplus. Formally, this means that the animal spirits increase when the rate of economic growth

---

4.   There is no spontaneous market-driven process that makes the rate of growth of wages equal to the rate of growth of labor productivity. The model assumes that workers have enough bargaining power to make $\widehat{w}_s = -\widehat{b}_s$. Empirically, this is not always the case. Indeed, since the late 1980s, wages failed to catch up with productivity in many developed and developing countries, giving rise to a fall of the wage share in GDP (OECD 2011).

5.   The term 'autonomous' indicates investment decisions that do not respond directly to changes in income levels. Such decisions depend on the capitalist's expectations on long-run growth (which in the model are driven by the external constraint). Although the model does not consider the role of fiscal policy, γ_0 may also vary as a function of fiscal deficits or surplus (for a discussion, see Neto and Porcile 2017).

    Journal compilation © 2019 Edward Elgar Publishing Ltd

with external equilibrium, given by equation (9), exceeds the effective rate of growth given by equation (12):

$$\widehat{\gamma_0} = \varphi \left(\underbrace{\left(\frac{\varepsilon_N(q,G)}{\varepsilon_S} \right) g_N + \frac{(\mu_N + \mu_S - 1)}{\varepsilon_S} \vartheta(\sigma_S(z) - \sigma_S^f)}_{g_s^*} \right.$$

$$\left. - \underbrace{\gamma_0 - \gamma_1 \left(\frac{\gamma_0 + \gamma_2(\sigma_S(z))}{(\sigma_S(z)) - \gamma_1} \right) - \gamma_2 \left(\sigma_S(z) \right)}_{g_s} \right). \tag{17}$$

The differential equations (16) and (17) form a dynamic system with state variables γ_0 and z (the RER and the animal spirits are the two state variables).

$$J = \begin{vmatrix} \partial \hat{z}/\partial z & \partial \hat{z}/\partial \widehat{\gamma_0} \\ \partial \widehat{\gamma_0}/\partial z & \partial \widehat{\gamma_0}/\partial \gamma_0 \end{vmatrix} = \begin{vmatrix} - & 0 \\ ? & - \end{vmatrix} \tag{18}$$

The trace of the Jacobian is negative and the determinant positive. Hence the system is unambiguously stable, even though the sign of $\partial \widehat{\gamma_0}/\partial z$ is not well defined. Taking the derivative of equation (17) with respect to z gives:

$$\frac{\widehat{\partial \gamma_0}}{\partial z} = \varphi \left(\left(\frac{g_N}{\varepsilon_S} \right) \frac{\partial \varepsilon_N}{\partial q} \frac{\partial q}{\partial z} + \frac{(\mu_N + \mu_S - 1)}{\varepsilon_S} \vartheta \left(\frac{\partial \sigma_S}{\partial z} \right) \right.$$

$$\left. - \gamma_1 \left(\frac{\left(\frac{\partial \sigma_S}{\partial z} \right) [\gamma_2 \sigma_S(z) - \gamma_2 \gamma_1 - (\gamma_0 + \gamma_2 \sigma_S(z))]}{(\sigma_S(z) - \gamma_1)^2} \right) - \gamma_2 \left(\frac{\partial \sigma_S}{\partial z} \right) \right). \tag{19}$$

The first term on the right-hand side of equation (19) is negative because a rise in z reduces the RER and this curbs diversification and the income elasticity of exports of the periphery; the second term is positive because a rise in z reduces the distance between the desired and the effective profit share, and hence the rate of growth of the mark-up and the inflation rate (assuming an initial condition $z^f > z$); the third and fourth terms combined ($\partial g^s/\partial z$) will be negative if the economy is profit-led, and positive if the economy is wage-led.

5   COMPARATIVE DYNAMICS: THE IMPACT OF CHANGES IN COMPETITIVENESS AND GLOBAL GROWTH

5.1   The profit-led economy

We first address *the medium run*, when the technology gap is given (technology changes occur at a slower pace than investment decisions and changes in prices). Assume initially that the economy is profit-led. Assume, in addition, that the price elasticities of exports and imports are not very high, that is, $(\mu_N + \mu_S - 1) \cong 0$, and hence we can neglect the second term on the right-hand side of equation (19). If the economy is profit-led, then the derivative (19) will be unambiguously negative and the isocline $\widehat{\gamma_0} = 0$ downward-sloping. This means that lower levels of autonomous expenditure are required to keep zero net exports when the mark-up is high (and

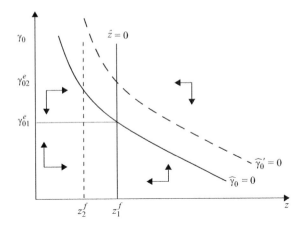

Figure 1   Growth, profit shares, and competitiveness in the medium run and in the long run

competitiveness is low). Figure 1 shows the phase diagram and the equilibrium values of the mark-up (z^f) and of 'autonomous' investment (γ_0^e).

The dynamics represented in Figure 1 offers several interesting insights. Assume that the monopoly power of firms in the periphery falls, which makes the capitalists accept a lower profit share as a target (moving the $\hat{z} = 0$ isocline to the left, from, say, the vertical line z_1^f to z_2^f). This move may arise out of a process of opening the economy to trade or adopting regulations that enhance competition in the domestic market or allow unions to capture a higher share of total income for given prices, curbing the market power of the capitalists. Since by assumption the economy is profit-led, a fall in the desired mark-up reduces the effective rate of growth g_S. However, at the same time, the real exchange rate increases, giving a boost to international competitiveness and hence reshaping the pattern of specialization. Some firms that were unable to compete with foreign firms with the old RER become competitive with the new one. The diversification of exports follows as firms in the periphery enter new external markets. As a result, expectations over future growth become more optimistic, the animal spirits are reinvigorated, and so is investment in the periphery (γ_0 goes up in the new equilibrium). The income elasticity of exports will be higher than it was before the fall in the monopoly power of the periphery firm (higher g_S^*).

In other words: the effective rate of growth reacts and converges to the new BoPC rate of growth. The short-run decline in growth turns into a higher medium-run equilibrium rate of growth as a result of the easing of the external constraint. At the same time, income distribution improves (the wage share increases because z falls). The short-run depression in the incentive to invest associated with a fall in the profit share is more than compensated by the subsequent rise in investment made possible by more optimistic expectations regarding future economic growth. This story is compatible with Blecker's observation that an economy may behave as being profit-led in the short run and wage-led in the long run (Blecker 2016).[6] The key for understanding why the increase

---

6.   In the case of the RER, Blecker observes that lower wages may provide just a temporary advantage compared to technological learning, which reshapes comparative advantages in the long run. We acknowledge this temporal dimension by assuming that the effect of a fall in z works in the medium run, while in the long run the driving force of convergence is the technological catching-up. More on this below.

    Journal compilation © 2019 Edward Elgar Publishing Ltd

in the profit share compromises growth in the long run is its negative impact on the RER and on the BoPC rate of growth.

The RER does not depend exclusively on the profit share. If wages lag behind productivity growth in the periphery, it is possible to have a rise in the profit share in the short run which does not reduce competitiveness in the medium run. In this case a worsening of income distribution may be compatible with both a positive short-run impact on economic growth (in a profit-led economy) and a medium-run rise in the equilibrium growth rate. Such a rise stems from export diversification based on the reduction of unitary wage costs. This case will not be addressed in this paper.

So far we have assumed that the technology gap is given. But in the *long run* the technology gap may change as a result of domestic efforts towards technical change and the international diffusion of technology (see Appendix 2). What happens if the periphery – for instance, by means of a new industrial and technological policy that reinforces what has been called the 'absorptive capabilities of the country' (Narula 2004, p. 8) – reduces the technology gap? The income elasticity of exports increases for any given value of z^f and the RER. The isocline $\widehat{\gamma_0} = 0$ shifts to the right, to $\widehat{\gamma_0}' = 0$. The result is a higher rate of growth with the same income distribution, as autonomous expenditures increase from γ_{01}^e to γ_{02}^e in equilibrium. This represents the concept of 'authentic competitiveness' set forth by Fernando Fajnzylber (1990), which is competitiveness based on technological learning and structural change, not in the depression of real wages. This is an enduring source of growth as increasing returns that reproduce technological asymmetries in the absence of industrial policy.

An effect similar to that of a fall in the technology gap comes out of a rise in the global demand for periphery goods – such as that represented by the rise of China in the past three decades – although these positive effects are usually confined to certain periods or cycles in commodity prices (the 'commodity lottery'). The shift in global patterns of demand in favor of the periphery, brought about by the new enhanced role of the Chinese in the international system, raises the equilibrium rate of growth of the periphery for a given degree of export diversification and for a given RER, by easing the external constraint on growth (Pérez Caldentey and Vernengo 2015; Moreno-Brid and Garry 2016; CEPAL 2018). This result may be less straightforward, however, than the reduction of the technology gap by faster technical change in the periphery. If the increase in global demand enhances the monopoly power of the exporting firms in the periphery (z^f increases and q goes down in equilibrium), then the degree of diversification may actually fall and – at least partially – hinder the expansionary stimulus provided by the international markets. Such stimulus will be limited by the loss of international competitiveness in sectors which are not the main beneficiaries of the export boom (as in the Dutch Disease phenomenon). Higher growth in global demand, if associated with enhanced power for highly concentrated exporters, may come hand-in-hand with a higher z^f and lower diversification.

5.2   The wage-led economy

Two different scenarios arise in a wage-led economy (in which $\left(\partial(g_s)/\partial z \right) < 0$). If the positive effect of a fall in the profit share on domestic demand is lower than its positive effect on export growth, then Figure 1 still adequately represents the adjustment process. The reason is that a high level of investment will be required to keep the external sector in equilibrium when competitiveness is high (low z^f), and hence the $\widehat{\gamma_0} = 0$ isocline continues to be downward-sloping.

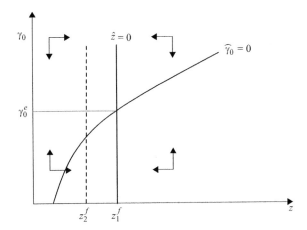

Figure 2   Growth, profit shares, and competitiveness in the medium run: wage-led in the short run and in the long run

A different scenario emerges when the response of domestic demand to a fall in the profit share is strong enough to overcome the positive increase in competitiveness produced by a lower z^f. This is the scenario represented in Figure 2. A fall in z^f increases exports, but it has such a strong effect on domestic consumption that a deficit in the trade balance emerges. Now the $\widehat{\gamma_0} = 0$ isocline has a positive slope. If z^f falls, γ_0 must fall too, to make more room for the expansion of consumption in total aggregate demand. Such an expansion of workers' consumption is made possible by the increase in competitiveness (and higher g_S^e) associated with a lower monopoly power and a higher RER.

6   CONCLUDING REMARKS

This paper presented a formal version of New Structuralism by including in a BoPC growth model (built in the spirit of the old Structuralism and Thirlwall's law) three specific assumptions about the process of adjustment between the effective rate of growth and the equilibrium rate of growth. First, changes in expectations about future growth bring about changes in investment decisions, reducing or increasing aggregate demand as a response to a deficit or a surplus in the trade balance. Second, the real exchange rate is defined by wage bargaining and the degree of monopoly in the labor and goods markets under imperfect competition. Third, the RER and relative technological capabilities in the center and periphery impact on the degree of diversification and the pattern of specialization, thereby shaping the ratio between the income elasticity of exports and imports.

The model gives support to some of the core policy recommendations associated with the New Structuralist approach to economic development. On the one hand, a policy for building technological capabilities and transforming the pattern of specialization is crucial for long-run growth. Otherwise, the efforts for boosting aggregate demand by means of traditional macroeconomic tools (for instance, an expansive fiscal

                    Journal compilation © 2019 Edward Elgar Publishing Ltd

policy) will be frustrated by the emergence of external disequilibria and an unsustainable debt. On the other hand, a competitive and stable RER is a necessary complement to policies for structural change. An industrial policy coexisting with a highly appreciated domestic currency would be totally ineffectual: all its positive effects on learning and productivity growth would be neutralized by the loss of competitiveness stemming from a low RER.

Rodrik (2008) has argued that in countries with poor institutional capabilities, a high and stable RER can work as a second-best option for industrial policy. However, using the RER as the single instrument to promote competitiveness has strong deficiencies. As put forward by Ribeiro et al. (2019), a high RER implies a lower real wage and therefore carries negative distributive implications (spurious competitiveness). In addition, technological learning shows high degrees of inertia, lock-in, and hysteresis phenomena There are slow-learning traps that cannot be overcome by market forces alone. Industrial and technological policies should invest in and encourage an institutional setting conducive to the interaction of public and private agencies (some profit-oriented, others working under different, non-market rules, as universities or research centers) engaged in innovation and the diffusion of technology (Mazzucato 2015). A macroeconomic policy concerned with competitiveness is a necessary complement to, but not a substitute for, this institutional setting.

Finally, the model makes several crucial assumptions in order to offer a simple account of what we see as the main tenets of New Structuralism. If some of these assumptions are removed, new questions and outcomes emerge that can be discussed within the framework of the New Structuralist model. First, if we allow for capital flows, then the RER and the external sector will be driven by the dynamics of the capital account (not only the trade balance), along with conflicting claims over income shares. Cycles of financial liquidity will appreciate the RER and lead to trade deficits which (for some time) the international financial system will be willing to finance. This process may end in major RER and debt crises compromising for a long period investment and growth in the periphery – see Botta (2018) for a formalization of this idea. Second, if we assume that the government deficit is part of γ_0, and if governments invest in critical areas for international competitiveness, then there may emerge interactions between γ_0 and the income elasticity of exports and imports – as put forward by Porcile and Spinola (2018). In both cases (capital flows and interactions between government expenditures and competitiveness), the stability of the system cannot be taken for granted. Cyclical patterns of growth may be observed, as well as explosive paths for the external debt.

REFERENCES

Agosin, M.R., R. Alvarez, and C. Bravo-Ortega (2012), 'Determinants of export diversification around the world: 1962–2000,' *The World Economy*, 35(3), 295–315.

Amable, B. and B. Verspagen (1995), 'The role of technology in market shares dynamics,' *Applied Economics*, 27(2), 197–204.

Baldwin, R. (1988), 'Hysteresis in import prices: the Beachhead effect,' *American Economic Review*, Z, 773–785.

Bhaduri, A. and S. Marglin (1990), 'Unemployment and the real wage: the economic basis for contesting political ideologies,' *Cambridge journal of Economics*, 14(4), 375–393.

Blecker, R.A. (2011), 'Open economy models of distribution and growth,' in E. Hein and E. Stockhammer (eds), *A Modern Guide to Keynesian Macroeconomics and Economic Policies*, Cheltenham, UK and Northampton, MA: Edward Elgar Publishing, pp. 215–239.

    Journal compilation © 2019 Edward Elgar Publishing Ltd

Blecker, R.A. (2016), 'Wage-led versus profit-led demand regimes: the long and the short of it,' *Review of Keynesian Economics*, 4(4), 373–390.

Bogliacino, F. and M. Pianta (2016), 'The Pavitt Taxonomy, revisited: patterns of innovation in manufacturing and services,' *Economia Politica*, 33, 153–180, available at: https://doi.org/ 10.1007/s40888-016-0035-1.

Botta, A. (2018), 'The long-run effects of portfolio capital inflow booms in developing countries: permanent structural hangovers after short-term financial euphoria,' ECLAC Production Development series (LC/TS.2018/96), available at: https://repositorio.cepal.org/ bitstream/handle/11362/44282/1/S1800998_en.pdf.

Bresser-Pereira, L.C. (2016), 'Reflecting on new developmentalism and classical developmentalism,' *Review of Keynesian Economics*, 4(3), 331–352, available at: https://doi.org/10.4337/ roke.2016.03.07.

Bresser-Pereira, L.C., J.L. Oreiro, and N. Marconi (2014), *Developmental Macroeconomics*, London: Routledge.

Caglayan, M. and F. Demir (2019), 'Exchange rate movements, export sophistication and direction of trade: the development channel and North–South trade flows,' *Cambridge Journal of Economics*, available at: https://doi.org/10.1093/cje/bez005.

CEPAL (2018), 'Desarrollo e igualdad: el pensamiento de la CEPAL en su séptimo decenio,' Textos seleccionados del período 2008–2018.

Cimoli, M. and J. Katz (2003), 'Structural reforms, technological gaps and economic development: a Latin American perspective,' *Industrial and Corporate Change*, 12(2), 387–411.

Cimoli, M., S. Fleitas, and G. Porcile (2013), 'Technological intensity of the export structure and the real exchange rate,' *Economics of Innovation and New Technology*, 22(4), 353–372, doi: 10.1080/10438599.2012.748504.

Cimoli, M., J.B. Pereima, and G. Porcile (2019), 'A technology gap interpretation of growth paths in Asia and Latin America,' *Research Policy*, 48(1), 125–136.

Colacelli, M. (2010), 'Intensive and extensive margins of exports and real exchange rates,' Mimeo, Barnard College, Columbia University.

Diao, X., M. McMillan, and D. Rodrik (2017), 'The recent growth boom in developing economies: a structural change perspective,' Working Paper No w23132, National Bureau of Economic Research.

Dixon, R. and A.P. Thirlwall (1975), 'A model of regional growth-rate differences on Kaldorian lines,' *Oxford Economic Papers*, 27(2), 201–214.

Dutt, A.K. (2002), 'Thirlwall's law and uneven development,' *Journal of Post Keynesian Economics*, 24(3), 367–390.

Elbadawi, I.A., L. Kaltani, and R. Soto (2012), 'Aid, real exchange rate misalignment, and economic growth in Sub-Saharan Africa,' *World Development*, 40(4), 681–700.

Fagerberg, J. and B. Verspagen (2002), 'Technology gap, innovation-diffusion and transformation: an evolutionary interpretation,' *Research Policy*, 31, 1291–1304.

Fagerberg, J., M. Srholec, and B. Verspagen (2001), 'Innovation and development,' in B. Hall and N. Rosenberg (eds), *Handbook of the Economics of Innovation*, Amsterdam: North Holland, ch. 20.

Fajnzylber, F. (1990), *Industrialization in Latin America: From the 'Black Box' to the Empty Box*, Cuadernos de la Cepal series, No 60, Santiago, Chile: ECLAC.

Felipe, J., U. Kumar, A. Abdon, and M. Bacate (2012), 'Product complexity and economic development,' *Structural Change and Economic Dynamics*, 23(1), 36–68.

Ffrench-Davis, R. (2012), 'Employment and real macroeconomic stability: the regressive role of financial flows in Latin America,' *International Labour Review*, 151(1–2), 21–41.

Ffrench-Davis, R. and J.A. Ocampo (2001), 'The globalization of financial volatility,' in R. Ffrench-Davis (ed.), *Financial Crises in 'Successful' Emerging Economies*, Washington, DC: Brookings Institution Press/ECLAC.

Frenkel, R. and M. Rapetti (2011), 'A concise history of exchange rate regimes in Latin America,' in J.A. Ocampo and J. Ros (eds), *The Oxford Handbook of Latin American Economics*, Oxford: Oxford University Press, pp. 187–213.

Freund, C. and M.D. Pierola (2008), 'Export entrepreneurs: evidence from Peru,' World Bank Policy Research Working Paper 5407.

Freund, C. and M.D. Pierola (2012), 'Export surges: the power of a competitive currency,' *Journal of Development Economics*, 97(2), 387–395.

Gala, P. (2008), 'Real exchange rate levels and economic development: theoretical analysis and econometric evidence,' *Cambridge Journal of Economics*, 32(3), 273–288.

Gouvêa, R.R. and G.T. Lima (2010), 'Structural change, balance-of-payments constraint, and economic growth: evidence from the multisectoral Thirlwall's law,' *Journal of Post Keynesian Economics*, 33(1), 169–204.

Goya, D. (2014), 'The multiple impacts of the exchange rate on export diversification,' Cambridge Working Paper in Economics, available at: https://doi.org/10.17863/CAM.5841.

Goya, D. (2018), 'The exchange rate and export variety: a cross-country analysis with long panel estimators,' Working Papers No 2018-01, Escuela de Negocios y Economía, Pontificia Universidad Católica de Valparaíso.

Guzmán, M., J.A. Ocampo, and J. Stiglitz (2018), 'Real exchange rate policies for economic development,' *World Development*, 110, 51–62.

Ibarra, C.A. and R.A. Blecker (2015), 'Structural change, the real exchange rate and the balance of payments in Mexico, 1960–2012,' *Cambridge Journal of Economics*, 40(2), 507–539.

Lee, K. (2013), *Schumpeterian Analysis of Economic Catch-Up*, Cambridge, UK: Cambridge University Press.

Libman, E., J.A. Montecino, and A. Razmi (2019), 'Sustained investment surges,' Oxford Economic Papers, gpy071, available at: https://doi.org/10.1093/oep/gpy071.

Lima, G.T. and G. Porcile (2013), 'Economic growth and income distribution with heterogeneous preferences on the real exchange rate,' *Journal of Post Keynesian Economics*, 35(4), 651–674.

Marconi, N., E.C. Araújo, and J.L. Oreiro (2015), 'The exchange rate, income elasticities, and structural change: theoretical foundations and empirical evidence,' Paper presented at the 43rd Encontro Nacional de Economia da Anpec, Florianópolis, Brazil.

Mazzucato, M. (2015), *The Entrepreneurial State: Debunking Public vs. Private Sector Myths*, vol. 1, London: Anthem Press.

Mbaye, S. (2013), 'Currency undervaluation and growth: is there a productivity channel?' *International Economics*, 133, 8–28.

McMillan, M.S. and D. Rodrik (2011), 'Globalization, structural change and productivity growth,' Working Paper No w17143, National Bureau of Economic Research.

Missio, F.J., F.G. Jayme Jr, G. Britto, and J. Luis Oreiro (2015), 'Real exchange rate and economic growth: new empirical evidence,' *Metroeconomica*, 66(4), 686–714.

Moreira, M., M.D. Pierola, and D. Sánchez-Navarro (2017), 'Exchange rate devaluation and import substitution in Latin America and the Caribbean,' IDB Technical Note 1275, Inter-American Development Bank.

Moreno-Brid, J.C. and S. Garry (2016), 'Economic performance in Latin America in the 2000s: recession, recovery, and resilience?' *Oxford Development Studies*, 44(4), 384–400.

Narula, R. (2004), 'Understanding absorptive capacities in an innovation systems context: consequences for economic and employment growth,' DRUID Working Paper No 04-02, December.

Nassif, A., C. Feijó, and E. Araújo (2015), 'Structural change and economic development: is Brazil catching up or falling behind?' *Cambridge Journal of Economics*, 39(5), 1307–1332, available at: https://doi.org/10.1093/cje/beu052.

Nassif, A., C. Feijó, and L.C. Bresser-Pereira (2018), 'The case for reindustrialization in developing countries: toward the connection between the macroeconomic regime and industrial policy in Brazil,' *Cambridge Journal of Economics*, 42(2), 355–381, available at: https://doi.org/10.1093/cje/bex028.

Neto, A.S.M. and G. Porcile (2017), 'Destabilizing austerity: fiscal policy in a BOP-dominated macrodynamics,' *Structural Change and Economic Dynamics*, 43, 39–50.

Ocampo, J.A., C. Rada, and L. Taylor (2009), *Growth and Policy in Developing Countries: A Structuralist Approach*, Oxford: Oxford University Press.

OECD (Organisation for Economic Co-operation and Development) (2011), 'Divided we stand: why inequality keeps rising,' Report, Paris: OECD Publishing.

Otani, A., S. Shiratsuka, and T. Shirota (2003), 'The decline in the exchange rate pass-through: evidence from Japanese import prices,' Institute for Monetary and Economic Studies, Bank of Japan.

Otani, A., S. Shiratsuka, and T. Shirota (2006), 'Revisiting the decline in the exchange rate pass-through: further evidence from Japan's import prices,' *Monetary and Economic Studies*, 24(1), 61–75.

Pérez Caldentey, E. (2015), 'Una lectura crítica de'la lectura crítica'de la Ley de Thirlwall,' *Investigación Económica*, LXXIV(292), 47–65.

Pérez Caldentey, E. and M. Vernengo (2015), 'Towards an understanding of crisis episodes in Latin America: a post-Keynesian approach,' *Review of Keynesian Economics*, 3(2), 158–180.

Porcile, G. and D.S. Spinola (2018), 'Natural, effective and BOP-constrained rates of growth: adjustment mechanisms and closure equations,' *PSL Quarterly Review, Economia civile*, 71(285), 139–160.

Razmi, A. and R.A. Blecker (2008), 'Developing country exports of manufactures: moving up the ladder to escape the fallacy of composition?' *The Journal of Development Studies*, 44(1), 21–48.

Razmi, A., M. Rapetti, and P. Skott (2012), 'The real exchange rate and economic development,' *Structural Change and Economic Dynamics*, 23, 151–169.

Ribeiro, R.S., J.S. McCombie, and G.T. Lima (2019), 'Does real exchange rate undervaluation really promote economic growth?' *Structural Change and Economic Dynamics*, available at: https://doi.org/10.1016/j.strueco.2019.02.005.

Robinson, J. (1966 [1973]), 'The new mercantilism, an inaugural lecture,' in J. Robinson, *Collected Economic Papers*, vol. 4, Oxford: Basil Blackwell, pp. 1–13.

Rodríguez, O. (2006), *El estructuralismo latinoamericano*, Ciudad de México: Siglo XXI.

Rodrik, D. (2008), 'The real exchange rate and economic growth,' *Brookings Papers on Economic Activity*, 2008(2), 365–412.

Storm, S. and C.W.M. Naastepad (2015), 'Crisis and recovery in the German economy: the real lessons,' *Structural Change and Economic Dynamics*, 32, 11–24.

Sunkel, O. (1991), 'El desarrollo desde dentro. Un enfoque neoestructuralista para América Latina,' Ciudad de México: Fondo de Cultura Económica.

Verspagen, B. (1993), *Uneven Growth Between Interdependent Economies: An Evolutionary View on Technology Gaps, Trade and Growth*, Avebury, UK: Ashgate Publishing.

APPENDIX 1   THE ADJUSTMENT PROCESS IN THE ORIGINAL DUTT MODEL

It is interesting to contrast the determinants of investment and growth in the modified Thirlwall–Dutt model and in the original Dutt (2002) model. The critical theoretical question raised by equation (15) is which variables are responsible for leading the economy to its medium-run equilibrium. Dutt (2002) makes the investment rate in the periphery a positive function of the terms of trade, and hence a negative function of the RER. This allows this author to rewrite equation (15) by including q in the argument of the investment function as follows:

$$\hat{q} = [1/(\mu_S + \mu_N - 1)]\left(\varepsilon_S g_S(q) - \varepsilon_N g_N\right), \text{ with } (\partial g_S/\partial q) < 0. \tag{20}$$

The equilibrium solution is stable. The dynamics is driven by changes in the terms of trade, which in the model are the inverse of the RER. Assume that initially the RER is below equilibrium and g_S is above the equilibrium rate of growth, and hence $\varepsilon_N g_N < \varepsilon_S g_S(q)$. The periphery is experiencing a trade deficit. RER will be increasing ($\hat{q} > 0$) and g_S will be falling, along with the terms of trade, to balance the external sector.

In the modified model we suggested in the article, the forces at work are different. Assume for simplicity that the RER is always in equilibrium (that is, capitalists almost instantaneously set $z = z^f$). The dynamics of the modified Thirlwall–Dutt model boils down to:

$$\widehat{\gamma_0} = \varphi\{\varepsilon_{N(q,G)} g_N - \varepsilon_S[g_S(\gamma_0)]\}. \tag{21}$$

Changes in growth rely entirely on changes in the animal spirits. Nevertheless, the RER does play a role in the adjustment process: the higher the RER in equilibrium (the lower z^f), the more diversified the economy, and the higher the rate of investment in equilibrium.

Using equation (21) (or the dynamic system in the state variables γ_0 and z presented above) instead of equation (20) has some advantages. First, the empirical evidence we reviewed in Section 2 suggests that a higher RER in the long run tends to be related to a higher rate of economic growth and more rapid structural change. In equation (20), a lower RER boosts growth, while in equation (21) it has the opposite effect. Second, the idea that the adjustment takes place by changes in aggregate demand rather than by changes in prices is one of the key tenets of Thirlwall's law – and of the Structuralist tradition for that matter (Pérez Caldentey 2015). Last but not least, in many periphery countries the RER is the focal point of the bargaining process between workers and capitalists (Frenkel and Rapetti 2011). A rise in the real exchange rate has impacts on real wages and income distribution and triggers the distributive conflict. This implies that the RER does not respond exclusively to what is going on in the external sector, as in Dutt (2002), but is part and parcel of the bargaining process in the labor market and in the goods market (through mark-up pricing). Equation (20) cannot be easily reconciled with the Kaleckian model of inflation based on the distributive conflict.

APPENDIX 2   THE LONG RUN AND THE TECHNOLOGY GAP

In the long run, relative technological capabilities evolve as a result of different rates of innovation in the center and diffusion of technology in the international economy. The technology gap will vary up to the point at which the rate of innovation in the

                    Journal compilation © 2019 Edward Elgar Publishing Ltd

center equals the rate of diffusion of technology to the periphery (implying a stable technology gap).

To analyse the evolution of the technology gap ($G = T^C/T^P$) it is necessary first to define the forces that drive T^C (technological capabilities in the center) and T^P (technological capabilities in the periphery). The growth rate of the stock of knowledge in the North is exogenous, $\hat{T}^C = r$. The growth rate of the stock of knowledge in the South ($\hat{T}^P$) depends on two factors: (i) potential knowledge spillovers from the center; (ii) investments in the South to transform this potential into effective capabilities (Verspagen 1993). Potential spillovers (factor (i)) from the center increase with the technology gap G: the higher is G, the higher the opportunity for the periphery to learn from / imitate / improve on innovations that already exist in the center. G represents a stock of knowledge the periphery could tap into if it makes the necessary investments (factor (ii)). These investments strengthen the National System of Innovation (NSI), namely the set of institutions, firms, and agencies that encourage innovations and enhance the diffusion of foreign technology in the laggard economy (Fagerberg et al. 2001; Narula 2004).

The relationship between technological spillovers and the technology gap is non-linear, as suggested by Verspagen (1993). If G is low, an increase in the technology gap increases international technological spillovers from center to periphery; after some critical value of G, however, technological spillovers slow down because the gap becomes too large, making it more difficult for the laggard economy to absorb foreign technology. Formally:

$$\hat{T}^P = G(h - jG). \tag{22}$$

Therefore, the rate of growth of the technology gap is given by:

$$\hat{G} = \hat{T}^C - \hat{T}^P = r - G(h - jG). \tag{23}$$

The parameter r gives the rate of growth of innovation in the center, h reflects increasing returns to innovation in the center (factor (i)), while j represents the efforts at catching up in the periphery (factor (ii), a very crude proxy of the NSI). There are two equilibrium values for G (which make $\hat{G} = 0$), of which only G_0^e is stable (see Figure A1). Maximum spillovers are obtained when $G = h/2j \rightarrow \hat{T}^P max$.

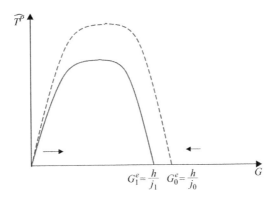

Figure A1   Strengthening the NSI in the periphery

   Journal compilation © 2019 Edward Elgar Publishing Ltd

The higher the technological efforts in the periphery, the lower the technology gap in equilibrium. Figure A1 shows the effect of a rise in j due to the strengthening of the technological policy in the periphery, from j_0 to j_1. In equilibrium the technology gap falls from G_0^e to G_1^e. The figure assumes for simplicity $r = 0$.

The take-away from this simple model of catching up / falling behind in technology is:

1. Foreign technology can be used to build up indigenous capabilities, but this becomes more difficult when the technology gap is too large (and impossible if the initial value of the technology gap is so high that it will increase without bounds).
2. The NSI (captured by j) enhances learning and diffusion of foreign technology across all periphery firms, reducing the technology gap.
3. The lower the technology gap, the higher the degree of export diversification and the higher the BoPC rate of growth.

                    Journal compilation © 2019 Edward Elgar Publishing Ltd

Review of Keynesian Economics, Vol. 7 No. 4, Winter 2019, pp. 111–127

Is Indonesia's growth rate balance-of-payments-constrained? A time-varying estimation approach*

Jesus Felipe**
Advisor, Economic Research and Regional Cooperation Department, Asian Development Bank, Mandaluyong, Philippines

Matteo Lanzafame***
Senior Economist, Economic Research and Regional Cooperation Department, Asian Development Bank, Mandaluyong, Philippines

Gemma Estrada****
Senior Economics Officer, Economic Research and Regional Cooperation Department, Asian Development Bank, Mandaluyong, Philippines

This paper analyses the performance of Indonesia's economy since the early 1980s using Thirlwall's balance-of-payments-constrained (BoPC) growth model, estimated in state-space form to take account of the varying nature of the income elasticities of demand for exports and imports. Results indicate that after peaking in the mid 1980s at above 10 percent, Indonesia's BoPC growth rate has declined significantly, to about 3 percent in recent years. This is the result of changes in the three components of this growth rate: the income elasticities of demand for exports and imports, and the growth rate of world income, all three significantly lower. Especially worrisome for Indonesia's future is the decline in the income elasticity of demand for exports, a variable that summarizes the non-price competitiveness of its exports. This is the consequence of the lack of progress in upgrading the export basket and increasing its sophistication, with natural resources and low value-added manufacturing still dominating the country's exports. Focusing on the two income elasticities, the analysis shows that their determinants are variables that proxy the economy's structural changes (for example, the manufacturing employment share) and within-sector productivity growth (for example, complexity of the economy, gross fixed capital formation as a share of GDP).

Keywords: *balance-of-payments-constrained growth rate, Indonesia, Kalman filter, Thirlwall's law*

JEL codes: *E24, E32, O14, O47, O53*

*   We are grateful to John McCombie, Tony Thirlwall, and a referee, for useful comments. The usual disclaimer applies. The paper represents the views of the authors and not necessarily those of the Asian Development Bank, those of its Executive Directors, or those of the member countries they represent.
**   Email: jfelipe@adb.org.
***   Email: mlanzafame@adb.org.
**** Email: gestrada@adb.org.

Journal compilation © 2019 Edward Elgar Publishing Ltd
The Lypiatts, 15 Lansdown Road, Cheltenham, Glos GL50 2JA, UK
and The William Pratt House, 9 Dewey Court, Northampton MA 01060-3815, USA

1   INTRODUCTION

This paper discusses Indonesia's growth performance since the 1980s using Thirlwall's (1979) balance-of-payments-constrained (BoPC) growth model. Indonesia was one of the eight economies featured by the World Bank (1993) in its analysis of East Asia's high-performing economies (for having achieved high growth rates during 1965–1990). The country was severely affected by the Asian Financial Crisis (AFC) of 1997–1998 and GDP growth since then has declined significantly. Although current growth remains high for world standards (slightly above 5 percent per annum in recent years), Indonesia is still today a lower middle-income economy.

Our interest in this economy lies in the fact that, after China, India, and the United States, Indonesia is the world's fourth most populous country in the world (about 260 million people) and it is well endowed with natural resources. It is somewhat puzzling that this large nation, which did very well for a couple of decades and was even dubbed a miracle economy, has not yet achieved upper middle-income status. The BoPC growth model helps us to understand this lack of progress: it is the result of the composition of Indonesia's exports and imports, summarized in the income elasticities of demand for exports and imports. Their low values today are the result of the country's 'shallow export-led industrialization' (Dhanani and Hasnain 2001, p. 133). Nevertheless, Indonesia has received much less attention in the development literature than China or India, its larger regional neighbors. This paper intends to fill this gap.

The rest of the paper is structured as follows. Section 2 provides a historical overview of Indonesia's economy. Section 3 presents the BoPC growth model formally, including the state-space form used to obtain time-varying estimates of the key parameters. Section 4 discusses the estimation results. Section 5 analyses the determinants of Indonesia's BoPC growth rate. Section 6 concludes.

2   AN OVERVIEW OF INDONESIA'S ECONOMY

Indonesia obtained independence in 1945. It was still very poor by the early 1960s, and when former President Suharto assumed power in 1966, its economy was in a shambles after two decades of economic stagnation (with GDP growth at 1.8 percent during 1957–1966, and GDP per capita growth at –0.6 percent during the same period), successive wars, revolution, brief economic recovery, political turbulence, and economic decline (Boediono 2016). Prominent scholars thought that Indonesia's prospects to achieve economic growth were meagre, and some considered it a 'basket case' (Myrdal 1968) or a 'chronic dropout' (Hill 1995). Until the mid 1960s, the modern industrial sector that existed in Indonesia was dominated by a few large enterprises, subsequently taken over by the state as part of the 1957–1958 series of nationalizations.

With the arrival of President Suharto, Indonesia started growing much faster, reaching 10.9 percent in 1968 (Boediono 2016). The country began to experience rapid industrialization following major political changes and economic reforms in 1966–1967. Indonesian industrial development policy can be divided into three phases until the AFC (Dhanani and Hasnain 2001):

  (i) 1965–1975: this was an open-door period. The government had to tackle a high debt-ridden and chaotic economy. The objective was to maximize growth by relying on international corporate capital.

(ii) 1975–1981: buoyed by high oil prices, Indonesia embarked on an industrialization strategy. The event that truly spring-boarded the Indonesian economy was the Organization of the Petroleum Exporting Countries' (OPEC) price hike of 1974, when oil prices quadrupled. The objective was to develop a national heavy-industry capacity based on major resource projects in steel, natural gas, oil-refining, and aluminium. This industrialization proceeded initially in an environment of import substitution. Indeed, the bonanza of this period meant that the country turned toward a slightly more statist, nationalistic, and inward-looking strategy than in previous years. Efforts were made to increase non-oil exports and in 1978 the rupiah was devalued 34 percent to increase the competitiveness of non-oil exports. Hill (1995, p. 778) argues that during this period 'there was a discordance between macro and microeconomic policies, reflecting divided authority in the realm of economic and particular industrial policy at that time.'

Indonesia grew by over 7 percent per year during the 1970s, implying that the economy doubled in size. The percentage of people living below the poverty line fell dramatically, from about 57 percent in 1970 to less than 40 percent in 1980. Rice output doubled between 1974 and 1987 and Indonesia became self-sufficient. However, despite the rapid growth in manufacturing from the late 1960s onwards and a shift towards a more diversified industrial structure from the 1970s onwards – away from the earlier dominance of simple consumer goods and resource processing – a dynamic manufacturing sector was slow to develop in Indonesia.

(iii) 1980s to the AFC: it wasn't until the 1980s that Indonesia became a significant industrial exporter. In 1982, oil prices collapsed and the government decided to restructure the Indonesian economy in a less protectionist environment. At the start of the 1980s, exports of manufactured goods represented less than 5 percent of total merchandise exports, which stands in stark contrast to the early specialization in manufacturing of other Asian countries. The delay in moving toward exporting resource- and labor-intensive goods was likely due to the presence of significant natural resources, most notably oil, but also rubber and others. At the peak of the boom, oil accounted for around three-quarters of export earnings and more than 60 percent of government revenues.

In 1982, economic expansion came to a halt when oil prices dropped, and the balance of payments deteriorated significantly. The government responded to this situation with a new stabilization program. An export-led industrialization strategy was adopted but without renouncing to protect several industries serving the domestic market. The rupiah was again devalued 28 percent in 1983 (and 30 percent in 1986, followed by a managed 5 percent annual devaluation against the dollar in the following years) and a major export promotion package was passed (for example, low interest rates for export credits). Other significant reforms were introduced, such as deregulation of the banking and financial sector.

It was not until 1985–1986 that 'both macro and microeconomic policy began to pull in the same direction ... [and] manufactured exports and the private (domestic) sector became the major engines of economic growth' (Hill 1995, p. 779). 'The major thrust of the reforms was not "pro-export" and they did not generally involve government promotion in the sense of subsidy. Rather, the reforms were designed to achieve more straightforward and predictable policy environment, in which firms

were less encumbered by complex, costly and often unenforceable business regulations' (ibid., p. 779). While there is agreement that the macroeconomic reforms of
the mid 1980s worked, there is less agreement on the impact of industrial policy.
For example, Hill (1995) argues that the impact of this policy was not significant,
while Rock (1999) argues that the view that industrial policy was incoherent, subject
to rent-seeking and irrelevant is an oversimplified conclusion. In his view, industrial
policy played a crucial role in the development of Indonesian manufacturing since
the 1960s, and must be credited for the increase in diversification of the economy.

Dhanani and Hasnain (2001, p. 136) argue that the efforts produced disappointing
results because by 1984 manufacturing exports had reached only 11 percent of total
exports. However, the reality is that the economy became more broadly based, that is,
more diversified toward manufactures of all types (and of higher value added), in particular textiles, plywood, iron and steel, footwear, sporting goods, toys, glass, electronics,
and furniture. Manufactured exports represented a meagre 2 percent of total exports in
1980. This share increased to 35 percent in 1990 and to 53 percent in 1993. During this
period, manufactures of clothing, woven fabrics, footwear, and electronics increased significantly. Plywood was a major item in Indonesia's exports. This product's phenomenal
growth resulted from the prohibition of log exports (unprocessed timber) introduced in
the early 1980s. The ban was introduced to exploit Indonesia's market power in the
industry and to increase domestic value added. Clothing and textiles were also very
large, in part propelled by the Multi-Fiber Arrangement, an international trade agreement
in effect from 1974 until 2004. The assigned quotas under the arrangement allowed
Indonesia to compete with the newly industrializing economies (NIEs). The increase
in these exports reflected Indonesia's comparative advantage in labor-intensive and
resource-based activities. Indonesia showed amazing rates of manufacturing growth,
of about 30 percent per year in real terms between 1980 and 1993.

The fact that Indonesia was following an export-led growth (ELG) model led some
authors to argue that, from the mid 1980s, Indonesia finally began to follow the standard
path of labor-intensive outward orientation of other East Asian countries, with labor-
intensive exports becoming a significant engine of growth (Hill 1995). Despite this,
Indonesia had an extensive negative list of sectors closed to foreign investment,
which was only gradually reduced, and there was a requirement to form partnerships
with local firms.

The 1985 Plaza Accord realignment sent many Japanese companies, especially in
the consumer electronics and automotive industries, to Southeast Asia. Indonesia benefitted enormously from restructuring in Japan, which led to a massive shift of its
labor-intensive industries. The NIEs also restructured their economies and sent their
production of footwear and garments to Indonesia.

By the end of the 1980s the economy was growing fast again (6–7 percent) and this
lasted until 1996. In 1993, the World Bank included Indonesia as part of the group of
'high-performing Asian economies.' Its achievements became so well documented that
it became part of the *The East Asian Miracle* report (World Bank 1993) and many econ-
omists became convinced that it was following the Japanese–Korean development
model. As in the case of the NIEs, the World Bank attributed its success to 'getting
prices right,' macroeconomic stability, export orientation, and the use of functional inter-
ventions or horizontal policies in the form of public goods such as infrastructure, education, and public health. Industrial policies were deemed incoherent and unsuccessful.

In the years before the AFC, some analysts started to question the country's status as
a miracle economy, arguing that not everything was rosy in the Indonesian economy:
the volume of bad loans mushroomed, cronyism between government, banks, and

   Journal compilation © 2019 Edward Elgar Publishing Ltd

businesses had led to growing inefficiency, and corruption had become rampant. Moreover, notwithstanding the country's progress, Indonesia could not create a thriving manufacturing sector like those of the NIEs, or even like those of Malaysia and Thailand.

Over the period 1990–1996, Indonesia's non-oil and gas sector grew at an average rate of 12 percent per year and contributed one-third to overall GDP growth. This contributed decisively to the transformation of Indonesia's economy. Today, manufacturing employs over 14 million Indonesians (about 15 percent of total employment) and contributes about 20 percent to GDP.

During this period, and more precisely in 1994, a new foreign investment regulation lifted the local partner requirement, allowing foreign firms to hold 100 percent equity in Indonesia. The negative list was also reduced considerably. Foreign direct investment (FDI) surged during 1994–1997, but manufacturing export growth began to slow down during this period, in particular manufacturing exports of plywood, textiles, garments, and footwear (the four major exports) (Dhanani and Hasnain 2001).

The next episode in Indonesia's development was the Asian Financial Crisis of 1997–1998, which devastated the country. Investment collapsed (as a result of the reversal in FDI inflows) and export growth (especially manufactures) declined significantly. Not without reason, Hill (1995, p. 787) concluded that: 'the World Bank may not have done the country a service by including it in the "miracle club".' Indonesia experienced a deep economic contraction. As noted, FDI inflows collapsed and most manufacturing sectors were severely affected (transport and equipment were the exception), particularly export-driven sub-sectors such as textiles, clothing and footwear, and wood products. These sectors' activities fell into a 'growth recession' and their contribution to GDP growth declined considerably (World Bank 2012). Lower domestic demand and a deteriorating business environment in the years following the AFC were major drivers of this decline. At the same time, rising commodity prices induced a shift in Indonesia's exports, away from manufactures and toward resource-based manufacturing and commodities. The result was that the transformation of the economy took a different direction after the AFC, with natural resource-based sectors (for example, food, beverages and tobacco, fertilizer, chemicals, and rubber) increasing, and the labor-intensive sectors (for example, textiles, leather and footwear, and wood and wood products) decreasing in importance. The shares in total value-added of sectors such as transport equipment and machinery and apparatus increased. Likewise, the shares of exports of natural resource-based commodities increased.

The result is that today Indonesia is still highly dependent on imported raw materials and components, low value-added generated in resource-based and labor-intensive industries, a virtually non-existent capital goods sector, a limited range of export products and markets, remarkable specialization in labor-intensive and demand-inelastic manufactures, low productivity in small and medium-sized enterprises, high market concentration, weak human resources, weak technology support systems, and weak domestic capabilities of domestic manufacturing firms (Asian Development Bank 2019).

Average GDP growth in Indonesia slowed down after the AFC. Average annual GDP growth was 5.3 percent in the 2000–2017 period, down from 7.2 percent over 1990–1997 and 5.8 percent in the 1980s. This worsening growth performance has also weakened the pace of Indonesia's progress towards better living standards, as annual per capita GDP growth decreased to about 4 percent in 2000–2017, down from 5.50 percent during 1990–1997. Against this backdrop, the question of whether Indonesia can improve its long-run growth performance and go back to growing on average 6 percent or more becomes critical – and, indeed, is at the centre of the country's next National Medium-Term Development Plan (RPJMN) covering 2020–2024 (ibid.). For instance, since annual population growth is projected at about 1 percent over 2018–2024, average GDP growth at 6 percent would imply a per capita GDP level about 10 percentage points higher in 2024 with respect to what it would be with annual GDP growth at 5 percent over the same period.

3   BALANCE-OF-PAYMENTS-CONSTRAINED GROWTH RATE ESTIMATION: A STATE-SPACE MODEL WITH TIME-VARYING PARAMETERS

Before achieving its potential growth rate, an economy's actual growth performance can be curtailed by macro constraints. For emerging economies like Indonesia, the external constraint associated with the current account balance is particularly significant, given these countries' dependence on the availability of foreign exchange to finance their imports. Current account deficits can be sustainable and, indeed, necessary in the short-run – especially when they allow faster capital accumulation. However, countries cannot finance ever-growing current account deficits in the long run, as there is a limit beyond which the deficit becomes unsustainable (or is perceived as such by the financial markets) and a balance-of-payments (BoP) crisis ensues. Therefore, countries that find themselves in BoP problems may be forced to constrain growth while the economy still has surplus capacity and surplus labor – that is, while the actual growth rate is still below the potential growth rate.

To formally consider the implications of this situation for Indonesia's long-run growth performance, we start from the contention that, in the long run, economies cannot grow faster than the rate consistent with current account balance. This rate is the so-called balance-of-payments-constrained (BoPC) growth rate. The concept of the BoPC growth rate was put forward by Thirlwall (1979) and has given rise to a large theoretical and empirical literature (for example, Guarini and Porcile 2016; Lanzafame 2014; Mayer 2017).

Thirlwall (1979) proposed a model of BoPC growth based on the notion that persistent current account deficits are not endlessly sustainable, so that growth must be consistent with a balanced current account in the long run. As such, the BoPC growth rate approach encapsulates the Keynesian view that growth is demand-driven, as a country's performance in external markets may ultimately constrain the growth of the economy to a rate below that which domestic supply-side conditions would warrant.

The model assumes the following specifications for the export and import demand functions:

$$X_t = \alpha \left(\frac{P_{dt}}{P_{ft}} \right)^{\eta} Z_t^{\varepsilon} \tag{1}$$

$$M_t = \beta \left(\frac{P_{dt}}{P_{ft}} \right)^{\theta} Y_t^{\kappa}, \tag{2}$$

where t indicates time, α and β are constants, X, M, Y, and Z are, respectively, the flows of exports, imports, domestic income, and world income (in real terms); P_d and P_f are domestic and foreign prices (measured in a common currency); $\eta < 0$ and $\theta > 0$ are the price elasticities; and $\varepsilon > 0$ and $\kappa > 0$ are the income elasticities of exports and imports. In a growing economy, the long-run constraint imposed by BoP equilibrium requires

                              Journal compilation © 2019 Edward Elgar Publishing Ltd

that exports and imports grow at the same rate, that is, $x_t = m_t$. Log-linearizing equations (1) and (2) and differentiating with respect to time, the equilibrium condition $x_t = m_t$ can be written as:

$$\eta(p_{dt} - p_{ft}) + \varepsilon z_t = \theta(p_{dt} - p_{ft}) + \kappa y_t, \tag{3}$$

where lower-case letters denote the growth rates of the relevant variables. If purchasing power parity (PPP) holds, so that relative prices measured in a common currency do not change over the long-run (that is, $p_{dt} = p_{ft}$), equation (3) can be rearranged to give:

$$y_B = \frac{\varepsilon}{\kappa} z_t. \tag{4}$$

Given that $\varepsilon z_t = x_t$, equation (4) can also be expressed as:

$$y_B = \frac{x_t}{\kappa}, \tag{5}$$

so that y_B is given by the ratio of the growth rate of exports to the income elasticity of imports.[1] Equations (4)–(5) are known as 'Thirlwall's law.' The BoPC growth rate represents an upper limit to long-run growth, which becomes binding and, therefore, constrains actual growth when a country's y_B is lower than its potential growth rate.

What do expressions (4) and (5) mean? In the long run, actual growth faster than the BoPC growth rate results in a persistently worsening current account balance, which puts constant pressure on the exchange rate and the financial system. Evidence shows that flexible exchange rates can support a short-run adjustment, but in the long run, the adjustment process occurs through slower growth to rebalance the current account. Given this, the long-term constraint associated with the BoPC growth rate is not affected by the price elasticities. Rather, it depends on the income elasticities for exports and imports. The latter capture the (non-price) competitiveness of a country's goods relative to the alternatives available in international markets; as such, the value of these elasticities depends on the type, quality, variety, etc., of the country's goods, as well as on the features (for example, reliability, speed of delivery) of its distribution network. These elasticities determine a country's BoPC growth rate and, consequently, its relative growth performance in the long run. Specifically, for any given value of the income elasticity of imports, the BoPC growth rate will be higher the faster exports grow as a result of the growth of the world economy – that is, the higher the income elasticity of exports.

Using these insights, an estimate of the BoPC growth rate can be constructed as the product of (trend) world economy growth times the ratio of the exports to imports income elasticities (equation (4)). The latter two can be obtained from the estimation of standard export and import functions. A simpler and equivalent formulation produces the BoPC growth rate as the ratio of a country's trend growth rate of exports with respect to the income elasticity of imports (equation (5)).

---

1.   An alternative assumption that can be imposed on the equilibrium condition (3), which results in specification equations (4)–(5), is that the Marshall–Lerner condition for a successful depreciation or devaluation (that is, $|\eta| + \theta > 1$) is only just met. In this case, even large rates of change of relative prices will have no effect on the BoPC growth rate.

3.1   The model in state-space form

Since the BoPC growth rate represents a long-run limit to growth, empirical studies in the literature usually consider it to be constant over time. However, unless x_t or z_t are constant, a simple look at equations (4) and (5) shows that, even ignoring short-term variations, the value of y_B will change over time because of changes in the trend growth rate of exports. More importantly, the long-run value of y_B will also be time-varying if the income elasticities of exports and/or imports are not fixed parameters but, rather, are subject to changes over time. Since ε and κ capture non-price competitiveness and, more generally, an economy's structural characteristics (for example, sectoral composition of output, resource endowments, etc.), their values are bound to be time-varying, and this is particularly so for emerging economies like Indonesia, which have undergone and/or are still undergoing substantial structural change. Given this, we adopt an empirical approach that allows the estimation of time-varying export and import income elasticities, so that we obtain a time-varying BoPC growth rate for Indonesia.

The estimation methodology relies on Kalman filtering techniques, and is based on a model that can accommodate and account for changes in the economy's structural features and trade elasticities. To avoid problems with the possible non-stationarity of the variables involved in the log-level specifications of the export and import demand functions, the estimates reported in this paper are based on the growth-rate versions of equations (1) and (2). The latter are specified in state-space models with time-varying parameters and estimated relying on the Kalman filter recursive algorithm. Hence, for instance, in the case of the export demand function our model consists of the following system of equations, with the export growth relation in (6) being the measurement equation, and (7)–(8) the two state equations:

$$x_t^T = \theta_t rp_t + \varepsilon_t z_t^T + u_t \tag{6}$$

$$\theta_t = \theta_{t-1} + \upsilon_t \tag{7}$$

$$\varepsilon_t = \varepsilon_{t-1} + \nu_t, \tag{8}$$

where lowercase letters denote growth rates, $rp_t = (p_{dt} - p_{ft})$ and the terms υ_t and ν_t are independent normally distributed errors, with zero mean and constant variance. The parameters θ_t and ε_t are, respectively, the time-varying price and income elasticities of exports.[2] Since the BoPC growth rate is held to be a long-term constraint on

---

2.   Some authors have used recursive estimation (that is, the use of an increasing window to re-estimate the model) or rolling regressions (that is, the use of a fixed window to re-estimate the model) of the export and import equations. Though these methods are related to the Kalman filter, they are different. All of them are recursive estimators designed to minimize the squared errors between a 'true' value and an estimate. The Kalman filter is a general algorithm to estimate the latent states of a system through a vector of observable signals. These states evolve in time according to a 'state equation' and are related to the signals through a 'measurement equation.' The state and measurement equation define a 'state-space model.' Estimation is based on maximum likelihood. The recursive least squares algorithm is a particular case of the Kalman filter, when applied to a specific state-space model. In this model, the state equation shows how the regression parameters change in time, and the observation equation describes how the dependent variable is related to the parameters by the regression model. Estimation is based on least squares or weighted least squares. See McCombie and Thampanich (2013) for an example of estimation of Thirlwal's law (export and import elasticities) using rolling regressions.

                                   Journal compilation © 2019 Edward Elgar Publishing Ltd

growth, the estimated $\hat{\varepsilon}_t$ and the relationship between the growth rates of exports and output need purging from short-run fluctuations. Thus, to estimate equation (6), we rely on x_t^T and z_t^T, which denote the trend growth rates of exports and world output, respectively, obtained via the commonly used Hodrick–Prescott filter. The same approach is applied to the growth-rate version of the import demand function in (2) to produce a time-varying estimate of the income elasticity of imports $(\hat{\kappa}_t)$.

Having obtained the two time-varying estimates $\hat{\varepsilon}_t$ and $\hat{\kappa}_t$, the estimate of Indonesia's time-varying BoPC growth rate (y_{Bt}) is then constructed as specified in equation (4′):

$$y_{Bt} = \frac{\hat{\varepsilon}_t}{\hat{\kappa}_t} z_t^T, \tag{4′}$$

where all variables are as previously defined.

4   ESTIMATION RESULTS AND DISCUSSION

We estimate Indonesia's BoPC growth rate for the period 1982–2014, using annual data from two data sources: the World Bank's 'World Development Indicators' (WDI), and the database 'Merchandise: trade value, volume, unit value, terms of trade indices and purchasing power index of exports' from the United Nations Conference on Trade and Development (UNCTAD). To discuss the results of our analysis, we refer to the six panels in Figure 1, which report: (a) the income elasticity of exports; (b) the income elasticity of imports; (c) the ratio of exports to imports income elasticity; (d) Indonesia's trend growth rate as a ratio the world's trend growth rate; (e) Indonesia's BoPC growth rate and actual growth rate; and (f) the actual and trend current account balance as a share of GDP.

The two income elasticities display a fairly similar and increasing trend in the 1980s but, after peaking at about 3.65 in 1991, the income elasticity of exports decreased rapidly after the mid 1990s, stabilizing only in the early 2000s at around an average of about 0.5. The value of the income elasticity of imports, on the other hand, peaked only in 2005 (at about 1.65) and declined rather quickly afterwards. As a result, both elasticities are estimated at about 0.34–0.35 in 2014. Tables 1 and 2 show Indonesia's top 10 exports and imports (average 2012–2014), together with the complexity ranking (out of 5111 products), and the shares in total exports and imports.[3] The tables show that these products, especially exports, are mostly natural resources, low complex products with low export and import elasticities.

The outcome of these different dynamics is reflected in panel (c) in Figure 1, where we report the ratio of the two income elasticities. The $\frac{\hat{\varepsilon}_t}{\hat{\kappa}_t}$ ratio increased from about 1 to 4 in the mid 1980s, and though it displayed a negative trend thereafter, it remained above 2 until the late 1990s. This is consistent with the view that the productive diversification and manufacturing development experienced by Indonesia in the 1980s and during the pre-AFC years led to gains in international competitiveness. This, however, seems to have been lost throughout the following two decades as, while other Asian countries (primarily, but not only, China) excelled, Indonesia gradually became laggard in the

---

3.   Complexity is an index that combines information of a country's diversification (number of products exported with comparative advantage) and how unique the products it exports are (how many countries export a given product). To derive complexity, we use a database that contains information on 5111 products for 150 countries.

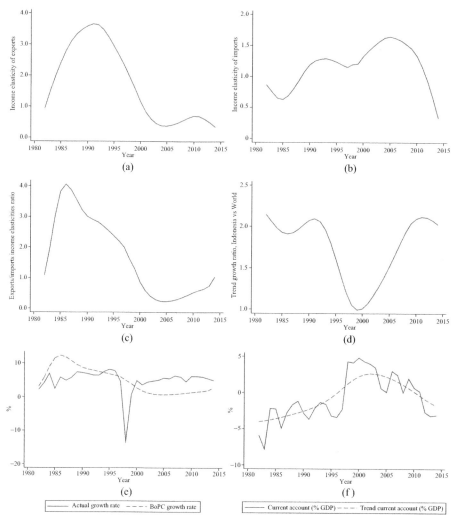

Source: Authors.

Figure 1   Indonesia's exports and imports income elasticities, and BoPC growth rate

competitiveness race: the ratio of the two elasticities fell to about 0.26 in the mid 2000s, before returning to a value of about 1 again in 2014. Interestingly, panel (d) in Figure 1 shows that Indonesia's average growth rate was about twice as high as the growth rate of the world economy both in the pre-AFC period and from the mid 2000s onwards, once the recovery was completed. However, while in the 1980s and 1990s the economy enjoyed high international competitiveness (reflected in an income elasticity of exports much higher than the income elasticity of imports), this has not been the case in the post-AFC years, when the $\frac{\varepsilon_t}{\kappa_t}$ ratio fell below (or was at most equal to) 1. The upshot of all this is shown in panel (e) in Figure 1. In the pre-AFC 1981–1996 years, Indonesia's BoPC growth rate was very high (on average, about 8.5 percent) and almost always higher than

                              Journal compilation © 2019 Edward Elgar Publishing Ltd

Table 1   Indonesia's top 10 exports by value, 2012–2014

HS code	Product description	Complexity ranking	Share in 2014 exports (%)
271111	Petroleum gases and other gaseous hydrocarbons; liquefied, natural gas	5098	5.84
270119	Coal (other than anthracite and bituminous), whether or not pulverized but not agglomerated	4598	5.11
270900	Oils; petroleum oils and oils obtained from bituminous minerals, crude	5111	4.85
270112	Coal; bituminous, whether or not pulverized, but not agglomerated	3827	4.90
151190	Vegetable oils; palm oil and its fractions, other than crude, whether or not refined, but not chemically modified	4841	6.05
400122	Rubber; technically specified natural rubber (TSNR), in primary forms or in plates, sheets or strip (excluding latex and smoked sheets)	5079	2.41
151110	Vegetable oils; palm oil and its fractions, crude, not chemically modified	4961	2.63
271121	Petroleum gases and other gaseous hydrocarbons; in gaseous state, natural gas	4956	2.42
271000[a]	Petroleum oils and oils from bituminous minerals, not crude; preparations n.e.c., containing by weight 70% or more of petroleum oils or oils from bituminous minerals; these being the basic constituents of the preparations; waste oils	5102	2.01
270210	Lignite; whether or not pulverized, but not agglomerated, excluding jet	3210	1.26

Note: a. Only 4-digit product descriptions are available from https://www.foreign-trade.com/reference/hscode.htm.

the actual growth rate, so that the country was able to sustain high actual growth without incurring in BoP problems. Meanwhile, the BoPC growth rate decreased significantly and is estimated to be always lower than the actual growth rate in the post-AFC period. Panel (f) in Figure 1 shows how these BoPC and actual growth patterns translate into the dynamics of Indonesia's current account balance as a share of GDP. The positive trend of the 1980s and 1990s when, on average, the BoPC growth rate was higher than the actual growth rate turned negative after the AFC when the BoPC growth rate became lower than the actual growth rate. Since 2012 this negative trend has led to current account deficits of about 2–3 percent of GDP which, while far from worrying in the short run, do indicate that Indonesia's growth performance may run up against the BoP constraint in the medium to long term.

To sum up, the dynamics of Indonesia's BoPC growth rate shown in panel (e) in Figure 1, and the additional information included in Figure 1, seem to fit very well the narrative illustrating the country's macroeconomic development reported in Section 2. In particular, the fast growth during the 1980s and early 1990s can be suitably explained when considering that the export-led industrialization strategy adopted by Indonesia in those years boosted its BoPC growth rate. Similarly, the post-AFC growth slowdown becomes less puzzling when compared to the concomitant decline in the BoPC growth rate, underpinned by a shift away from manufacturing exports.

Table 2   *Indonesia's top 10 imports by value, 2012–2014*

HS code	Product description	Complexity ranking	Share in 2014 imports (%)
271000[a]	Petroleum oils and oils from bituminous minerals, not crude; preparations n.e.c., containing by weight 70% or more of petroleum oils or oils from bituminous minerals; these being the basic constituents of the preparations; waste oils	5102	14.59
270900	Oils; petroleum oils and oils obtained from bituminous minerals, crude	5111	6.83
852520[a]	Transmission apparatus for radio-broadcasting or television, whether or not incorporating reception apparatus or sound recording or reproducing apparatus; television cameras, digital cameras and video camera recorders	1767	1.54
880240	Aeroplanes and other aircraft; of an unladen weight exceeding 15 000 kg	3748	0.94
100190[a]	Wheat and meslin	3978	1.15
230400	Oil-cake and other solid residues; whether or not ground or in the form of pellets, resulting from the extraction of soya-bean oil	3919	1.04
271113	Petroleum gases and other gaseous hydrocarbons; liquefied, butanes	5104	0.85
854230[a]	Electronic integrated circuits	1314	0.77
170111[a]	Cane or beet sugar and chemically pure sucrose, in solid form	5018	0.66
520100	Cotton, not carded or combed	5095	0.78

Note: a. Only 4-digit product descriptions are available from https://www.foreign-trade.com/reference/hscode.htm.

In other words, this descriptive evidence indicates that Indonesia's growth performance can be properly understood through the lens of the BoPC growth model. In the next section, we provide empirical evidence to support this view.

4.1   Tests of Thirlwall's law

How relevant is Thirlwall's law to explaining Indonesia's long-run growth? Or, in other words, has Indonesia's actual growth rate been balance-of-payments-constrained? A number of tests of the law have been proposed and widely applied in the literature. These include those by Alonso (1999), McCombie (1989), McGregor and Swales (1985), and Thirlwall (1979).

In this paper we develop a new time-series approach to investigate empirically the relevance of Thirlwall's law. The intuition underlying our testing procedure is as follows. Theory indicates that the actual growth rate will not deviate from the BoPC growth rate in the long run or, equivalently, that $y_t - y_{Bt} = ydiff_t = 0$. Similarly, since $y_{Bt} = \frac{\hat{\varepsilon}_t}{\hat{\kappa}_t} z_t^T$, the hypothesis that $y_t = y_{Bt}$ implies that $\frac{y_t}{z_t^T} = \frac{\hat{\varepsilon}_t}{\hat{\kappa}_t}$, or $ydiff_t^{REL} = \frac{y_t}{z_t^T} - \frac{\hat{\varepsilon}_t}{\hat{\kappa}_t} = 0$, in the long run. That is, a country's growth rate relative to the world's trend growth rate will reflect the ratio of the export to the import income

   Journal compilation © 2019 Edward Elgar Publishing Ltd

elasticities in the long run. These implications of the theory are consistent with the following hypotheses:

Hypothesis 1   *$ydiff_t$ and $ydiff_t^{REL}$ are stationary, mean-reverting processes. This is a necessary, but not sufficient, condition that we test relying on standard unit root tests.*

Hypothesis 2   *$ydiff_t$ and $ydiff_t^{REL}$ are zero-mean processes. This hypothesis is tested by modeling $ydiff_t$ and $ydiff_t^{REL}$ as autoregressive (AR) processes, that is,*

$$ydiff_t = \theta + \sum_{i=1}^{l} \lambda_i ydiff_{t-i} + \upsilon_t \text{ and } ydiff_t^{REL} = \theta + \sum_{i=1}^{l} \lambda_i ydiff_{t-i}^{REL} + \upsilon_t.$$

For the theory to be supported by the data, the null hypothesis $H_0 : \theta = 0$ should not be rejected at the usual significance levels.

Table 3 reports the results of the tests of Hypotheses 1 and 2. Hypothesis 1 is supported by the data, as all unit root test results indicate that $ydiff_t$ and $ydiff_t^{REL}$ are stationary processes. Specifically, the ADF (Dickey and Fuller 1979) and DF-GLS

Table 3   Tests of Hypotheses 1 and 2

	Tests of Hypothesis 1 for $ydiff_t$: unit root tests on $ydiff_t$				
	ADF	DF-GLS	KPSS	CMR-AO	CMR-IO
	−3.706*	−3.321*	0.061	−2.394	−8.194**
	Tests of Hypothesis 1 for $ydiff_t^{REL}$: unit root tests on $ydiff_t^{REL}$				
	ADF	DF-GLS	KPSS	CMR-AO	CMR-IO
	−3.744*	−3.499*	0.064	−2.374	−8.215**
	Tests of Hypothesis 2 for $ydiff_t$: test based on $ydiff_t = \theta + \sum_{i=1}^{l} \lambda_i ydiff_{t-i} + \upsilon_t$				
$ydiff_{t-1}$		0.864**	1.065**	1.042**	
$ydiff_{t-2}$		–	−0.203^	−0.220*	
$ydiff_{t-3}$		–	–	0.051	
Constant		−0.333	−0.200	−0.265	
R-squared		0.771	0.800	0.800	
Half-life		4.760	4.690	5.102	
	Tests of Hypothesis 2 for $ydiff_t^{REL}$: test based on $ydiff_t^{REL} = \theta + \sum_{i=1}^{l} \lambda_i ydiff_{t-i}^{REL} + \upsilon_t$				
$ydiff_{t-1}^{REL}$		0.871**	1.063**	1.036**	
$ydiff_{t-2}^{REL}$		–	−0.194	−0.211^	
$ydiff_{t-3}^{REL}$		–	–	0.053	
Constant		−0.116	−0.074	−0.096	
R-squared		0.781	0.806	0.806	
Half-life		5.001	4.905	5.339	

Notes: **, * and ^ indicate, respectively, significance at the 1 percent, 5 percent and 10 percent level; lag-selection for the unit root tests performed with a general-to-simple procedure, setting the maximum number of lags to 3; half-life calculated as $Ln(0.5)/Ln(\sum_{i=1}^{l} \lambda_i)$ and expressed in years; the years 1997–1999 are excluded from the sample used for the tests of Hypothesis 2.

(Elliott et al. 1996) tests reject the null of a unit root at the 5 percent significance level, while the KPSS test (Kwiatkowski et al. 1992) does not reject the null of stationarity at any conventional statistical level. Moreover, contrary to the additive outlier version (CMR-AO), the innovational outlier one-break variety of the Clemente et al. (1998) test (CMR-IO) strongly rejects the null of a unit root as well, while also signaling the presence of a significant structural break associated with the onset of the AFC in 1997.[4] In the case of Hypothesis 2, the evidence supports the long-run equivalence between actual and BoPC growth rates in Indonesia: independently of the lag order considered, and both for $ydiff_t$ and $ydiff_t^{REL}$, the three AR specifications in Table 3 return estimates of the constant that are not significantly different from zero.

To sum up, the evidence gathered supports the view that both $ydiff_t$ and $ydiff_t^{REL}$ are zero-mean stationary processes. This implies that actual growth in Indonesia tends to be equal to the BoPC growth rate on average, as short-term divergences between the two rates do not last in the long run. However, the calculated half-lives (between 4.8 and 5.3 years, depending on the AR specification considered) do indicate that deviations from the long-run equilibrium are very persistent.

5   THE DETERMINANTS OF INDONESIA'S BALANCE-OF-PAYMENTS-CONSTRAINED GROWTH RATE

The analysis of Indonesia's BoPC growth rate naturally raises the policy-relevant question of which factors may drive its dynamics. To investigate this issue, we carry out an empirical assessment of the determinants of Indonesia's BoPC growth rate, focusing on the two key elements in the framework – the export and import income elasticities. Note that, given the short time-series dimension of the data used, the analysis can at best be considered as a first exploratory inquiry into the proximate drivers of BoPC growth in Indonesia.

The two elasticities are modeled as a function of changes in sectoral employment shares (to control for structural change effects), as well as of a number of additional variables typically selected in the literature as possible determinants of a country's competitiveness on international markets. Specifically, we consider various measures of innovative activity, physical capital accumulation, trade openness, economic complexity, etc. Since the aggregate demand (AD) components are typically characterized by different import intensities, in the case of the import income elasticity we also take account of AD composition effects. The selection of a robust set of determinants and appropriate specifications (for example, in terms of lag orders) is carried out via a general-to-specific methodology. The outcome of this selection process is reported in Table 4. All data used are retrieved from the WDI dataset, except for the index of current account openness (which is the KAOPEN index by Chinn and Ito 2006) and the economic complexity index ECI+ constructed by Albeaik et al. (2017). Significance tests are based on heteroskedasticity-robust White–Huber standard errors, while the VIF test indicates that the estimates are not affected by multicollinearity. Moreover, the Durbin–Watson test (Durbin and Watson 1950; 1951) and Durbin's (1970) alternative test suggest the possible presence of serial correlation in the residuals only for the import income elasticity equation. However, the

---

4.   We also performed the two-break version of the Clemente et al. (1998) test: the results, available from the authors upon request, did not change. Taking account of this outcome, the years 1997–1999 are excluded from the empirical analysis in the remaining part of the paper.

    Journal compilation © 2019 Edward Elgar Publishing Ltd

resulting loss of efficiency does not weigh heavily on the significance of the coefficient estimates, while the latter remain consistent and unbiased in this static model even in the presence of serial correlation.[5]

While there is no evidence of a significant impact from FDI, we find that the income elasticity of exports is significantly and positively correlated with manufacturing-biased structural change, gross physical capital formation, current account openness, as well as improvements in economic complexity (proxied by the index ECI+) and the share of manufacturing exports. This outcome is in line with the view that trade expansion can foster Indonesia's BoPC growth rate when complemented by product diversification and upgrading.

Turning to the final set of estimates in Table 4, we can see that a positive change in ECI+ *decreases* the income elasticity of imports – all else constant, a one standard deviation in the change of ECI+ is correlated with a decline of about 1.3 points in the income elasticity of imports. Consequently, the picture that emerges from these results is consistent with the view that, for any given growth rate of the world economy, a rise in Indonesia's economic complexity is associated with an increase in exports, a reduction in imports, and, thus, a boost to the BoPC growth rate. Furthermore, in line with the evidence indicating that investment and exports are the two most import-intensive components of aggregate demand, exports as a share of GDP and capital accumulation are positively and significantly correlated with the income elasticity of imports. Finally, higher government consumption reduces the import elasticity, a result which is consistent with a significant 'home-bias' effect in public spending.

Table 4 Determinants of Indonesia's income elasticities of exports and imports, 1982–2014

	Exports income elasticity	Imports income elasticity
Lag of change in manufacturing employment share	0.176*	–
Lag of gross physical capital formation as a share of GDP	0.078**	–
Lag of change in gross physical capital formation as a share of GDP	–	0.040*
Change in FDI as a share of GDP	0.126	–
Change in manufacturing exports as a share of total merchandise exports	0.104**	–
Standardized change in ECI+ index	–	−1.257***
Lag of standardized change in ECI+ index	4.088*	–
Current account openness index	5.159**	–
Government consumption as a share of GDP	–	−0.085*
Lag of exports as a share of GDP	–	0.021^
Constant	−4.449**	1.434**
R^2	0.96	0.79
Observations	19	27

Notes: **, * and ^ indicate, respectively, significance at the 1 percent, 5 percent and 10 percent level; White–Huber standard errors; the years 1997–1999 are excluded from the sample.
Source: Authors.

5.   The results for the VIF, Durbin–Watson and Durbin alternative tests are available from the authors upon request.

    Journal compilation © 2019 Edward Elgar Publishing Ltd

Taken at face value, these results have important policy implications. The BoPC growth model indicates that Indonesia's key constraint on long-run growth is on the demand side and depends on the country's production and trade structures, based on non-complex products characterized by a low income elasticity of demand. Since there is little scope for further expansion of manufacturing based on domestic natural resources and a narrow range of labor-intensive and resource-based products, broader and technologically more resilient industrial development requires a comprehensive industrial strategy to strengthen the competitiveness of firms and spans the patterns of investment, innovation, industrial organization, and structure. This calls for a policy design aimed at transforming the manufacturing sector, in the context of open, deregu-lated, and increasingly liberalized markets. The challenge is how to channel domestic investment resources, attract more FDI, and direct more technology and other support infrastructure to transform the country's industrial sector. The government can play an important role in this endeavor (Mishra 2015), complementary to the market, and directed at improving the business environment, physical and human capital endow-ments, and also at implementing concrete and practical private–public measures to directly improve the competitiveness of manufacturing firms in Indonesia.

6   CONCLUSIONS

Indonesia's economy performed well between the mid 1960s and the mid 1990s. It achieved macroeconomic stability, high growth rates, and began industrializing (that is, the share of manufacturing increased both in GDP and in total employment, and the economy diversified out of natural resources). This process ended abruptly with the AFC of 1997–1998, and, since then, Indonesia's growth rate, at 5.0–5.5 percent, though high by world standards, has been significantly lower than that prior to the AFC (and much lower than that of China). This paper has argued that Indonesia's actual performance can be well explained by the fact that its BoPC growth rate increased significantly, reaching 9.5 percent in 1995–1996, and then declined to about 3 percent today. The fact that its BoPC growth rate is below the actual growth rate manifests itself in a current account deficit. What lies behind this performance is a significant decline in the ratio of the income elasticity of demand for exports to the income elasticity of demand for imports, a sign of significant loss in non-price competitiveness. Moving forward, as its actual growth rate appears to be balance-of-payments-constrained, Indonesia needs to upgrade its export structure to attain higher growth rates.

REFERENCES

Albeaik, S., M. Kaltenberg, M. Alsaleh, and C.A. Hidalgo (2017), 'Improving the Economic Complexity Index,' arXiv Working Paper, arXiv:1707:1–21, available at: https://arxiv.org/abs/1707.05826v3.

Alonso, J.A. (1999), 'Growth and the external constraint: lessons from the Spanish case,' Applied Economics, 2, 245–253.

Asian Development Bank (2019), 'Policies to support the development of Indonesia's manufac-turing sector during 2020–2024: a joint ADB-BAPPENAS report,' Manila.

Boediono (2016), Ekonomi Indonesia: Dalam Lintasan Sejarah, Bandung: PT Mizan Pustaka.

Chinn, M.D. and H. Ito (2006), 'What matters for financial development? Capital controls, insti-tutions, and interactions,' Journal of Development Economics, 81(1), 163–192.

Clemente, J., A. Montanes, and M. Reyes (1998), 'Testing for a unit root in variables with a double change in the mean,' *Economics Letters*, 59, 175–182.

Dhanani, S. and S.A. Hasnain (2001), 'Indonesia: beyond shallow, export-led industrialization,' in A. Chowdhury and I. Islam (eds), *Beyond the Asian Crisis: Pathways to Sustainable Growth*, Cheltenham, UK and Northampton, MA: Edward Elgar Publishing, pp. 132–165.

Dickey, D.A. and W.A. Fuller (1979), 'Distribution of the estimators for autoregressive time series with a unit root,' *Journal of the American Statistical Association*, 74, 427–431.

Durbin, J. (1970), 'Testing for serial correlation in least-squares regressions when some of the regressors are lagged dependent variables,' *Econometrica*, 38, 410–421.

Durbin, J. and G.S. Watson (1950), 'Testing for serial correlation in least squares regression: I,' *Biometrika*, 37, 409–428.

Durbin, J. and G.S. Watson (1951), 'Testing for serial correlation in least squares regression: II,' *Biometrika*, 38, 159–177.

Elliott, Gr., T.J. Rothenberg, and J.H. Stock (1996), 'Efficient tests for an autoregressive unit root,' *Econometrica*, 64, 813–836.

Guarini, G. and G. Porcile (2016), 'Sustainability in a Post-Keynesian growth model for an open economy,' *Ecological Economics*, 126, 14–22.

Hill, H. (1995), 'Indonesia: from "chronic dropout" to miracle?' *Journal of International Development*, 7(5), 775–789.

Kwiatkowski, D., P.C.B. Phillips, P. Schmidt, and Y. Shin (1992), 'Testing the null hypothesis of stationarity against the alternative of a unit root: how sure are we that economic time series have a unit root?' *Journal of Econometrics*, 54, 159–178.

Lanzafame, M. (2014), 'The balance of payments-constrained growth rate and the natural rate of growth: new empirical evidence,' *Cambridge Journal of Economics*, 38, 817–838.

Mayer, J. (2017), 'How could the South respond to secular stagnation in the North?' *The World Economy*, 40, 314–335.

McCombie, J.S.L. (1989), 'Thirlwall's law and balance of payments constrained growth: a comment on the debate,' *Applied Economics*, 21, 611–629.

McCombie, J.S.L. and N. Tharnpanich (2013), 'Balance-of-payments constrained growth, structural change, and the Thai economy,' *Journal of Post Keynesian Economics*, 35(4), 569–597.

McGregor, P. and K. Swales (1985), 'Professor Thirlwall and balance of payments constrained growth,' *Applied Economics*, 17, 17–32.

Mishra, S. (2015), 'The economy in Indonesia's ascent: making sense of it all,' in C. Roberts, A. Habir, and L. Sebastian (eds), *Indonesia's Ascent: Power, Leadership, and the Regional Order*, London: Palgrave Macmillan, pp. 40–68.

Myrdal, G. (1968), *Asian Drama: An Inquiry into the Poverty of Nations (Volumes, I, II and III): A Twentieth Century Fund Study*, New York: Pantheon.

Rock, M.T. (1999), 'Reassessing the effectiveness of industrial policy in Indonesia: can the neoliberals be wrong?' *World Development*, 27, 691–704.

Thirlwall, A.P. (1979), 'The balance of payments constraint as an explanation of international growth rate differences,' *Banca Nazionale del Laboro Quarterly Review*, 32(128), 45–53.

World Bank (1993), *The East Asian Miracle: Economic Growth and Public Policy*, Washington, DC: World Bank.

World Bank (2012), 'Picking up the pace: reviving growth in Indonesia's manufacturing sector,' Reports Series, Jakarta: The World Bank Office.

                    Journal compilation © 2019 Edward Elgar Publishing Ltd

Review of Keynesian Economics, Vol. 7 No. 4, Winter 2019, pp. 128–141

Thoughts on balance-of-payments-constrained growth after 40 years

A.P. Thirlwall*
Professor of Applied Economics, University of Kent, Canterbury, UK

This paper considers how Thirlwall's balance-of-payments-constrained growth model has fared over the preceding 40 years. Issues dealt with include how the model fits into Harrod's closed-economy dynamic model; whether the model is a tautology; the role of the exchange rate and terms of trade in influencing the long-run growth rate, and whether capital inflows make any difference to the long-run predictions of the model. The conclusion is that it is mainly the structure of production and trade that determines the long-run growth rate of countries, within a balance-of-payments equilibrium framework, as determinants of the income elasticities of demand for exports and imports.

Keywords: *open-economy macroeconomics, balance-of-payments-constrained growth, the Harrod trade multiplier, Thirlwall's law*

JEL codes: *F41, F43*

1 INTRODUCTION

Recently I received a letter from a student in India, who wrote:

> I was absolutely thrilled when my professor worked through the math to arrive at Thirlwall's Law, especially when the entire complex looking equation collapsed to just three variables. It was one of the few moments during my economics education when everything just came together and started to make sense. Seeing the Marshall–Lerner condition, and the Law of One Price all come together in one equation was a great feeling.[1]

Naturally I was delighted to receive the letter, not least because it endorses my Occam's Razor approach to economics which is 'the simpler the better', and that 'to get a lot out of a little' is the essence of good economics!

When I wrote my 1979 paper, I never imagined it would still be discussed 40 years on; and I would like to thank the editors of *ROKE* for organising this anniversary symposium, as well as all the contributors for their thoughtful contributions. To put the paper into context, I had always been unhappy with orthodox Neoclassical growth theory (*à la* Solow 1956), particularly for understanding the *actual* growth experience of countries which, for the most part, are open economies in which not only domestic demand but also foreign demand (exports) matter for long-run economic performance.

---

* Email: at4@kent.ac.uk. I am very grateful to Professor Kevin Nell and to Professor John McCombie for helpful comments on an early draft of the paper.
1. Letter dated 19 May 2019 from Advait Moharir, Azim Premji University, Bengaluru, India.

Journal compilation © 2019 Edward Elgar Publishing Ltd
The Lypiatts, 15 Lansdown Road, Cheltenham, Glos GL50 2JA, UK
and The William Pratt House, 9 Dewey Court, Northampton MA 01060-3815, USA

I was also unhappy with the underlying assumptions of the orthodox model that the supplies of labour and capital, and technical progress, are exogenously determined when we know that labour supply is very elastic to demand, and that investment and productivity growth, to a large extent, depend on the growth of output itself.

To make progress, there was no point in tinkering with the orthodox model; a completely new approach was required which recognised the importance of demand, and that in the real world, national economies are open to trade. I had in the back of my mind the United Kingdom (UK) economy, and I had been concerned with the fragility of the UK's balance of payments (BoP) long before 1979 (see Thirlwall 1970; 1974). Every time the UK economy had attempted to grow faster, the BoP deteriorated, and the currency came under attack.

The initial stimulus to the formulation of the 1979 model came from Kaldor's 1970 regional export-led growth model (Kaldor 1970) in which growth is demand-driven by export growth, initiating a virtuous circle of growth sustained by the induced impact of output growth on productivity growth known as Verdoorn's law (Verdoorn 1949). Dixon and I (1975) formalised the model, but it contained no BoP constraint because regions using a common currency don't suffer BoP problems in the usual sense of having an exchange rate to defend.[2] It occurred to me, however, that if the same model was applied to countries, the growth rate determined by the variables and parameters of the model may generate a faster growth of imports than exports which may be unsustainable because of a limit to the current-account deficit to GDP, or export, ratio beyond which financial markets get nervous and borrowing becomes impossible. It was a short step from that insight to realising that the Kaldor model could be augmented by an import growth function and, since import growth is partly a function of output growth, it would be possible, setting import growth equal to export growth, to solve for the growth of output consistent with BoP equilibrium on current account. Given long-run current-account equilibrium, and no change in the real exchange rate (or real terms of trade), the predicted long-run growth rate is $g = \varepsilon w/\pi = x/\pi$, where x is export growth determined by world income growth (w) and the income elasticity of demand for exports (ε), and π is the income elasticity of demand for imports. This result turns out to be the dynamic analogue of Harrod's static foreign-trade multiplier (Harrod 1933) – see below.

Given how well the BoP-constrained growth rate fits the experience of many countries (see Thirlwall 2011 for a dated survey), my thinking now is the following sequence: the BoP-constrained growth rate determines the long-run actual growth rate, and the actual growth rate determines the long-run potential growth rate (or the natural rate of growth as Harrod 1939 originally called it) because the determinants of the natural rate – labour force growth and labour productivity growth – are endogenous to demand.[3] The most convincing research to show this, at least for a selection of OECD countries, is Lanzafame (2014). The model could be replicated for other groups of countries.

---

2. This does not mean, of course, that regions don't suffer balance-of-payments problems in other ways such as slow growth and high unemployment, as in some of the eurozone countries today (see Thirlwall 1980).

3. There are now many empirical studies of the endogeneity of the natural rate of growth, for example, Leon-Ledesma and Thirlwall (2002) for OECD countries; Perrotini and Tlatelpa (2003) for NAFTA countries; Libanio (2009) and Vogel (2009) for Latin American countries; Dray and Thirlwall (2011) for a selection of Asian countries; and Lanzafame (2010) for Italian regions.

The basic model (and its many extensions) raises several issues which contributors highlight in this symposium, some of which I discuss below. The model also has many policy implications, but in my view the most important one concerns a country's structure of production and trade because different goods have different production and demand characteristics. This obvious point is totally missing from the one-good aggregate closed-economy models of mainstream growth theory so prevalent in textbooks. Countries growing slowly need to examine carefully the types of goods they produce and export. 'What you export matters' is the evocative title of the paper by Hausmann et al. (2007), in which they show the clear association across countries between the technological sophistication of goods and export growth, determined by the income elasticity of demand for exports, and GDP growth. Pacheco-Lopez and Thirlwall (2014) also show the close association across countries between the growth of manufacturing output, export growth and GDP growth, which is an alternative (open-economy) interpretation of Kaldor's first growth law of manufacturing industry as the 'engine' of growth (Kaldor 1967). In many ways, the BoP-constrained growth model is an export-led growth model based on the crucial role of manufacturing and exports in the development process (Mathews 2019).

2   HARROD'S TRADE MULTIPLIER AND DYNAMIC ANALYSIS

The main result that the long-run growth of countries is likely to be approximated by the growth of exports relative to the income elasticity of demand for imports ($g_b = x/\pi$) turned out to be the dynamic analogue of Harrod's (1933) static foreign-trade multiplier result, $Y = X/m$, derived on the same assumptions as the dynamic result (where Y is the level of output, X is the level of exports and m is the marginal propensity to import), although I didn't realise it at the time. I had never read Harrod's 1933 book, *International Economics*, in which the foreign-trade multiplier, $1/m$, appears, but when I showed my result to my colleague at the University of Kent, Charles Kennedy (a former Oxford friend of Harrod), he immediately recognised the correspondence of the static and dynamic result. McCombie (1985) has also shown how the dynamic Harrod trade multiplier result can be interpreted as the Hicks supermultiplier because only exports can pay for the import content of other components of demand such as consumption, investment and government expenditure, which therefore allows them to grow faster in tune with export growth without a country running into a BoP constraint. Exports are a unique component of aggregate demand in this respect, which is often forgotten because, by relating imports to income in conventional income multiplier analysis, the import content of expenditure is missing. The correct approach to the foreign-trade multiplier in macro-analysis is to relate imports to expenditure, not income, allowing the import content of different items of expenditure to differ (Kennedy and Thirlwall 1979).

It will remain a mystery why Harrod himself did not realise that his static foreign-trade multiplier had a dynamic equivalent. If he had realised, he could have added the BoP equilibrium growth rate (g_b) to his dynamic analysis of the relation between the actual growth rate (g_a), the warranted growth rate (g_w) and the natural growth rate (g_n) (Harrod 1939). Despite Harrod's later promises to consider 'whether the problem of external balance gives rise to further conflicts [between g_w and g_n]' (Harrod 1973, p. 123), he failed to recognise the dynamic analogue of his static foreign-trade multiplier, and its implications. Whether the BoP position helps or hinders growth equilibrium depends on the precise initial configuration of g_b, g_w and g_n (Thirlwall 2001). There are four interesting scenarios to consider:

1. $g_w > g_n > g_b$. A country in this case would be in a dire situation with excess saving and a tendency to BoP deficits before the capacity growth rate is reached. Capital inflows would worsen the inequality between g_w and g_n. The challenge would be to convert excess saving into exports.
2. $g_w > g_n < g_b$ and $g_w > g_b > g_n$. In this scenario there is no BoP constraint, and capital outflows would reduce g_w to g_n. On the other hand, $g_b > g_n$ could pull up g_n through the endogeneity of the natural rate of growth, thereby worsening the inequality between g_w and g_n.
3. $g_w < g_n > g_b$ and $g_w < g_b < g_n$. This situation could characterise many developing countries where $g_n > g_w$, causing structural unemployment and inflationary pressure because planned investment is greater than planned saving. The country would likely have a BoP problem, and capital inflows would raise g_w towards g_n. The growth of the country would be constrained by its BoP, despite surplus labour. The challenge is to convert excess domestic resources into tradable goods.
4. $g_w < g_n < g_b$. In this case, the BoP equilibrium growth rate exceeds the capacity to grow. Surpluses on the BoP will arise, and capital outflows will reduce g_w further below g_n. This situation describes many oil-producing countries. The solution lies in raising domestic saving and importing more.

It is an interesting question where individual countries lie within this framework and whether disequilibrium between g_b and g_n is self-correcting or self-aggravating. This is the issue that Perrotini-Hernández and Vázquez-Muñoz (2019) attempt to address in their innovative contribution to this symposium, for the countries of Argentina, Brazil, Chile and Mexico. They calculate g_b and g_n for each country and then estimate the elasticity of the two growth rates to the degree of capacity utilisation in the economies. Two scenarios are postulated: (i) where g_b is more elastic than g_n to capacity utilisation, in which case initial disequilibrium is reduced; and (ii) where g_n is more elastic than g_b, in which case initial disequilibrium is aggravated. In all four countries, the relationship between g_b, g_n and capacity utilisation is positive and generally g_b is more elastic than g_n, but not always. Over quite a long interval of time, sometimes the disequilibrium is self-correcting, but sometimes it is aggravated. There is more interesting work to be done on this topic for other samples of countries.[4]

3   IS THE HARROD TRADE MULTIPLIER AN IDENTITY?

One misconception that needs to be buried for good is that the dynamic Harrod trade multiplier result that $g_b = x/\pi$ is based on an identity, or is a tautology, because in the long run the growth of exports is bound to equal the growth of imports. This canard

4.   Palley (2003) and Setterfield (2006) have previously addressed this issue in a different way. If $g_b \neq g_n$, does g_b adjust to g_n or g_n to g_b to avoid ever-increasing over- or under-capacity utilisation? For Palley, g_b adjusts to g_n through variations in the income elasticity of demand for imports (π), so long-run growth approaches g_n – the supply side rules. For Setterfield, g_n adjusts to g_b through variations in the Verdoorn coefficient (linking productivity growth to output growth), so long-run growth approaches g_b – the demand side rules. In practice, both effects are likely to operate.

was originally raised by McCombie (1981), but he soon changed his mind as a result of my response to him (Thirlwall 1981). The misconception has had an unfortunate reincarnation in the works of Blecker (2016) and Razmi (2016), among others. The result would reflect an identity if the income elasticity of demand for imports (π) is measured as m/g, where m is the growth of imports and g is actual output growth, but it is *not*. The income elasticity of demand for imports in all the empirical work I know (including the original estimates of π that I used in the 1979 paper, taken from Houthakker and Magee 1969) is estimated econometrically, controlling for changes in the real exchange rate, or the real terms of trade. It is perfectly possible, therefore, that π is not significantly different from zero, and the hypothesis that $g = x/\pi$ is refutable. McCombie shows this brilliantly in his paper in this symposium, in which he runs five simulations, all of which assume $x = m$ over the long run, but where sometimes the rule $g = x/\pi$ is accepted and at other times it is not. As McCombie (2019, p. 441) writes,

> the test of the law is an econometric matter and this, by itself, is sufficient to show that the law is not a tautology. There is nothing, *a priori*, to stop the estimates of both the income elasticities and price elasticities being statistically insignificant. This would empirically refute the law and, of course, a tautology cannot be refuted.

4   THE EXCHANGE RATE AND LONG-RUN GROWTH

The basic BoP-constrained growth rate prediction of $g = x/\pi$ has been criticised many times for neglecting the role of the exchange rate in determining the economic performance of nations. For the exchange rate to matter, the *real* exchange rate would have to change significantly over time, and the Marshall–Lerner condition would also have to be satisfied; that is, the sum of the price elasticities of demand for exports and imports would have to sum to greater than unity in absolute value. A property of the original 1979 model was that the export and import demand functions were specified as multiplicative (or log-linear), with constant price and income elasticity parameters. This implied that if the exchange rate was to affect the *growth* of exports and imports permanently, it would have to change continuously. A one-shot devaluation, for example, could not affect the *growth* of exports and imports permanently (and therefore output growth), only the *level* of exports and imports at the time the devaluation takes place. I then argued that a long-run change in the *real* exchange rate is unlikely for a number of different reasons depending on a country's economic circumstances. Firstly, a nominal devaluation could pass through into rising domestic prices; secondly, competitors may 'price to market'; thirdly, the law of one price may hold; and, fourthly, even without devaluation, relative domestic prices may be sticky because competition, at least among industrial producers, takes the form of non-price competition. In the end, this is an empirical question whether price adjustment is an efficient BoP adjustment mechanism. Alonso and Garcimartin (1998) find that it is not, at least for a group of ten OECD countries. From the evidence we have, it clearly cannot be an efficient adjustment mechanism for any country if the hypothesis that $g = x/\pi$ holds in the long run. It is income growth that adjusts to preserve long-run BoP equilibrium, not relative price changes.

Recently, however, there has been a different line of attack on the model relating to the multiplicative, constant elasticity, specification of the export and import demand functions. It has been argued that the *level* of the exchange rate is important for export performance, and that an undervalued exchange rate can initiate a virtuous circle of growth relating to investment and structural change. In the extreme (Razmi 2016), exports are perfectly elastic at the 'correct' exchange rate, and the growth of world trade and the income elasticity of demand for exports plays no part in determining a country's export performance. This is diametrically opposed to the demand-oriented explanation of growth at the heart of the BoP-constrained growth model.[5]

The first point to make in response is that making the *growth* of exports a function of the *level* of the exchange rate implies a very peculiar demand function for exports. It would certainly not be a constant elasticity function. The price elasticity would vary according to the changing ratio of the growth of exports to the price level. This is not satisfactory theoretically. The second important point to make is that while a currency devaluation may initiate a growth acceleration, it is unlikely to sustain it.[6] The impetus of the initial depreciation is likely to peter out. This is where it is crucial to stress that the BoP-constrained growth model is meant to be applied to the long run; it is unsuitable for predicting growth over a short span of years not only because exchange-rate changes may only have temporary effects, but also because there can be nominal terms-of-trade shocks and volatile capital flows in and out of countries in response to, for example, interest-rate differentials between countries. These shocks can cause large deviations of actual growth from that predicted from the simple BoP-constrained model, but these shocks cannot, and do not, last forever, in which case the long-run growth rate will be determined by the structural characteristics of a country, reflected in the income elasticities of demand for exports and imports. This distinction between the short run and the long run shows up very nicely in the paper by Mhlongo and Nell in this symposium on growth transitions in South Africa. What the authors show is that it is misleading to evaluate the simple growth law, $g = x/\pi$, across a single regime because it provides no information on the sustainability of growth transitions.

Three growth regimes are identified: 1960–1976, when the annual average growth of GDP was 4.63 per cent; 1977–2003 with average growth of 1.74 per cent, and 2004–2017 with average growth of 3.01 per cent. Over the whole period 1960–2017, the simple growth law is rejected, but once regime changes are controlled for, the growth law provides valuable information on the sustainability of South Africa's different growth accelerations. In the period 1977–2003, the current-account-to-GDP ratio was virtually in balance and the rate of change of the real terms of trade was virtually zero. The growth acceleration in the period prior to that was related to FDI inflows (which did not last); and the growth acceleration afterwards proved unsustainable because of the short-term nature of the inflows. In the post-1973 period the economy has been converging to the rate predicted by the simple growth rule. Razmi (2016) and Blecker (2016) have used the empirical evidence of the literature on growth transitions to argue that the *level* of the real exchange rate matters for long-run growth. Mhlongo and Nell (2019) point out that the authors who have contributed to this literature (for example, Rodrik 2018) themselves acknowledge that an undervalued exchange rate cannot sustain growth transitions indefinitely. Ultimately growth reverts to the simple law.

Another way of coping with the understanding of growth fluctuations and transitions is not to work with a single import elasticity (π) estimated over a long period,

5.   For a full critique of the Razmi (supply-side) model, see the papers by McCombie and by Mhlongo and Nell in this symposium.
6.   Equally, a devaluation could ossify a production structure by making countries more competitive in goods that caused BoP problems in the first place. There are more direct and efficient ways of inducing structural change.

                    Journal compilation © 2019 Edward Elgar Publishing Ltd

as in Mhlongo and Nell (2019), but to estimate a time-varying import elasticity (and export elasticity as well), and attempt to analyse why the elasticities might have changed. This is what Felipe, Lanzafame and Estrada (2019) do in their interesting paper in this symposium, which applies the BoP-constrained growth model to Indonesia, whose economic fortunes have fluctuated considerably over time. Over the long period 1982–2017, the actual growth rate and the BoP-constrained growth rate virtually coincide, but within the period there is wide variation in growth performance. In the 1980s, GDP growth averaged 5.8 per cent per annum. From 1990 to 1997, it averaged 7.2 per cent, and in the period 2000–2017 it fell to 5.3 per cent. The authors use a Kalman filter to make time-varying estimates of the income elasticities of demand for exports and imports, and hence time-varying estimates of g_b. What they show is that the deceleration of growth since 2000 has been the result of a dramatic fall in the ratio of the income elasticity of demand for exports to imports largely associated with the poor performance of the manufacturing sector in world trade. McCombie and Tharnpanich (2013) found the same for Thailand.

5   TERMS OF TRADE

The full BoP-constrained growth model contains an expression for the terms of trade; and both the direct and indirect effect of terms-of-trade changes on BoP-constrained growth can be estimated with knowledge of the price elasticities of demand for exports and imports, or as a residual after the effect of world income growth and capital flows (see later) have been calculated. Nureldin Hussain (1999) took this second approach for a sample of 29 African and 11 East Asian countries during the 1980s and 1990s and found terms-of-trade effects small for the vast majority of countries relative to the effect of differences in the income elasticities of demand for exports and the effect of capital flows. Africa grew more slowly than Asia because of its specialisation in primary commodities with a low income elasticity of demand.

It is true, however, that short-term terms-of-trade movements can cause large temporary deviations of actual growth from the long-run predicted growth rate from the BoP-constrained model. Africa in the 2000s is the most recent example where the commodity price boom caused the continent to be the fastest-growing on the planet for a short period of time (see Bagnai et al. 2016). Many studies have documented cyclical fluctuations in commodity prices and the terms of trade. Cashin and McDermott (2002) and Cashin et al. (2002) go as far back as 1862 and show fluctuations against a background of a declining long-run trend in the terms of trade of primary commodities (the Prebisch–Singer thesis). They conclude that such fluctuations 'have serious consequences [for] commodity-dependent countries and have profound implications for the achievement of macroeconomic stabilisation'. Erten and Ocampo (2013) identify four super-cycles of real commodity prices over the period 1865 to 2010 ranging between 30 and 40 years. The mean of each super-cycle of non-oil commodity prices is generally lower than the previous cycle, supporting the Prebisch–Singer hypothesis.[7]

Apart from commodity price changes causing temporary fluctuations in the actual growth performance of countries, Pérez Caldentey and Moreno-Brid in their paper in this symposium are right that the long-term consequences have not been fully explored.

---

7.   Blattman et al. (2007) have looked historically at the relation between terms-of-trade volatility and GDP growth taking 35 countries over the period 1870–1939 and find a negative relation caused mainly by the deterrent to foreign direct investment (FDI).

As they say, 'the [balance-of-payments-constrained] growth literature has not yet explicitly considered the influence of the terms of trade given its potentially strong interrelations with the foreign-capital movements, the real exchange rate, the productive structure and its non-price competitiveness, and, thus, the long-term growth potential of an economy' (Pérez Caldentey and Moreno-Brid 2019, p. 478). The authors attempt to rectify this theoretically, but don't give evidence of its quantitative significance. In the period 2000–2012, the price of commodities rose significantly relative to manufactured goods, but what was the impact on the real exchange rate of countries and capital flows? It is well known that improvements in the terms of trade may lead to an appreciation of the real exchange rate – the Dutch Disease – leading to adverse consequences for the tradable goods sector and the premature 'deindustrialisation' of countries. Resources shift into commodity production where the linkages with other sectors of the economy are weak, undermining a country's growth potential. The impact on capital flows is uncertain. Pérez Caldentey and Moreno-Brid consider the case where an improvement in the terms of trade allows a higher current-account-deficit-to-GDP ratio to be financed by capital inflows, but I doubt in practice whether this is likely over the long term. Financial markets will still be nervous about the size of debt and whether the terms-of-trade improvement is permanent or not. If history is a guide, the evidence suggests that improvements are transitory and not the basis for sustained borrowing. The experience of Latin America, and the debt crisis of the 1980s, offers a salutary warning that countries and creditors can find themselves in deep trouble, borrowing and lending on the back of a commodity boom.

6   CAPITAL FLOWS

While writing the 1979 paper, I realised that the simple model might not fit very well many developing countries that often run large balance-of-payments deficits for a considerable period of time financed by a variety of short- and long-term capital inflows. In 1982, Nureldin Hussain and I extended the basic current-account model to include capital flows. This essentially meant working within the framework of an identity because the sum of the current account and capital account must equal zero. We showed that it is possible to disaggregate any country's growth rate into four component parts: (i) a pure terms of trade effect; (ii) the effect of real exchange-rate changes on the volume of exports and imports; (iii) the effect of world income growth determined by the income elasticity of demand for exports; and (iv) the impact of real capital flows – all deflated by the income elasticity of demand for imports. A major weakness of the extension to the basic model, however, was that no limit was imposed on the size of the current-account deficit that could be financed by capital inflows; nor were interest payments on debt considered, except implicitly as a negative component of capital inflows. It was not until much later that these important weaknesses were rectified by, among others, McCombie and Thirlwall (1997), Moreno-Brid (1998; 2003) and Barbosa-Filho (2001). Without considering interest payments, and assuming no change in the terms of trade, the growth rate consistent with a sustainable debt-to-GDP ratio is $g_D = (\Theta x)/[\pi - (1 - \Theta)]$, where Θ is the share of the import bill financed by exports, and $(1 - \Theta)$ is the share of the import bill financed by capital inflows. With no deficit, $\Theta = 1$, and the growth rate gives the simple rule $g = x/\pi$. The remarkable fact about this result, however, is that even if exports cover only 90 per cent of the import bill and 10 per cent is financed by capital inflows, the predicted growth rate hardly changes. For $x = 10$ per cent and $\pi = 2$, the simple rule yields

    Journal compilation © 2019 Edward Elgar Publishing Ltd

5 per cent growth, while the modified model with $\Theta = 0.9$ gives $g_D = 4.73$ per cent. Export growth reigns! With interest payments on debt considered, the debt-constrained growth rate becomes: $g_{Di} = (\Theta x - \Theta_i)/[\pi - (1 - \Theta - \Theta_i]$, where i is the growth of real net interest payments abroad, and Θ_i is the share of foreign exchange devoted to interest payments. Now the growth rate is more significantly affected. If $i = 5$ per cent and Θ_i is 0.3, with $x = 10$ per cent, $\pi = 2$ and $\Theta = 0.1$, the predicted growth rate is 3.4 per cent compared to 5 per cent from the simple model.[8]

Bhering, Serrano and Freitas (2019), in their important paper in this symposium, criticise me and others, and rightly so, for measuring debt sustainability by the current-account-deficit-to-GDP ratio and not the debt-to-export ratio, because the latter is the true measure of the capacity to pay off external liabilities – otherwise there is a currency mismatch. The authors remind me that in a paper in 1983 (Thirlwall 1983), I argued that to get my simple growth rule ($g = x/\pi$) 'the only assumptions needed to produce this result are that in the long run trade must be balanced on current account (or that there is a *constant ratio of capital flows to export earnings*) and that the real terms of trade … remain constant' (ibid., p. 250, emphasis added). Regrettably, McCombie and I (1997) did not adopt the constant ratio of capital flows to export earnings. But the interesting result that Bhering et al. derive is that while sustainable long-run capital inflows can positively affect the long-run *level* of output, they do not alter the *growth* rate consistent with BoP equilibrium because ultimately there has to be a balance between exports and imports. The first necessary condition for debt sustainability in this improved model is that the interest rate should be less than export growth. The second necessary condition is that the ratio between imports and exports should not grow, otherwise the trade deficit will grow faster than exports – although this is not a sufficient condition because there will be a debt maximum beyond which the financial system will no longer finance external deficits. It would have been interesting if the authors had given some numerical simulations showing by how much the level of output could be affected by different ratios of debt-to-export earnings.

7   CONCLUDING REMARKS: THE NEED FOR STRUCTURAL CHANGE

If terms-of-trade changes and capital flows can only have transitory, or short-term, effects, the only component left from the full 1979 BoP-constrained growth model determining the long-run growth of countries is how well the world economy is performing (w), and the structure of a country's production and trade which determines the income elasticity of demand for exports (ε) and imports (π); that is, growth will tend towards $g = \varepsilon w/\pi$. The growth-of-world-income variable facing an individual country will be a weighted average of the growth rates of all the countries that a country exports to; ε will be a weighted average of the income elasticity of demand of all the goods that a country exports; and π will be a weighted average of the income elasticity of demand for all the goods a country imports. This leads to two important extensions of the basic model.

The first is a 'generalised' model originally developed by Nell (2003), which disaggregates the world income growth variable and takes into account the different income elasticities of demand for exports and imports to and from each trading partner.

---

8.   McCombie and Roberts (2002) have shown in a different model that an increase in the sustainable debt-to-GDP ratio will raise the sustainable current-account-deficit-to-GDP ratio, allowing a transitional, but not a *permanent,* effect on growth.

Nell estimates the disaggregated model for South Africa, the rest of the Southern Africa Development Community (RSADC) and the OECD. Bagnai et al. (2016) have applied the model to 20 sub-Saharan African (SSA) countries trading with the rest of SSA, some Asian countries and the rest of the world. They are able to disaggregate how the BoP constraint on African countries has been affected by different factors from different sources. The policy message is plain that a country should orient its exports as far as possible to fast-growing markets and target import substitution from countries where the income elasticity of imports is high.

The second extension is a multi-sectoral model first developed by Araujo and Lima (2007) in which different exports and imports have different income elasticities. What this model highlights is that even if sectoral elasticities are constant and there is no change in world income growth, a country can grow faster by shifting resources to sectors with higher income elasticities of demand for exports and away from sectors with a high income elasticity of demand for imports. This is what export promotion and import substitution are supposed to achieve. Equally it shows that if there is an increase in world income, a country will benefit more the higher its sectoral income elasticities of demand for exports and the lower its sectoral income elasticities of demand for imports. From a policy point of view, this multi-sectoral specification of the model allows for the identification of key, strategic, growth-promoting tradable goods sectors of the economy.

This is where the supply side of an economy becomes extremely important because there is a growing body of evidence showing how the income elasticity of products is a positive function of the level of technology and the skill embodied in them. Gouvea and Lima (2010) test this multi-sectoral model for four Latin American and four Asian countries, distinguishing six sectors: primary products; resource-based manufacturing; low-technology manufactures; medium-technology manufactures; high-technology manufactures; and others. In general, technology-intensive sectors have a higher income elasticity of demand for exports, but for imports there is not much difference between sectors. Gouvea and Lima (2013) have also estimated sectoral export demand functions for a sample of 90 countries, and find that machinery has the highest income elasticity and primary products the lowest. Romero and McCombie (2016) estimate export-growth functions for different technological sectors in 14 OECD countries separately. Medium- and high-tech industries show higher income elasticities of exports than low-tech and primary commodities. Romero and McCombie (2018) use cross-product panel data to estimate export and import demand functions for four-digit product categories across 14 OECD countries. Income elasticities are always higher for high-tech sectors. Bottega de Lima and Romero (2019) estimate export demand functions for 15 countries on three continents measuring technology using patent data, and dividing the sample by technological groups. The income elasticity of demand for high-tech groups ranges from 1.1 to 2.0, while the income elasticity for low-tech groups ranges from 0.2 to 0.8. The evidence is overwhelming that the structure of production and trade matters for export growth and the growth of output in a BoP-constrained framework. Cimoli and Porcile (2014) and Gabriel et al. (2016) address the issue of the technological gap between poor and rich countries, and how it might be bridged. Porcile and Yajima in this symposium highlight the strong links between Structural, Keynesian and Schumpeterian approaches to development, with emphasis on the link between the structure of production and trade, and the external constraint on growth, based on the technical sophistication of goods and the diversity of production. They write: '[B]uilding technological capabilities and transforming the pattern of specialization is crucial for long-run growth. Otherwise, the efforts for boosting aggregate demand by means of traditional macroeconomic tools (for instance, an expansive fiscal policy) will be frustrated by the emergence of external disequilibria and an unsustainable debt' (Porcile and Yajima 2019, pp. 529–530).

Structural change almost certainly requires a country to design an industrial policy embracing a national innovation system to facilitate the flow of technological knowledge across all sectors of the economy. The market mechanism itself is unlikely to bring about the required structural changes needed. I am attracted to the concepts of growth diagnostics (Hausmann et al. 2008) and self-discovery (Hausmann and Rodrik 2003). Growth diagnostics involves locating the binding constraints on a country's economic performance and to target these directly, giving the most favourable outcome from the resources available compared to the 'spray gun' approach to economic policy-making which may not hit hard enough the binding constraints on growth that really matter. In the case of the BoP, it would involve targeting exports with growth potential, and identifying imports where there is import substitution potential. Government expenditure on R&D to enhance export quality could reap high returns. Self-discovery involves seeking out new areas of comparative advantage and then implementing the most appropriate policies to foster them. Hausmann and Rodrik point out that there is much randomness in the process of a country discovering what it is best at producing, and a lack of protection reduces the incentive to invest in discovering what goods and services they are. Governments need to encourage entrepreneurship and invest in new activities, but the first best policy is not by the traditional means of tariffs and quotas, but public sector credit and guarantees which reward the innovator (and not the copy-cats), and can be withdrawn if firms do not perform well after a certain period of time.

It will be interesting to see whether the BoP-constrained growth model will still be discussed in the next 40 years, but in my view there is really no substitute for structural change to improve the trade balance if countries are to improve their long-run growth performance consistent with current-account BoP equilibrium.

REFERENCES

Alonso, J.A. and C. Garcimartin (1998), 'A new approach to balance of payments constraint: some empirical evidence', *Journal of Post Keynesian Economics*, 21(2), 259–282.
Araujo, R.A. and G. Lima (2007), 'A structural economic dynamic approach to balance of payments constrained growth', *Cambridge Journal of Economics*, 31, 775–774.
Bagnai, A., A. Reiber and T. Tran (2016), 'Sub-Saharan Africa's growth, South–South trade and the generalised balance of payments constraint', *Cambridge Journal of Economics*, 40(3), 797–820.
Barbosa-Filho, N. (2001), 'The balance of payments constraint: from balanced trade to sustainable debt', *Banca Nazionale del Lavoro Quarterly Review*, 54, 381–400.
Bhering, G., F. Serrano and F. Freitas (2019), 'Thirlwall's law, external debt sustainability, and the balance-of-payments-constrained level and growth rates of output', *Review of Keynesian Economics*, 7(4), 486–497.
Blattman, C., J. Hwang and J.G. Williamson (2007), 'Winners and losers in the commodity lottery: the impact of terms of trade growth and volatility in the periphery 1870–1939', *Journal of Development Economics*, 82(1), 156–179.
Blecker, R. (2016), 'The debate over "Thirlwall's Law": balance of payments constrained growth reconsidered', *European Journal of Economics and Economic Policies: Intervention*, 13(3), 275–290.
Bottega de Lima, A. and J. Romero (2019), 'Innovation and export performance in different groups of sectors and countries', Unpublished Paper.

Cashin, P. and C.J. McDermott (2002), 'The long-run behaviour of commodity prices: small trends and big volatility', *IMF Staff Papers*, 49(2), 175–199.

Cashin, P., C.J. McDermott and A. Scott (2002), 'Booms and slumps in world commodity prices', *Journal of Development Economics*, 69(1), 277–296.

Cimoli, M. and G. Porcile (2014), 'Technology, structural change and BoP-constrained growth: a structuralist toolbox', *Cambridge Journal of Economics*, 38, 215–237.

Dixon, R.J. and A.P. Thirlwall (1975), 'A model of regional growth rate differences on Kaldorian lines', *Oxford Economic Papers*, 27(2), 2001–2014.

Dray, M. and A.P. Thirlwall (2011), 'The endogeneity of the natural rate of growth for a selection of Asian countries', *Journal of Post Keynesian Economics*, 33(3), 451–468.

Erten, B. and J.A. Ocampo (2013), 'Super cycles of commodity prices since the mid-nineteenth century', *World Development*, 44, 14–30.

Felipe, J., M. Lanzafame and G. Estrada (2019), 'Is Indonesia's growth rate balance-of-payments-constrained? A time-varying estimation approach', *Review of Keynesian Economics*, 7(4), 537–553.

Gabriel, L.F., F.G. Jayme and J. Oreiro (2016), 'A North–South model of economic growth, technological gap, structural change and real exchange rate', *Structural Change and Economic Dynamics*, 38, 83–94.

Gouvea, R. and G. Lima (2010), 'Structural change and balance of payments constraint and economic growth: evidence from the multi-sectoral Thirlwall's Law', *Journal of Post Keynesian Economics*, 33(1), 169–204.

Gouvea, R. and G. Lima (2013), 'Balance of payments constrained growth in a multi-sector framework: a panel data investigation', *Journal of Economic Studies*, 40(2), 240–254.

Harrod, R. (1933), *International Economics*, London: Macmillan.

Harrod, R. (1939), 'An essay in dynamic theory', *Economic Journal*, 49(1), 14–33.

Harrod, R. (1973), *Economic Dynamics*, London: Macmillan.

Hausmann, R. and D. Rodrik (2003), 'Economic development as self discovery', *Journal of Development Economics*, 72(2), 603–633.

Hausmann, R., D. Rodrik and J. Hwang (2007), 'What you export matters', *Journal of Economic Growth*, 12(1), 1–25.

Hausmann, R., D. Rodrik and A. Velasco (2008), 'Growth diagnostics', in J. Stiglitz and N. Serra (eds), *The Washington Consensus Reconsidered: Towards a New Global Governance*, New York: Oxford University Press, pp. 324–355.

Houthakker, H. and S.P. Magee (1969), 'Income and price elasticities in world trade', *Review of Economics and Statistics*, 51(2), 111–125.

Kaldor, N. (1967), *Strategic Factors in Economic Development*, Ithaca: Cornell University Press.

Kaldor, N. (1970), 'The case for regional policies', *Scottish Journal of Political Economy*, 17(4), 336–348.

Kennedy, C. and A.P. Thirlwall (1979), 'The input–output approach to the foreign trade multiplier', *Australian Economic Papers*, 18(1), 173–180.

Lanzafame, M. (2010), 'The endogeneity of the natural rate of growth in the regions of Italy', *International Review of Applied Economics*, 24(5), 533–552.

Lanzafame, M. (2014), 'The balance of payments constrained growth rate and the natural rate of growth: new evidence', *Cambridge Journal of Economics*, 38(4), 817–838.

Leon-Ledesma, M. and A.P. Thirlwall (2002), 'The endogeneity of the natural rate of growth', *Cambridge Journal of Economics*, 26(4), 441–459.

Libanio, G. (2009), 'Aggregate demand and the endogeneity of the natural rate of growth: evidence from Latin American countries', *Cambridge Journal of Economics*, 33(5), 967–984.

Mathews, J.A. (2019), 'Latecomer industrialisation', in E.S. Reinhert, J. Ghosh and R. Kattel (eds), *Handbook of Alternative Theories of Economic Development*, Cheltenham, UK and Northampton, MA: Edward Elgar Publishing, pp. 613–636.

McCombie, J.S.L. (1981), 'Are international growth rates constrained by the balance of payments? A comment on Professor Thirlwall', *Banca Nazionale del Lavoro Quarterly Review*, 34(139), 455–458.

McCombie, J.S.L. (1985 [2004]), 'Economic growth, the Harrod trade multiplier and the Hicks super-multiplier', in J.S.L. McCombie and A.P. Thirlwall (eds), *Essays on Balance of Payments Constrained Growth*, London: Routledge, pp. 41–57.

McCombie, J.S.L. (2019), 'Why Thirlwall's law is not a tautology: more on the debate over the law', *Review of Keynesian Economics*, 7(4), 429–443.

McCombie, J.S.L. and M. Roberts (2002), 'The role of the balance of payments in economic growth', in M. Setterfield (ed.), *The Economics of Demand-Led Growth*, Cheltenham, UK and Northampton, MA: Edward Elgar Publishing.

McCombie, J.S.L. and N. Tharnpanich (2013), 'Balance of payments constrained growth, structural change and the Thai economy', *Journal of Post Keynesian Economics*, 35(4), 569–595.

McCombie, J.S.L. and A.P. Thirlwall (1997), 'Economic growth and the balance of payments constraint revisited', in P. Arestis, G. Palma and M. Sawyer (eds), *Markets, Unemployment and Economic Policy*, Cheltenham, UK and Northampton, MA: Edward Elgar Publishing, pp. 498–511.

Mhlongo, E. and K.S. Nell (2019), 'Growth transitions and the balance-of-payments constraint', *Review of Keynesian Economics*, 7(4), 498–516.

Moreno-Brid, J. (1998), 'On capital flows and balance of payments constrained growth models', *Journal of Post Keynesian Economics*, 21(2), 283–298.

Moreno-Brid, J. (2003), 'Capital flows, interest payments and the balance of payments constrained growth model: a theoretical and empirical analysis', *Metroeconomica*, 54(2–3), 346–365.

Nell, K. (2003), 'A generalised version of the balance of payments growth model: an application to neighbouring regions', *International Review of Applied Economics*, 17(3), 249–267.

Nureldin Hussain, M. (1999), 'The balance of payments constraint and growth rate differences amongst African and East Asian countries', *African Development Review*, 11(1), 103–137.

Nureldin Hussain M. and A.P. Thirlwall (1982), 'The balance of payments constraint, capital flows and growth rate differences between developing countries', *Oxford Economic Papers*, 34(3), 498–510.

Pacheco-Lopez, P. and A.P. Thirlwall (2014), 'A new interpretation of Kaldor's first law of growth for an open developing economy', *Review of Keynesian Economics*, 3, 384–398.

Palley, T. (2003), 'Pitfalls in the theory of growth: an application to the balance of payments constrained growth model', *Review of Political Economy*, 15(1), 75–84.

Pérez Caldentey, E. and J.C. Moreno-Brid (2019), 'Thirlwall's law and the terms of trade: a parsimonious extension of the balance-of-payments-constrained growth model', *Review of Keynesian Economics*, 7(4), 463–485.

Perrotini, I. and D. Tlatelpa (2003), 'Crecimiento Endogeno y Demanda en las Economias de America del Norte', *Momento Economico*, 128, 10–15.

Perrotini-Hernández, I. and J.A. Vázquez-Muñoz (2019), 'Endogenous growth, capital accumulation and Thirlwall's dynamics: the case of Latin America', *Review of Keynesian Economics*, 7(4), 444–462.

Porcile, G. and G.T. Yajima (2019), 'New Structuralism and the balance-of-payments constraint', *Review of Keynesian Economics*, 7(4), 517–536.

Razmi, A. (2016), 'Correctly analysing the balance of payments constraint on growth', *Cambridge Journal of Economics*, 40(6), 1581–1608.

Rodrik, D. (2018), 'An African growth miracle', *Journal of African Economies*, 27(1), 10–27.

Romero, J. and J.S.L. McCombie (2016), 'The multi-sectoral Thirlwall's law: evidence from 14 developed European countries using product level data', *International Review of Applied Economics*, 30(3), 301–325.

Romero, J. and J.S.L. McCombie (2018), 'Thirlwall's law and the specification of export and import demand functions', *Metroeconomica*, 69, 366–395.

Setterfield, M. (2006), 'Thirlwall's law and Palley's pitfalls: a reconsideration', in P. Arestis, J.S.L. McCombie and R. Vickerman (eds), *Growth and Economic Development: Essays in Honour of A.P. Thirlwall*, Cheltenham, UK and Northampton, MA: Edward Elgar Publishing, pp. 47–59.

Solow, R.M. (1956), 'A contribution to the theory of economic growth', *Quarterly Journal of Economics*, 70(1), 65–94.

Thirlwall, A.P. (1970), 'Another autopsy on Britain's balance of payments 1958–1967', *Banca Nazionale del Lavoro Quarterly Review*, 23(94), 308–325.

Thirlwall, A.P. (1974), 'The panacea of the floating pound', *National Westminister Bank Quarterly Review*, August, 16–28.

Thirlwall, A.P. (1980), 'Regional problems are balance of payments problems', *Regional Studies*, 14(5), 419–425.

Thirlwall, A.P. (1981), 'A reply to Mr McCombie', *Banca Nazionale del Lavoro Quarterly Review*, 34(139), 458–459.

Thirlwall, A.P. (1983), 'Foreign trade elasticities in centre–periphery models of growth and development', *Banca Nazionale del Lavoro Quarterly Review*, 36(146), 249–261.

Thirlwall, A.P. (2001), 'The relationship between the warranted rate of growth, the natural rate and the balance of payments equilibrium growth rate', *Journal of Post Keynesian Economics*, 24(1), 81–88.

Thirlwall, A.P. (2011), 'Balance of payments constrained growth models: history and overview', *PSL Quarterly Review*, 64(259), 307–351.

Verdoorn, P.J. (1949), 'Fattori che Regolano lo Sviluppo della Produttivita del Lavoro', *L'Industria*, 1, 3–10.

Vogel, L. (2009), 'The endogeneity of the natural rate of growth: an empirical study for Latin American economies', *International Review of Applied Economics*, 23(1), 41–53.